PRESSURE GROUPS
AND POWER ELITES
IN PERUVIAN POLITICS

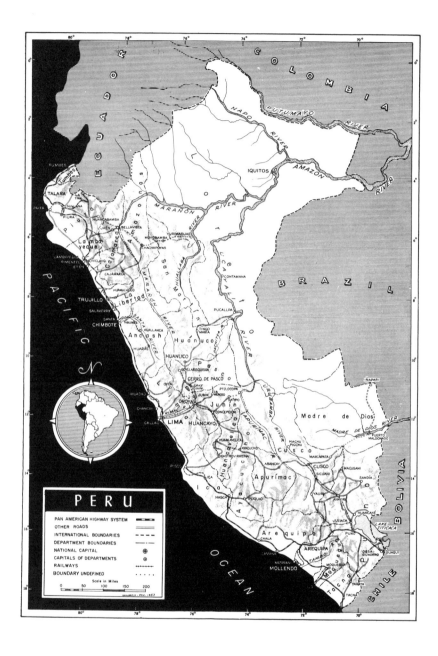

PERU

PRESSURE GROUPS AND POWER ELITES IN PERUVIAN POLITICS

BY CARLOS A. ASTIZ

CORNELL UNIVERSITY PRESS

ITHACA AND LONDON

Standard Book Number 8014-0538-6

Library of Congress Catalog Card Number 74-87012

PRINTED IN THE UNITED STATES OF AMERICA
BY VAIL-BALLOU PRESS, INC.

To María Teresa

without whose encouragement
this book would not have been written

Foreword

Little more than a decade ago, studies of Latin American politics were notable for their superficiality and lack of analytical sophistication. Much of the research was essentially descriptive in character, preoccupied mainly with historical development, institutional evolution, and chronological tabulation of constitutions, regimes, coups, revolutions, and juntas. Latin America was often treated as a homogenized whole (aside from Brazil and Mexico) characterized by chronic political instability, continuous social turbulence, and persisting economic retardation.

The special merit of Carlos A. Astiz's stimulating book is that it analyzes an important Latin American country, Peru, whose political processes and institutions have been largely neglected. Furthermore, he does not confine himself to the traditional practice of describing institutions and legal-constitutional development. Instead he seeks to reveal the underlying factors of continuity and stability in Peruvian politics hitherto concealed by the bewildering permutations of the political superstructure.

He successfully avoids two pitfalls: that of macroanalysis (excessive and premature abstract conceptualization) and that of microanalysis (obsessive preoccupation with minutiae). He attempts to develop an analytical framework combining the broad insights gained by an examination of the class structure of Peru and the detailed empirical knowledge afforded by interest-group analysis. Professor Astiz cautiously warns that he is not offering a theory of Latin American politics, which he considers premature at this stage. But his study has clear implications for studies of political behavior not only in other Latin American countries but in underdeveloped and semideveloped countries generally.

In analyzing the complex revolutionary patterns evolving in the underdeveloped countries of the world, a modified class-analysis framework is often more likely to provide an accurate image of social and practical reality than a contextual framework consisting largely of impersonal descriptive categories like "poverty," "ignorance," "misery," and "hunger," and employing equally irrelevant verbal confrontations like "freedom vs. slavery," "democracy vs. dictatorship," "the rule of law vs. chaos and violence," and "free elections vs. subversive takeovers." Sentiment, humanistic concern, and moral self-righteousness are often necessary to arouse and impel action, but they cannot be surrogates for effective analysis. Professor Astiz sedulously avoids this confusion, although his rigorous analysis obviously has been motivated by social concern. He observes strict impartiality in the organization of his data, but he is hardly indifferent to the moral and political implications of the conditions in Peru or of his analysis.

But even a modified form of class analysis is not sufficiently calibrated to cope with the bewildering and shifting mosaic of conflicting, intersecting, and harmonizing interests in Peruvian society. Class analysis is notoriously deficient in its ability to explain in sophisticated detail the patterns of interest-group aggregation, articulation, and behavior on the subclass or intraclass level, particularly where ethnic and racial divisions intersect and clash with social and political formations. And while interest-group analysis appears on the surface to be eminently equipped to deal with both infinitely divisible groups and endlessly proliferating formations, it betrays a consistent inability to define the ideological parameters of a given sociopolitical order or to explain the basic rules of conflict and cooperation that govern a particular system.

Interest-group analysis functions most efficiently in highly variegated social and political systems where the great fundamental issues of power and ideology have been largely resolved in a broad and relatively stable consensus. In societies of this character, the major preoccupation of politics is the selection of alternative means and options to achieve agreed-upon normative goals. Conflict is generated not only because of differing values and aspirations, but more pertinently because the identical ends might be achieved through alternative paths that promote the interests of some groups at the expense of others. But even in stable societies, such as the United States, interest-group analysis fails when the ideological parameters of the system become ill-defined and the social consensus begins to erode, as appears to be happening in the area of race relations.

The most pressing issues in Latin America generally, and in Peru specifically, are those concerned with the fundamental character of the social order itself, not whether this or that group should be favored by a particular policy that will achieve common goals. Interest-group analysis thus enables us to understand the politics of subclass, transclass, and intraclass groupings during a long period of transitional stability, but it is a modified system of class analysis that enables us to comprehend why the current order in Peru is transitional and what directions Peruvian society may assume as it moves from temporary order, through equally temporary disorder, to another order.

In the underdeveloped world, in Latin America, in Peru, leaders continue to analyze social and political issues in terms of class categories, not because they are necessarily Marxists, but because the social and political realities of a society searching for consensus can be better understood and analyzed within a context of class categories and the conflict of social classes. In many Middle Eastern and Latin American countries, varying approximations of the Marxist "ruling class" are realities and not figments of the imagination. And while many Western scholars have been woefully incapable of discovering or even defining a "ruling class," the members of "ruling classes" in Latin America have little difficulty in either discovery or definition. Class conflict, along with subclass and intraclass conflict, is a real experience for millions, as is the exploitation of class by class, and this must be understood instead of being brushed aside as artificial constructs of revolutionary intellectuals.

Professor Astiz's study reveals the basic interconnection between

class formations and interest-group formations, whether such
groups are institutional or functional, associational or structural,
amorphous or latent. Interest groups in Peru cannot be defined in-
dependently of class and social structure, for many interest groupings, indeed, are simply intraclass or subclass formations, while
others overlap across class lines; but they are neither outside,
above, nor independent of class divisions. It is within this contextual framework that Professor Astiz provides new and imaginative
insights concerning the political behavior of the Church, the military, the trade unions, the Aprista party, and the various components of the "ruling class" and its instruments of political influence, manipulation, and control. Also within this framework Professor Astiz's study affords us a new appreciation of the political
role and potential of Peru's middle and professional classes, the racially mixed sectors of the population, and the physically ubiqui-
tous but politically invisible Indians. Furthermore, it enables us to
understand the complex patterns of social rigidity and political
fluidity in Peruvian society: the uncompromising persistence of
class lines, the relative impermeability of the "ruling class" from
below, combined with the accelerating proliferation and differentiation of intraclass, transclass, and subclass groupings and formations.

Professor Astiz also throws new light on the sociopolitical role of
the Peruvian military—both as an institution and as a constellation
of individual personalities and factions—as it functions ambiva-
lently and inadvertently as servant and disruptor of the social *status quo*. He deals with the agony of the Church in Peru in a
unique and imaginative way, showing how the eroding religious
commitment of the lower classes may force the Church into socially innovating and even revolutionary directions in order to retain the religious allegiance of its disillusioned flock. And finally,
he illuminates the ambivalent impact of American official and
business involvement in Peruvian politics and relates it convincingly to the pattern and behavior of domestic forces and institutions.

It was at one time fashionable to dismiss social classes as obsolete, and more recently we were informed that we had witnessed the "end of ideology," but Professor Astiz has graphically demonstrated that social classes, ideology, and interest groups are all alive and flourishing in Peru.

VERNON V. ASPATURIAN

University Park, Pennsylvania
April 4, 1969

Preface

I hope it will not be considered presumptuous for me to affirm that the study of Peruvian politics has been inadequate. Those few publications that exist are limited in scope. My objective is to present a view of Peruvian political reality through identifying and analyzing groups in Peruvian society. To this end I have discussed not only the traditional components of the social structure, but also four groups that have played a major, indeed crucial, role in the politics of most of the countries of Latin America, and certainly of Peru: the Roman Catholic Church, the military establishment, the political parties, and the outside "penetrators." Finally, an attempt is made to indicate how and to what extent the social classes actually articulate their interests and to explore the possibility of fundamental structural changes, which most scholars have come to desire.

One who undertakes a study of this type must confront the problem of Peru's backwardness (even by Latin American standards), and the secretiveness that surrounds many aspects of Peruvian society. The complete disregard (even contempt) felt by many Peruvians for the intellectual processes usually followed in the social sciences further complicates and frustrates the researcher. This disregard is reflected in the lack of relatively current and accurate statistics or in their unavailability to those interested in studies of this type. It is also evident in the absence of regularly published congressional records, authoritative electoral returns, reliable and up-to-date landholding information, and the like. This situation has made it impossible to document scholarly information obtained personally or through Peruvians whose identification could create problems for them.

I was faced with either publishing the present study on a subject that has been practically unexplored or maintaining the informational vacuum which now exists in the field of Peruvian politics. I feel that I must choose the first course and accept whatever criticism that choice may engender.

Of the many individuals and organizations which helped in this enterprise, I wish to single out Dr. Elnora Carrino, who read the manuscript and made substantive and stylistic suggestions; Mrs. Mary McCarthy, who put the manuscript together; Professor Helen Mayo, who made available important data; my assistants, Christina Zawisza and John McCarthy; and Dr. James Petras and Dr. Elton Atwater, both of the Pennsylvania State University. Deep gratitude is also expressed to Professor Vernon V. Aspaturian, whose influence on my intellectual formation is reflected throughout this study. I also wish to acknowledge the invaluable research support received from the Center for Inter-American Studies and from the library staff of the State University of New York at Albany.

CARLOS A. ASTIZ

State University of New York at Albany
January 1969

Contents

Tables

PRESSURE GROUPS
AND POWER ELITES
IN PERUVIAN POLITICS

1. Introduction to Peru

"Peru is a product of a feverish imagination; it belongs to a fantastic dream geography." Thus one of the most distinguished Peruvian scholars describes his country.[1] His expression would be considered quite accurate by anyone familiar with Peru.

Peru is located in the Southern Hemisphere, from just south of the Equator to the 18th degree, and from the 68th to the 81st degree west of Greenwich, thus falling within the tropical region. It has the Pacific Ocean on the west, Ecuador and Colombia on the north, Brazil on the east, and Bolivia and Chile on the south. The most easily perceived characteristics of the country are its long coastline (over 1,400 miles) and the Andean and pre-Andean ranges, which run more or less parallel to the coast and divide the country into three distinct regions (some geographers say four). The Andes are also a prime factor in determining the amount of rain that the various regions of the country receive, which in turn determines their viability, at least in terms of agricultural activities.

The three regions identified by most writers are: the Costa (coastal area), which varies in width from a few to 130 miles; the Sierra (highlands), which is usually considered to be anything more than 3,000 feet above sea level; and the Selva (jungle) located between the eastern part of the Andes and the Brazilian boundary. These regions show clearly differentiated features and play different roles in the national polity. Tables 1 and 2 show clearly the distribution of the population in these regions, as well as by legal subdivisions.

[1] Luis E. Valcárcel, *Ruta Cultural del Perú*, p. 13.

Table 1. Regional distribution of the
population (in per cent)

Region	1940	1950	1961
Costa	25	27	39
Sierra	62	60	52
Selva	13	13	9

Sources: Perú, Dirección Nacional de Estadística y Censos, *Sexto Censo Nacional de Población, vol.* I, sec. I; Banco Central de Reserva del Perú, *Renta Nacional del Perú,* 1958, 1960.

The Costa

Generally speaking, Peruvian geographers define the Costa as that region "where the influence of the sea is visible, either in the climate, the products, the fog, or the attitude of its inhabitants. Under these circumstances, the width of the coastal lands is extremely variable." [2] The region, really a narrow strip no more than 100 miles wide in most places, runs from north to south and is bordered by the Pacific Ocean on the west and the Andean ranges on the east. It is usually considered as having three sections: The northern coast extends approximately from the Ecuadorian boundary to the city of Trujillo; it is the widest and flattest area and is populated by more than 1,100,000 inhabitants engaged in agriculture and industry. The central coast extends between the cities of Trujillo and Nazca, with a width of no more than thirty miles to the foot of the Andes; it includes Lima and contains approximately 2,500,000 inhabitants in a combination of desert land and valleys which are fertile from irrigation and the short rivers which come down from the mountains. The southern coast is even drier and naturally more hostile to human habitation than the central coast; it runs from Nazca to the Chilean border and has only 130,000 inhabitants, who crowd the few fertile valleys and the *lomas* located beyond the coastal hills. The possibility of refining the minerals (copper, iron) being extracted from the sierras behind it has given new hope to its dwellers.

[2] Emilio Romero, *Geografía Económica del Perú,* p. 11.

Table 2. Population of Peru by legal subdivision and region, 1961

Legal subdivision	Total inhabitants	Inhabitants in		
		Costa	Sierra	Selva
Dept. of Amazonas	118,439	–	65,452	52,987
Dept. of Ancash	582,598	125,819	456,779	–
Dept. of Apurimac	288,223	–	288,223	–
Dept. of Arequipa	388,881	86,019	302,862	–
Dept. of Ayacucho	410,772	–	399,797	10,975
Dept. of Cajamarca	746,938	45,271	637,189	64,478
Constitutional Province of Callao	213,540	213,540	–	–
Dept. of Cuzco	611,972	–	541,691	70,281
Dept. of Huancavelica	302,817	3,854	287,300	11,663
Dept. of Huánuco	328,919	–	280,990	47,929
Dept. of Ica	255,930	251,048	4,882	–
Dept. of Junín	521,210	–	464,294	56,916
Dept. of La Libertad	582,243	303,466	278,777	–
Dept. of Lambayeque	342,446	329,358	13,088	–
Dept. of Lima	2,031,051	1,885,749	145,302	–
Dept. of Loreto	337,094	–	–	337,094
Dept. of Madre de Dios	14,890	–	–	14,890
Dept. of Moquequa	51,614	19,120	32,494	–
Dept. of Pasco	138,369	–	115,670	22,699
Dept. of Piura	668,941	543,506	125,435	–
Dept. of Puno	686,260	–	667,102	19,158
Dept. of San Martín	161,763	–	–	161,763
Dept. of Tacna	66,024	44,033	21,991	–
Dept. of Tumbes	55,812	55,812	–	–
Total	9,906,746	3,906,595	5,129,318	870,833

Source: Sexto Censo Nacional de Población, vol. I, sec. I, p. v.

Note: It has been estimated that approximately 500,000 inhabitants were omitted, 100,000 of whom lived in the Selva (see Instituto de Estudios Políticos para América Latina, *Perú,* p. 1).

The imperfect and limited statistical data available confirm the impressionistic reaction of most visitors—namely, that the coastal region is the most highly developed area of the country. This is the area of Peru where the first Spaniards built their rudimentary huts and from which they gained control of the highly developed Inca

Empire and took over its almost inexhaustible wealth. This is also the region of the modernly organized cotton and sugar plantations, which produce almost exclusively for the export market, and where the center of political, economic, and administrative power —Lima—is located.

There is a very important reason for this area's being the most highly developed of the country: the sea, which gave it a readily accessible natural highway. But the sea gave the coastal area of Peru much more than relatively easy and inexpensive transportation; the sea gave it guano—the excrement of various types of birds which live on the islands along the Peruvian coast—and the raw material for the country's new and growing fish-meal industry. The factories and fishing boats engaged in this industry can be found in the northern section, where the urban areas, of which Chimbote is perhaps the best example, have encountered new vitality and appear to be growing by the hour in spite of recent financial difficulties. These two products have provided new and important sources of income to new entrepreneurs and, indirectly, to the traditional upper class of the region. This occurred at a time when alternative sources were badly needed if the upper class were to maintain the control of the political, economic, and even social life of the nation, which they gained immediately after they were practically forced to become independent. Guano in the nineteenth century and fish meal in the twentieth century provided the needed boosts.

The central part of the coastline, with fertile valleys and the Lima-Callao urban complex, offers enough riches to make up for the lack of vegetation in the spaces between the well-irrigated valleys, although there is probably not enough arable land for all the people in the area.

The situation worsens as one moves toward the south. Rains are almost unknown south of Pisco, and the southern coast is a long, narrow desert; human life is possible only where a river comes down from the mountains. The distinguished Peruvian intellectual, Luis Alberto Sánchez, has effectively described the impression that the southern coast of Peru makes on the visitor:

It offers an overwhelming vision of barrenness: majestic, because of its loneliness. Gray, with a yellowish gray, a golden yellow, a bright gold, the Peruvian coast is a transcription of the African deserts. . . . As soon as one moves away from the point where the river enters the ocean and toward the interior, the dryness begins. Contradictory winds pick up clouds of fine sand which, capriciously, pile up and then fly away again, organizing armies of dunes which make the horizon more concave and the sealine less precise. As in Africa, one is surprised by the arrogance of a palm tree beyond a sandy hill. Around the palm tree a fearful and very limited green. Armies of *algarrobos* give the heavy blood of their veins. Anemic cactuses dot a few places. Again then, sand, sand, sand, vastness. Nothing grows there, but, could anything grow tomorrow? [3]

The few southern valleys, unlike those of the northern and central regions, are deep and narrow because of the erosion caused by rivers which have cut through the Coastal Mountain Range and the plateaus located east of it, up to the Western Andean Range. Adequate utilization of these rivers would require costly irrigation works, not yet available in the area; this explains the difference in population between the southern coastal region and the other two.

The Sierra

This region is generally considered to begin at 3,000 feet above sea level. Nevertheless, the most casual observer would acknowledge that altitude is only one of the factors which distinguish the Sierra from the Costa. The vegetation, the climate, and, to a certain extent, the inhabitants contribute to its identification. Distance from the sea is of varying significance; outside Lima the sea is thirty miles away, and in the north it is 120 or 130 miles away. Some geographers prefer to use as the limit the dividing line of river waters along the Western Andean Range. There is, however, no agreement, and most Peruvians, as well as the government, tend to include as part of the Sierra all the territory which shows the presence of the Andean Mountains. The classification process

[3] *El Perú: Retrato de un País Adolescente,* p. 23–24.

is subjective—and often arbitrary. What may be the beginning of the Sierra for somebody who comes from Lima may be part of the Costa to a person from Cuzco.

The Sierra has some basic characteristics which set it apart from the rest of the country. The terrain is highly irregular, as a consequence of the geologic process that formed the Andes. Progressive climatic variations in accordance with the altitude above sea level, and large high plateaus through which the rivers run peacefully add to the Sierra's variety. Two different sectors can be identified: the *páramo* (humid highland), which runs from the Ecuadorian border to the Cajamarca area, where it becomes fragmented (parts of it reach as far south as Huánuco) and the *puna* (dry highland) which begins in the central part of the country and moves down to its southern borders. The southeastern *puna* sector, near Bolivia, is known as Puna Salada, because the presence of salt, borates, and saltpeter has actually burned the terrain.

This is the region where most of the population of Peru has lived since prehistoric times (although its relative share is decreasing, as shown in Table 1). It is the region with the greatest agricultural potential and the most important mineral resources, but it is also the most difficult to live in because of its geographic irregularity. Finally, it is the most traditional area of Peru, both culturally and politically.

The Selva

This region, located to the east of the Andes and mostly unexplored and thinly populated, is Peru's frontier, even today. Some Peruvians prefer to call it "the region of the great rivers," because the rivers are, for all practical purposes, the only lines of communication with the rest of the world.[4] Since these rivers (such as the Amazon) run toward the Atlantic Ocean, the Peruvian Selva communicates much more easily with Brazil than with the rest of Peru. Iquitos, the largest Peruvian city of the region, receives ships from different parts of the world, but they come through the Brazilian Amazon region; Iquitos can be reached from Peru only by plane, and the service is not reliable.

[4] Romero, *Geografía*, p. 18.

One observer points out with surprise that "it can be said that there are three jungles superimposed on each other." Most of the Indians who live in this region are completely uncivilized and have not been included in national censuses. The same observer reports that in the years 1956 and 1957 certain tribes killed a number of Brazilian and American explorers and attacked the town of Requena, where they killed and stole women. Airplanes are sometimes attacked with arrows.[5]

The Selva, which Peruvians also call "the *montaña*," could provide the nation with a frontier of limitless possibilities, if and when enough modern technology can be brought into the region. Around the turn of the century it was controlled by a group of rubber barons, who at one time thought of achieving independence from Peru. When the central government got around to dispatching forces to quell the revolt, they had to take such a long trip through strange territories that by the time they arrived peace had been re-established.[6] This physical separation has continued to exist, except for the presence of limited air service, which obviously can be enjoyed only by a tiny minority of the population. This area constitutes a hope and a potential solution to some of the country's present problems, particularly that of population pressure. But at this time it is only an unexplored region and is apparently considered unattractive even by the landless peasants who overpopulate the highlands: governmental attempts to encourage them to migrate to the Selva have not achieved a great deal of success. It is no surprise that the most rigorous penal colonies of the country are located there.[7]

Land Scarcity

Although the over-all population density of Peru—19.9 persons per square mile—cannot be considered threatening when compared either with other countries of the world or with its Latin American neighbors, the matter becomes less clear after a more

[5] Rafael Girard, *Indios Selváticos de la Amazonia Peruana*, pp. 17, 18.

[6] Sánchez, *El Perú*, p. 38.

[7] Both felons and political prisoners are sent there; for a description of one of the penal colonies, known as Sepa, see Genaro Ledesma Izquieta, *Complot*, ch. 10.

careful analysis.[8] According to the most reliable calculations, approximately 60 per cent of the Peruvian labor force is engaged in agriculture, and only 1.8 per cent of the total area is currently under cultivation, with an estimated maximum possible figure of 10 per cent; [9] the present ratio, then, is less than one acre per person engaged in agriculture. If the uneven distribution of land (94 per cent of those earning a livelihood through agriculture do not own any land),[10] the extreme concentration of income indicated in Table 3, and the low consumption patterns are also taken into account, the inescapable conclusion is that population density in the rural areas of Peru is extremely high in relation to the available fertile land, even if we ignore its distribution.

Table 3. Yearly distribution of income in the rural sector
of the Sierra, 1956

Group	Percentage of total rural population	Per capita income (in Peruvian sols)
Landless peasants	95.0	900
Small landowners	3.4	1,080
Large landowners and well-paid employees	1.6	22,800

Source: Virgilio Roel Pineda, *La Economía Agraria Peruana* . . . , I, 18; Augusto Salazar Bondy and others, *La Encrucijada del Perú,* p. 48; and Ricardo Letts Colmenares, *Reforma Agraria Peruana: Justificación Económica y Política,* p. 50.

While reluctant to recognize that their country is overpopulated, Peruvian writers, generally speaking, have pointed out that the "better" (meaning more rewarding) regions have more people than they can adequately support at the present time. Romero

[8] A specific definition of a "threatening percentage" has been avoided, since it depends on such factors as quality of the population, degree of capitalization, alternative economic activities, etc. See Peter Tomas Bauer and Basil S. Yamey, *The Economics of Underdeveloped Countries,* p. 61 ff.

[9] USDA/ERS, *Land Tenure and Holding Information: Peru,* p. 2.

[10] Oscar Delgado, "Revolución, Reforma y Conservatismo: Tipos de Políticas Agrarias en Latinoamérica," Table 4, p. 247.

mentions the coastal valleys and the departments surrounding Lake Titicaca, but he does not accept the idea of actual rural over-population. Other writers include different regions of the country, such as the Cuzco area, and trace recent political problems to scarcity of arable land.[11] According to Luis E. Valcárcel:

A primitive agriculture, on eroded lands, with eventual risks and frequent droughts, determine a meager production. The poorly administered *latifundia*, without investments, lacking technology, cultivates only a portion of its area, and leaves unexploited large portions of it, while there are millions of men without land.[12]

This scarcity is compounded by the pattern of land distribution shown in Table 4. It is clear that, as long as 1.4 per cent of the

Table 4. Distribution of agricultural land in Peru, by region, 1960

No. of acres	No. of holdings	% of total holdings	Area (in acres)	% of total area
Costa				
Up to 25	40,821	89.37	194,565	10.23
26–250	3,856	8.65	264,450	13.89
251–1,250	692	1.58	384,337	20.20
More than 1,250	181	.40	1,059,520	55.68
Sierra				
Up to 75	26,866	94.46	344,267	31.45
76–500	1,217	4.28	101,570	18.41
501–1,250	258	.91	142,060	12.99
More than 1,250	99	.35	416,607	37.15
Selva				
Up to 25	8,362	61.07	103,830	.84
26–250	4,124	30.13	318,942	2.30
251–2,500	905	6.61	603,210	4.92
More than 2,500	300	2.19	11,259,990	91.64

Source: Perú, Comisión para la Reforma Agraria y la Vivienda, *La Reforma Agraria en el Peru,* p. 13 (also reproduced in César Guardia Mayorga, *La Reforma Agraria en el Perú,* p. 169).

[11] Romero, *Geografía,* pp. 230–31. See also Instituto de Estudios Políticos para América Latina, *Perú,* p. 8; and Hugo Neira, *Cuzco: Tierra y Muerte, passim.*

[12] Luis E. Valcárcel, "La Vida Rural en el Perú," p. 3.

owners (approximately 3,000) control 62.8 per cent of the productive land, this scarcity will continue, since the very high cost of opening up whatever usable land there may be in the largely unexplored Selva makes it at best a long-term process that does not even keep up with the population growth. While the significance of the concentration of landownership will be explored in a later chapter, it should be indicated here that this scarcity has provided the "push" factor in the migration toward the urban areas; this migration is clearly demonstrated by the fact that, from 1940 to 1961, the urban population increased by 96.7 per cent, while the rural population increased only by 47.4 per cent. During the same period, certain cities more than tripled their population, as indicated in Table 5.

Table 5. The largest cities of Peru and their rate of growth

City	1961 Population	Average yearly growth rate since 1940
Lima	1,436,231	8.4%
Callao	155,953	5.9%
Arequipa	135,358	5.8%
Trujillo	100,130	8.1%
Chiclayo	95,667	9.7%
Cuzco	79,857	4.6%
Huancayo	64,153	6.7%
Vitarte	62,971	127.0%
Chimbote	59,990	62.2%
Iquitos	57,777	3.9%
Ica	49,097	6.4%
Piura	42,555	5.9%
Sullana	34,501	3.0%

Source: Prepared by the author from raw data in *Sexto Censo Nacional de Población*, vol. I, sec. I, pp. 13–16.

Nevertheless, this movement from the rural to the urban areas, which has been observed in most of the Latin American countries, will not suffice to solve the problem of scarcity of arable land in the Peruvian countryside. Furthermore, this migration creates new problems in the urban areas.[13] Whatever the eventual outcome of this migration, it will not alter the fact that not enough productive land is available in Peru today, and the situation is likely to persist in the near future.

The miseries of a high population density in terms of productive land are compounded by the lack of adequate transportation. It is obvious to anyone who knows the region that the Andes constitute a formidable barrier, but no one will claim that the problem cannot be solved. The fact is that the governments of Peru have done little to build highways and railroads, and even air facilities are still quite backward.

The railroads can presently be divided into three categories: (1) a group of seven lines owned by the Government, the longest of which runs for approximately 168 miles; (2) a group of five lines, the longest of which runs for 582 miles, owned by the "Peruvian Corporation," a syndicate of British investors; (3) a number of lines owned and operated by mining concerns or plantations, most of which are less than 100 miles long (the longest is the 151-mile Cerro de Pasco Corporation railroad). There is a total of 2,-554 miles of track, although not all lines are currently in operation; furthermore, many of the lines owned by industrial concerns are not normally open to anyone but their owners and do not carry passengers. It can be estimated that all the lines open to the general public carry an average of 6 million passengers and 4.5 million tons of freight a year. Because of the short distance covered by most lines, however, they average 340 million ton-miles and 180 million passenger-miles a year, not a very impressive figure even by Latin American standards.[14]

The highway situation does not appear to be any better, al-

[13] The political significance of this migration will be explored in a later chapter. For an analysis of urbanization in Peru see José Matos Mar, "The *Barriadas* of Lima: An Example of Integration into Urban Life," and Luis Dorich T., "Urbanization and Physical Planning in Peru," both in Philip M. Hauser (ed.), *Urbanization in Latin America,* pp. 170–90 and 280–93, respectively.

[14] Data assembled by the author from Ministerio de Hacienda y Comercio, *Boletín de Estadística Peruana,* various issues, and Sociedad Geográfica de Lima, *Anuario Geográfico del Perú,* various issues.

though the priority of building roads was established as early as 1926. In fact, mileage has quadrupled since that year although the base was not very impressive to begin with. According to the latest available information, there are 2,700 miles of paved highway, mostly in the coastal area; to that, 5,400 miles of "improved" roads should be added; finally, the statistics mention approximately 6,-600 miles of "unimproved" roads and around 8,800 miles of trails. Needless to say, the roads included in the last three categories are not necessarily open all year.

Although a look at the map gives the impression that the sea could be Peru's natural highway, at least for the coastal region, the fact is that its coast is rough and lacks natural harbors. In most cases cargo has to be transferred to barges before it can reach shore. The Peruvian government has built two ports: Callao, which receives 75 per cent of the value of the country's imports and sends out 30 per cent of its exports, and Salaberry, which handles 2 per cent of imports and 5 per cent of exports. There are three other important ports developed by foreign investors: San Juan and San Nicolás (considered as one in official statistics) account for almost 10 per cent of the country's exports, mostly iron ore; Ilo, located in the extreme south, was developed by the Southern Peru Copper Corporation and receives more than 10 per cent of total imports.[15]

River transportation does not provide a solution either. The Amazon River, which is formed in northeastern Peru, provides an exit to the Atlantic Ocean through Brazil. In the process, however, it increases the isolation of the Selva from the rest of Peru. Lake Titicaca constitutes a waterway between Peru and Bolivia, and a few rivers provide limited transportation for small vessels.

Population

Tables 1, 2, and 6 indicate that the majority of the Peruvian population is still located in the Sierra, where the Inca empire developed. But the statistical data also show that this majority is stead-

[15] Data extracted by the author from David A. Robinson, *Peru in Four Dimensions,* pp. 280–82.

ily diminishing, at least in relative terms, and that the overwhelming majority of those who migrate move to the coastal region, where many of them join the fast-growing urban masses. This migration tends to diminish the racial cleavage which has existed in Peru since the first Spanish conquistadors set foot in the country.

Table 6. Population, area, and density of the three main
regions, 1961

Region	Population Absolute	%	Area Square miles	%	Density (Persons per square mile)
Costa	3,906,595	39.4	62,028.25	12.5	62.9
Sierra	5,129,318	51.8	149,860.25	30.2	34.2
Selva	870,833	8.8	284,337.50	57.3	3.1
Total	9,906,746	100.0	496,226.00	100.0	

Source: Prepared by the author with data from *Sexto Censo Nacional de Población,* vol. I, sec. I, Introduction.

Despite population movements, the cleavage is still evident throughout the country, although somewhat distorted in the coastal areas and particularly in the two largest cities, Lima and Arequipa. Figures are difficult to obtain, but the white population of Peru has been estimated as no more than 20 per cent (the lowest estimate is 6.4 per cent); mestizos amount to approximately 32 per cent; 46 per cent are Indians, and 2 per cent have been placed in other categories.[16]

The complete separation between whites and Indians is obvious, no matter which set of statistics one uses. The predominantly Indian areas show the highest levels of poverty, disease, illiteracy, malnutrition, and inequality. The mestizos, called "cholos," lack clear identification and are often considered either whites or Indians, depending on the individual and the region. The separation that exists between whites and Indians has become a highly sensi-

[16] These figures are given by Angel Rosemblat in *La Población Indígena y el Mestizaje en América,* I, 159–60, and by Romero in *Geografía,* pp. 227–29. It is interesting that the latest census ignored racial differences.

tive topic for Peruvians, regardless of their point of view. In dealing with this, the well-known Peruvian intellectual Augusto Salazar Bondy wrote:

It is not necessary to perform a profound sociological analysis to determine that there exists in Peru, on the one hand, a traditional world with ancestral and quite rudimentary norms and values, a world which is ignored and interfered with by what we can call the official country; which slowly loses its vitality because it is disconnected from the channels of modern existence, but which nevertheless, serves as the only backstop for the autonomous conscience of the masses. On the other hand, there is a sector of modern living which encloses a minority of the population and which, divorced as it is from the basic community, comprises an unattached world of superficial life, polarized toward purely imitative ideals and values, incapable of feeding an autonomous cultural personality.[17]

Other writers attempt to minimize or downgrade the racial differences, often by emphasizing that there are really very few pure Indians and whites in Peru after four centuries of interracial relations. While this may be an anthropological fact, it does not appear to be self-evident, either to the casual observer or to the scholar interested in the social, economic, or political structure of the country. José Varallanos, in expressing this view, says:

We maintain that the Indian-Spanish *mestizaje*, under the Crown, took place not only as a simple union of blood, but also as a union of spirits. It was, at the same time, ethnic and cultural *mestizaje*, as a consequence of the social revolution which was implied in the Spanish Conquest of these lands. This, the mixture, the symbiosis, the transculturation of that which is Spanish and that which is Indian, is precisely what characterizes the cholo and that which is cholo and, consequently, Peru and that which is Peruvian.

And he concludes:

If ethnically there exists a cosmopolitan mixture—because no people of America blends as Peru, in its sons, the blood of all the races of this

[17] "Imagen del Perú de Hoy," in Augusto Salazar Bondy and others, *La Encrucijada del Perú*, p. 25.

earth—the Indo-Spaniard or Indo-white mestizo and his descendants constitute the widest demographic sector. . . . The Indian does not constitute the national majority, but only one of our majority groups.[18]

Whatever the ideological preconceptions of those who choose to emphasize that the gap does not exist (hoping, perhaps, that somehow it will go away, or that at least its effects will not be felt), the available data show the cleavage, although they are less clear as to its source. The political role and implications of the Indian presence, introduced in Salazar Bondy's words, above, will be discussed in later chapters.

The Indians further increase the educational problem that has existed in Peru since independence; they have shown a marked unwillingness or inability to speak Spanish (the majority speaks Quechua, a few Aymara). The educational lag is also compounded by a population growth rate of 3.36 per cent a year and by the fact that 43.3 per cent of the Indian population are 15 years of age or younger.[19] Illiteracy is high (recent estimates are contradictory, but they near the 50 per cent mark), particularly in the Sierra, where the majority of the Indian population lives. The number of university and secondary school students, while increasing impressively, is very low both absolutely and when compared with most of the other Latin American countries. The basic reason is indirectly suggested by a keen observer:

The fact that the creation of schools and the appointment, transfer, and dismissal of the staff is due in good measure to the demands of Representatives and Senators, is a backward custom, a crucial vice, and an attempt against the country's interest, the quality of public education, and the security and dignity of the educators.[20]

Naturally, since the Indians have little or no political leverage with the legislators, and only slightly more influence at the execu-

[18] José Varallanos, *El Cholo y el Perú. Perú Mixto,* pp. 12, 199.

[19] Gregorio Garayar Pacheco, "Demografía Peruana," in *La Universidad y el Pueblo,* I, 159. See also Perú, Dirección Nacional de Estadística y Censos, *Sexto Censo Nacional de Población,* vol. 1, sec. 1, p. xiv.

[20] Emilio Barrantes, "Aspectos Educativos," in *Breve Introducción al Estudio de la Realidad Nacional,* pp. 183–84.

tive level (as discussed in Chapters 5 and 9), they are bound to be at the bottom of any priority list. Furthermore, most Peruvian educators do not seek assignment to the areas where Indians predominate but pressure their superiors and the legislators to obtain alternative assignments.

If items such as an average nutrition pattern clearly below minimum standards (approximately 2,000 calories per person per day), a low ratio of available medical services (4.7 physicians and 22 hospital beds per 10,000 inhabitants), and an enormous housing deficit documented by the presence of seemingly endless shantytowns around most urban areas are added to the picture, a clear view of underdevelopment, indeed backwardness, appears.[21] This situation is compounded by an extremely uneven distribution of socioeconomic rewards, which few find possible to deny. This is the background against which Peruvian political reality will be explored.

[21] Data on nutrition are from Virgilio Roel Pineda, "La Agricultura en la Economía Peruana," in Salazar Bondy and others, *La Encrucijada,* p. 34. Data on available medical services are from United Nations Economic Commission for Latin America, *The Economic Development of Latin America in the Post-war Period,* p. 60.

2. Conceptual Framework

In an often-quoted article, Merle Kling reminds his readers that "a theory of power and political instability in Latin America is not a substitute for empirical research." [1] This study is carried out in complete agreement with that view. It is not a secret for political scientists (of whatever nationality) who have adventured in the Latin American jungle that even some of the most basic types of research still remain to be carried out. Thus, it seems a little early to embark on comprehensive typologies and all-inclusive frameworks which encompass the most important characteristics of the politics of Latin America, as some writers have done.[2] There is, of course, nothing to be lost and much to be gained by identifying and relating political characteristics common to the Latin American states; [3] but, because of the dearth of basic information on

[1] "Toward a Theory of Power and Political Instability in Latin America," in James Petras and Maurice Zeitlin (eds.), *Latin America: Reform or Revolution,* p. 78. The article originally appeared in 1956 in the *Western Political Quarterly* and has also been reprinted in John D. Martz (ed.), *The Dynamics of Change in Latin American Politics,* pp. 130–39. It is interesting that even the title of Mr. Kling's theoretical effort has been challenged by Claudio Veliz, who wrote that "perhaps the principal contemporary problem of Latin America is excessive stability." He was, however, dealing with both political and social stability; see his "Introduction" to Veliz (ed.), *Obstacles to Change in Latin America,* p. 1.

[2] See, for instance, Karl M. Schmitt and David D. Burks, *Evolution or Chaos: Dynamics of Latin American Government and Politics,* ch. 6; Jorge Graciarena, *Poder y Clases Sociales en el Desarrollo de América Latina,* ch. 2; and Roger Vekemans and J. L. Segundo, "Essay of a Socioeconomic Typology of the Latin American Countries," in Egbert de Vries and José Medina Echavarría (eds.), *Social Aspects of Economic Development in Latin America,* I, 67–93.

[3] This course has been recommended by Robert L. Peterson in his article

most of the countries, he who does so will find himself discoursing at such a level of generality that his contribution may be of extremely limited value or, if specific enough, subject to factual challenges which, significant or not, tend to cast doubts over the validity of the scheme.

It is one of the basic tenets of this study that it is still too early to attempt such theoretical endeavors. Furthermore, it is important to remember that the countries of Latin America comprise twenty different political units, and that, whether analysts like it or not, the nation-state is still the basic political unit. This is not to imply that intersystem factors are unimportant or can be dismissed lightly, but even these factors operate within the nation-state framework. In accordance with these premises, this broad study of Peruvian politics is carried out in the hope that it and others will provide the "raw material" which will make it possible for political scientists to construct valid typologies and comprehensive lists of interrelated phenomena.

The weaknesses of these macropolitical studies have led scholars in recent years to what may be considered the other extreme: micropolitical research, in which a certain aspect of a country's politics (a political party, the military establishment, the senior public officials, the land reform program, the industrialists, the judiciary) is studied in great detail, but very often to the exclusion of other elements in the country's political environment, as if whatever is being analyzed existed in a vacuum. This procedure, true enough, answers the objection raised in the previous paragraph, but at the very great risk of ignoring the other societal factors which have contributed to making the item under study what it is. Furthermore, by abstracting a political institution or group, the researcher involved in its study tends to make it, either directly or by implication, more important than it usually is when seen in the dynamic give-and-take of a political system in operation. Nevertheless, it is explicitly recognized here that no study, no matter how comprehensive and accurate, will fully convey the whole picture of a pol-

---

"Social Structure and the Political Process in Latin America: A Methodological Re-examination."

itical system in action. Yet attempts have been made in the past, mostly with regard to the more developed and stable Western nations, and the author has felt encouraged to try it with Peru.

Social Structure and Political Power

In exploring the limited number of studies on Peruvian politics, or even on the country in general, the researcher is immediately impressed by the emphasis on the recording and description of events, rather than on their analysis and systematic explanation: the writers seem to have concentrated on the "what" and, to a certain extent, on the "who," as opposed to the "why" and the "how." Furthermore, descriptive studies usually tend to treat superficially those situations and events which are only partially made public, or which are left unexplained by the actors. In an attempt to go beyond the surface of political action, the author intends to pay preferential attention to the political role played by Peru's social classes and by certain power elites—such as the Catholic Church and the military establishment—which seem to stand out by themselves when it comes to the exercise of power, as reflected in the internal distribution of social, political, and economic rewards.[4]

In trying to carry out what could be called an "in-depth" analysis of the Peruvian political system, the writer has tried to remain aloof from exclusive commitment to any one approach to the study of politics. At the same time, he has borrowed freely from different approaches when he has felt that they could make a positive contribution to the project. This initial lack of commitment should not be interpreted as a rejection of the existing approaches or as a dissatisfaction with the present state of the discipline. The writer simply wanted to "keep all his intellectual options open" and felt that commitment to any one line of thought would constitute a sort of

---

[4] A recently published essay exemplifies the type of descriptive study which this work *is not* trying to emulate; it begins with the premise that the changes that have occurred in Peru in the last two decades convert it into "one of Latin America's most dynamic contemporary political systems," a statement which goes undocumented throughout the paper (Marvin Alisky, "Peru," in Ben G. Burnett and Kenneth F. Johnson [eds.], *Political Forces in Latin America: Dimensions of the Quest for Stability,* p. 289).

straight jacket in pursuing his unexplored topic. In doing so, he kept in mind the tongue-in-cheek invitation made by a Peruvian intellectual: "Let us search for the 'theory' of the Peruvian system of government. Let us search for it, as the scholars want it, either as a comprehensive and preconceived theory, or as a justification *a posteriori* and in a pragmatic way." [5]

The apparent declaration of independence from any one school in the preceding paragraph does not imply that this study is purposely going out to collect a series of facts, causes, and processes, in the hope of being able to put them together at the end. The author believes, first and foremost, that in a given polity every individual member is pursuing what he perceives to be his interest, either alone or by joining with others. This apparently obvious assumption becomes significant when coupled with a realization that this goes beyond self-preservation and into self-improvement, self-extension, and self-aggrandizement. As some of these individual objectives conflict with each other—an inescapable fact in a political environment with a plurality of actors and a scarcity of rewards—individuals will resort to their reservoir of power to achieve their objectives.

That power among men is unevenly distributed is a truism. Since such diverse things as wealth, beauty, property, physical strength, education, intelligence, information, the possession of and willingness to use weapons, imagination, and charisma—to mention just a few—are ingredients of power, and since these ingredients vary in "weight" according to the specific circumstances, an even distribution of power over a given period of time is extremely difficult to effect, particularly in national societies. While these ingredients must be considered not in isolation but as interrelated elements, the ownership of property and, particularly, of real estate and related commercial activities has been found to be paramount in almost all underdeveloped countries, and Peru is not an exception. In fact, as will be demonstrated, the ownership of land has meant and still means power over those who work in the

[5] Arturo Salazar Larraín in his introduction to Enrique Chirinos Soto, *Cuenta y Balance de las Elecciones de 1962*, p. vi.

agricultural sector, as well as over merchants in small towns. And if the significance of owning large haciendas is diminishing, that of owning tracts of land near the urban centers is increasing more than proportionately. To put it briefly, property can be easily and rapidly converted into power, simply because "it is more directly connected with the means of livelihood and can be exchanged for the services of those who have access to other sources of power." [6] Consequently, private ownership of property often can be considered equivalent to power. As one student of Latin American politics has put it:

probably nothing provides a better indication of the power structure than the class structure conceived in a dynamic sense, that is to say, considering at the same time the relations between classes. A power structure is, after all, a special form of relations between classes, relations which are asymmetric by definition, that is, which imply the predominance of a controlling class over the rest. This predominance may take different forms or shapes and, in general, translates the different levels of power existing between the classes; it also contributes to the definition of the style with which power is exercised. The nature of the class structure, in the framework of its mutual relationships, is therefore essential to outline the features of the power structure and, consequently, the degrees of autonomy enjoyed by those who participate in it, either as active agents or as relatively passive objects of the power actions.[7]

Interest Groups and Social Classes

Individuals and groups tend to pursue power according to their perception of it and of the best road to achieve it; they may do so consciously or intuitively, in the process of moving toward their more immediate objectives. It does not take very long for individuals seeking certain political objectives to realize that, in a large society, their task would be made easier by joining with others on the basis of a community of interests and goals; the product, regardless of the specific name (or lack of it), is the interest group,

[6] Vernon V. Aspaturian, "Social Structure and Political Power in the Soviet System," p. 4.

[7] Graciarena, *Poder y Clases Sociales,* p. 51.

broadly understood to refer to "a number of individuals who interact with one another in accordance with certain regular behavioral
patterns." [8] The expression includes parties, single-issue groups,
ideological organizations, occupational groups, and the like.

An acceptable definition of what constitutes a class may be
quite difficult to arrive at, as witnessed by the disagreements
among the most distinguished sociologists. Borrowing again from
Robert L. Peterson, it could be said that "class is the totality of
people in any particular society who occupy a similar position in
regard to social, economic, and political status." [9] This definition,
general as it is, emphasizes the fact that human beings who have
similar roles, carry out like functions, and have access to the same
level of means belong to the same social class. A nation-state class
structure thus becomes a sociopolitical arena in which all other
processes take place. Social groups, being by definition narrower
entities whose members have certain common characteristics providing the basis for a degree of communication and identification,
can either develop within a given social class or recruit and operate across class lines.[10]

The author hypothesizes that groups recruited solely from
within one class tend to reinforce the existing class structure,
while interclass groups tend to weaken it. It is noteworthy that the
role of politically active groups has not been studied in most Latin
American countries, including Peru; this is true in spite of the fact
that the most superficial observation indicates that these groups,
particularly of the intraclass variety, play a crucial role in recruitment, communication, interest aggregation, and interest articula-

[8] Peterson, "Social Structure," p. 891n. For full treatment of this subject
see Robert K. Merton, *Social Theory and Social Structure,* pp. 285–86; Gabriel
A. Almond, "Introduction: A Functional Approach to Comparative Politics,"
in Almond and James S. Coleman (eds.), *The Politics of the Developing
Areas,* pp. 3–64; Gino Germani, *Política y Sociedad en una Época de
Transición: De la Sociedad Tradicional a la Sociedad de Masas,* pp. 15–47;
and Robert T. Golembiewski, "The Group Basis of Politics: Notes on Analysis
and Development."

[9] Peterson, "Social Structure," pp. 887–88. See also Pitirim A. Sorokin,
Social and Cultural Mobility, especially ch. 1.

[10] This definition is from Germani, *Política y Sociedad,* p. 29.

tion. This situation is not confined to the Latin American countries, but it is accentuated in many of them by the absence of even *pro forma* universal channels for those functions.

Social Class as a Tool of Analysis

The usefulness of the concept of social class as an analytical tool is derived from the fact that it directs the researchers' attention to the specific aspirations of clearly identified groups and serves as a most effective bridge in the study of the relationship between the political process and the social structure. It must be remembered that social classes exist in a highly dynamic context, sensitive to sociopolitical changes and fluctuations. This is particularly true in highly stratified societies such as those existing in most Latin American countries, where class membership at birth brings with it fairly strict social, economic, and political boundaries which accompany everyone through life.[11] This study hypothesizes that an analysis of interclass struggles and tensions, and perhaps intraclass ones as well, provides an insight into the political processes taking place in most Latin American countries, and particularly in Peru. Yet we must not forget that the objects of this study are human beings and human society, always subject to unpredictable and unexpected changes. But these possible changes (in goals, methods, environment) take place within the social structure, not outside it. In all but a truly classless society, change may affect the composition and characteristics of one or more strata, but certainly not the validity of the concept as a tool.

Recent studies of Latin American politics appear to indicate the rebirth of class as an analytical tool, although some authors stubbornly refuse to allow the word "class" to enter their vocabulary.[12]

[11] The opposite point of view is expressed by Kalman H. Silvert in *The Conflict Society: Reaction and Revolution in Latin America,* ch. 1. Mr. Silvert's experience in Argentina, where the urban middle class is much larger and more influential than in the rest of Latin America, may have influenced his views too heavily. For yet another opinion, also drawing heavily on Argentina, see Graciarena, *Poder y Clases Sociales, passim.*

[12] Even such scholars as Germani (*Política y Sociedad*) and John J. Johnson (*Political Change in Latin America: The Emergence of the Middle Sectors*) have made special efforts to avoid using this term.

The reason, or at least one of the most important reasons, is very simple: the concept of class as an analytical tool was popularized by Marxism and readily adopted by communism; individuals and groups who have felt and feel threatened by this ideology and who have become "professional anti-Communists" have usually been quick to associate the use of class analysis with a commitment to the methods and goals of Marxism-Leninism. To avoid this indiscriminate branding and whatever consequences it may have, students of Latin American politics who were not in full agreement with what José Nun calls "dogmatic Marxism" tended to stay away from class analysis, and this extremely important tool was mostly left in the hands of "action men," whose main objective was to serve their ideology regardless of the facts.[13] In reality, however, many of those who have been born in any one of the Latin American countries have been made aware of the importance of class membership by their immediate environments long before they knew of Marx, if they ever did. They have also been made aware of the necessity of keeping this perception to themselves lest the "professional anti-Communist" should pronounce them guilty by association. Vernon V. Aspaturian puts it very precisely when he writes:

Thus, in the underdeveloped world, leaders and intellectuals continue to analyze social and political issues in terms of class categories, not because they are Marxists, but because the social and political realities of a world searching for an ideological consensus can be better understood and analyzed within class categories and the conflict of social classes. . . . Class conflict is a real experience for millions, as is the exploitation of classes in the underdeveloped world, and this must be clearly understood instead of being brushed aside as an artificial consequence of Communist machinations and agitations.[14]

[13] José Nun, "Los Paradigmas de la Ciencia Política: Un Intento de Conceptualización." Jean Paul Sartre, *Crítica de la Razón Dialéctica*, p. 30. It is interesting to point out that one of the few Marxist activists who refused to place ideology above his perception of reality, the Peruvian writer José Carlos Mariátegui, was rejected as a "Trotskyist" by the Communist Conference held in Montevideo in 1929.

[14] "Strategies of the Status Quo and Revolutionary Change in Underdeveloped Countries," pp. 15–16. A shorter version of this penetrating essay

It has been emphasized elsewhere that even in affluent societies some individuals will tend to feel relatively deprived, at least in terms of prestige or status, as long as unequal distributions of socioeconomic rewards take place.[15] This feeling of deprivation causes class tensions, since class membership is important in determining one's prestige or status. It is not too daring to maintain that the socioeconomic situation in the Latin American countries, which are far from affluent, makes for highly increased tensions. In most of these countries, then, "just as in traditional societies, the pattern of political relationships is largely determined by the pattern of social and personal relations. Power, prestige, and influence are based largely on social status." [16]

A somewhat different approach will be followed in dealing with two institutional groupings which stand out in the political life of most but not all Latin American countries: the armed forces and the Roman Catholic Church. Their pre-eminent political role (discussed in Chapters 7 and 8) makes it unrealistic to consider them in the same category with groups such as labor unions and business organizations; they really do not have to pressure in order to obtain favorable responses from the formal decision-makers; their policy choices, if they are willing to exercise their maximum influence, are tantamount to adoption in a majority of these countries.[17] These two groups will be identified as "power elites," in recognition of the special role they play, although some authors employ the expressions "power factors" or "force groups." The political significance of the military establishments becomes obvious

---

appeared in Laurence W. Martin (ed.), *Neutralism and Nonalignment: The New States in World Affairs,* pp. 165–95.

[15] The point is made by Seymour Martin Lipset in *Political Man: The Social Bases of Politics,* p. 408.

[16] Lucian W. Pye, "The Non-Western Political Process," p. 468.

[17] This treatment of the armed forces and the Catholic Church has come from Latin American authors; see Germán J. Bidart Campos, *Grupos de Presión y Factores de Poder,* particularly ch. 3; Carlos S. Fayt, *Teoría de la Política,* particularly pp. 181 ff.; Hugo E. Alvarez Natale, *Contribución al Estudio de los Grupos de Interés;* and Alberto Antonio Spota, *El Poder Político y los Grupos de Fuerza y de Presión en la Crisis Contemporánea de la República Argentina.*

after even a superficial review of Latin American history, but few people have been more explicit than the Argentine General Toranzo Montero who, in an open letter to the then Secretary of War (General Fraga), wrote: "you joined the cabinet, *at my request,* not without making the implicit commitment beforehand to influence the government to obtain *the fulfillment of the demands which I presented* on behalf of the army." [18]

The identification of the Catholic Church as a power elite is more difficult because of the elusiveness of its role. Most students of Latin American politics place the Church in this category, but perhaps the best argument for this school of thought comes from the words of one of the most influential Latin American cardinals, Antonio Cardinal Caggiano, who carefully stated:

The truth is that I do not find a concept which responds exactly, in this case, to what I have to say and which has already been expressed, if not with the words "power factor." . . . In this sense, the Church . . . is a "preponderant factor" in the achievement of the public good, social peace, and the solution of the great national problems. [19]

A class analysis of Peruvian politics is intended to answer the questions of "who," "why," and hopefully "how" in regard to the distribution of societal rewards. The following chapters will deal in detail with the historical background, the current socioeconomic structure, the political parties, the power elites, and the articulation of interest on a class basis; finally, the results of the investigation will be analyzed in terms of the prospects for change. The writer knows of no comprehensive study of the type being developed here. The few discussions of Peruvian politics available in the English language are either chapters of more general books or are too narrow in scope and somewhat outdated. [20] The projects

[18] His letter was published in *La Nación* (Buenos Aires), March 26, 1961, p. 5 (emphasis added).

[19] This speech was published in *La Nación,* December 31, 1960, p. 1.

[20] For examples of the first kind, see Ronald J. Owens, *Peru,* and Thomas Robert Ford, *Man and Land in Peru.* Among the second type of studies are Harry Kantor's *The Ideology and Program of the Peruvian Aprista Movement,* which was completed in the early 1950's and deals only with one political party; James L. Payne's *Labor and Politics in Peru: The System of Political*

now in progress seem to refer to specific institutions or groups rather than to their interaction in the dynamic realities of the country's politics.

Bargaining, which covers the role played by middle- and lower-class unions; and James C. Carey's *Peru and the United States, 1900–1962*, which is a diplomatic history of Peru–United States relations.

3. Historical Development
of Peruvian Society

When the first Spanish explorers, led by Francisco Pizarro and Diego de Almagro, arrived in what is today Peruvian territory, they encountered a rather advanced civilization, which had been in existence for a long time. At the beginning of the Spanish conquest (1532) the Inca Empire extended from the southern part of what is today Colombia to the northern sections of Argentina and Chile. It included most of the present territory of Ecuador, Peru, and Bolivia and was centered about the Andean ranges. In fact, the city of Cuzco, capital of the Inca Empire, is located on the southern Peruvian Andes, at an altitude of 11,375 feet. The best archeological evidence indicates that different national groups originally inhabited the empire; numerous languages were spoken and different religious cults existed. Quechua, Lolla, Cajamarca, Huaras, and Huamachuco were among the most important tribes. These subdivisions of the Inca Empire had attained approximately the same level of development, although they had limited commercial and social contacts. As farming, crafts, irrigation, and architecture improved and as population increased, uniformity within the groups and diversity between them became more pronounced. Regionalism and political rivalries developed, and it appears that the northern valleys were able to obtain a certain degree of pre-eminence, partly due to their superior sources of irrigation. In some areas, such as the Lake Titicaca region, a certain amount of political unification seems to have been achieved through confederation.

War became more and more common, and this Hobbesian state

of political affairs seems to have paved the way for the take-over of all the subdivisions by one of the more advanced groups, the Incas. Although this group had been in control of the highland area around Cuzco for more than 200 years, it was not until the middle of the fifteenth century that they started their conquest and developed their empire. By the time the conquistadors arrived, the Incas were in firm control.

Unquestionably, Inca domination provided numerous benefits to the previously autonomous subdivisions. First, that of a single common language: the rulers forced most subjects to speak Quechua (Aymara continued in use in the southern sector, around Lake Titicaca). Second, it provided a highly structured social organization, with fixed and clearly determined roles, powers, privileges, and statuses. Third, the Incas developed an effective road network and an empire-wide messenger system (the messengers were called *chasquis*), which made it possible for the rulers to receive information rapidly and for their troops to reach remote areas on relatively short notice.

Since the Inca, besides being the emperor, was also recognized by the official religion as the supreme deity on earth (son of the sun), the faith became one more instrument employed in the integration and legitimation of the system. A member of the royal family held the position of Supreme Priest and directed the rites. The Incas did not forbid all local religions found in the subdivisions, but they incorporated them into their own, in a subordinate role.[1]

On the basis of an agricultural economy, the Incas developed a caste system, with the supreme ruler above the nation and the laws. One of the better-known Incas, Atahualpa, is believed to have said, "If I gave the order, even the birds would cease flying."

[1] This elite was even reported to have a language of its own, which was not understood by those who were not members of the nobility. For these and other details of the Inca Empire see Gustavo Valcárcel, *Perú—Mural de un Pueblo: Apuntes Marxistas sobre el Perú Prehispánico;* Louis Baudin, *A Socialist Empire: The Incas of Peru;* Burr Cartwright Brundage, *Empire of the Incas;* Hiram Bingham, *Inca Land;* Horacio Urteaga, *El Fin de un Imperio;* Jorge Cornejo Bouroncle, *Túpac Amaru: La Revolución Precursora de la Emancipación Continental;* Pedro de Cieza de León, *The Incas;* and Federico Kauffmann Doig, *El Perú Arqueológico.*

Immediately under the emperor three groups could be identified: the imperial family, a closed group whose main objective seems to have been to maintain itself apart from the rest of the population; the nobility, the old families of the Empire; and the regional bosses (*caciques* or *curacas*), leaders who had accepted the supremacy of the Incas without a struggle in exchange for privileges and protection.

There appear to have been elements which enjoyed an intermediate position; they were the public officials who ran the administrative machinery of the government, as well as the artisans and the military leadership. One important service provided by this stratum was that of controlling the statistical data collected at the local and regional levels. Other writers have emphasized that "the political and economic organization of the empire rested on statistical data.[2]

At the bottom of the social structure, and supporting it, was the lower class, which constituted the overwhelming majority of the population. They were located in rigidly subdivided and controlled communities. Movement away from the community was not allowed, and the statistical, economic, and military supervision of the bureaucracy made it almost impossible to change domicile. To facilitate this type of control, the inhabitants of each region were required to wear distinctive clothes. If the collective exploitation of the land is added to the legal prohibitions, it is not surprising to find that the subjects developed a sedentary tradition.

The basic economic unit of the Inca Empire was the community, called "ayllu". The land was owned collectively by the inhabitants and assigned to families, in accordance with their size, at the beginning of each agricultural year. Each family was responsible for working the plot assigned to it; however, the products were owned by the community, and need was an important consideration in distributing them. Besides the plots assigned to the families, there were parcels whose products were reserved for the Inca,

[2] Jorge G. Llosa P., *Visión Sintética del Perú*, p. 57. See also Gabriel A. Almond and G. Bingham Powell, Jr., *Comparative Politics: A Developmental Approach*, pp. 233–40.

the priests, and the community. These parcels were worked collectively, as a public duty. On occasion, the products from these parcels were used to take care of pressing needs, either in the same place or in nearby ayllus. Consequently, besides peace and security, the Inca provided his subjects with a minimum of economic well-being. It has been emphasized that the collective characteristics of the ayllu did not exclude the possibility of private landownership. For instance, there are reports of perpetuation of landholding by certain families, a sort of family ownership; quite often, the families in question provided political leadership, and there appears to be a relationship between it and landownership. In fact, at least one writer has maintained that the Inca Empire was evolving from collective to individual ownership and that the Spanish conquest altered the process.[3]

Whatever the truth of this assertion, the fact is that from the very beginning the conquistadors, led by Francisco Pizarro and Diego de Almagro, tried to modify the sociopolitical structure as little as possible. The divisions that existed within the empire, and even within the ruling elite made it possible for a few hundred conquistadors to acquire control of the empire after a few skirmishes. (A civil war to settle conflicting claims to the Inca throne was fought in the late 1520's, as the Spaniards were exploring the coastal area and were getting ready to colonize Peru.) The bizarre operation that led to the capture of the Inca Atahualpa, the murder of his brother and competitor, Huascar, the former's ransom for an enormous quantity of gold and silver, and finally his trial and execution by the Spaniards, have been told too many times and may not be particularly important to this study; but the fact is that after the sentence was carried out (on August 29, 1533):

the supreme authority of the Inca was replaced by that of the conqueror. But now the main activity was mining precious metals; and the communal welfare—the great mitigating element under the previous absolutism—was forgotten. Lands, together with Indians to work them, were given to the conquering soldiers, and over five million people,

[3] Roberto MacLean y Estenós, *Sociología del Perú*, p. 248.

members of a great and seemingly all-powerful empire, fell under the domination of 180 Spaniards.[4]

The conquistadors integrated themselves into the sociopolitical structure (obviously, at the top), selected a reliable Inca, and reorganized only those portions of society which were needed to intensify the production of precious metals and their diversion to Spanish hands. Their ambition resulted in struggles for control over the empire in which most of them, including Almagro and the Pizarro brothers, were killed, thus facilitating the take-over by bureaucrats sent by the Spanish Crown when it realized the wealth available in Peru.

The various reliable reports of unlimited quantities of precious metals and mines, the abuses committed in the name of the Crown to force the Indians to work on the Spaniards' behalf, and the internal quarreling prompted the king to make Peru one of the two viceroyalties in Spanish America (the other was Mexico). Lima, which had been founded by Pizarro on the coast as the "City of the Conquistadors," became the administrative center of the portion of South America under Spanish control. Spanish institutions, such as the Inquisition, had delegations in Lima, which also supervised all legal transactions between Spanish South America and Spain until the middle of the eighteenth century. To this city came

first the soldiers and later the successive immigratory waves of authorities, indoctrinators, colonists, and erudites. . . . Less than half a century after the city appeared, its aristocracy already existed. . . . Nobility, fortune and, thirdly, notoriety through arms or public service were the titles that the colonial oligarchy requested of those who hoped to enter it.[5]

The special attention enjoyed by Peru and the importance of Lima within the Spanish imperial system, plus the benefits placed at the disposal of the white society, more than explain the lack of interest shown by the Peruvian Creoles in any independence movement. Obviously, this attitude was not shared by the mestizos

[4] Ronald J. Owens, *Peru,* p. 24.
[5] Sebastián Salazar Bondy, *Lima la Horrible,* p. 29.

or, more particularly, by the Indians, who organized numerous revolts throughout the second half of the eighteenth century, of which the most important were those led by chiefs Condorcanqui (in different regions of the viceroyalty) and Pumacahua (mostly in the Cuzco area). Spaniards and Creoles acted diligently to stamp out these and other attempts, always with untold cruelty. It did not surprise many people when the movements for independence got under way after 1810 that Peru became the center of Spanish counterattack; when the Spaniards were finally defeated, in the early 1820's, it was by Argentine and Chilean troops led by San Martín, later joined by Venezuelan and Colombian troops led by Bolívar. It was only natural that many of the Peruvian Creoles fought on the Spanish side, since they could only fear the liberal ideologies which had developed in both extremes of South America. Evidence of the lack of Peruvian leadership on the pro-independence side was the fact that the first rulers of Peru were the Argentine General San Martín, the Colombian hero Sucre, and the Venezuelan leader Bolívar.

The danger of a Spanish comeback was eliminated, probably at the battle of Ayacucho in 1824. After this event a nationalistic reaction, and, more likely, the desire of seeing that the *status quo* suffered a minimum of alteration, encouraged Peruvian political and military leaders to assume control of the now independent country's affairs. Bolívar found it impossible to fulfill his obligations as Peru's ruler and withdrew to Colombia in 1826. The new national society was completely disorganized. The only institution with any degree of organization was the army:

It was only natural, therefore, that the military should occupy the power vacuum left by the Spaniards' departure, and that the early history of republican Peru is concerned with the super-party, the army, rather than with political parties, and with government by strong men rather than with strong government.[6]

The first two decades of the republican era were a succession of military *caudillos*, who fought brief civil wars for control of the

[6] Owens, *Peru,* p. 37.

national government and on occasion formed temporary alliances which never lasted very long. The unfortunate details of this period need not be recounted here, but one of the most distinguished Peruvian historians concluded that the first years of the republic had brought:

The cruelest deceit; the most complete disorder under the guise of the law; the most limitless despotism under the emblems of freedom, fraternity, and equality; the bankruptcy of the national treasury, under the mask of financial reform; the downfall and misery of the families; anarchy in government; desolation in our fields; backwardness for our people; ruins and more ruins.[7]

The domestic struggle between competing *caudillos* was compounded by attempts either to unite the country to or separate it from Colombia and Bolivia. The latter attempt produced the Peruvian-Bolivian Confederation, which appeared a number of times throughout the nineteenth century. Needless to say, an intimate relationship existed between civil encounters and international conflicts, since during the first decades it was difficult to distinguish between domestic and international politics. In any case, it is clear that neither the war of independence nor the numerous revolts and civil wars did anything to alter the socioeconomic structure left by the Spaniards. It may be, as Jorge Basadre maintains, that the upper class did not lead republican Peru at the beginning (after all, most of them favored the Spaniards), but the fact is that, except for the titles of nobility, it kept its status and sources of wealth.[8]

Slavery and the status of the Indian serve as illustrative examples. The Constitution of 1828 implicitly recognized the re-establishment of slavery in Peru by limiting citizenship to "free men" (Article 5, Section 1). Indians were important economically, as well as politically (they were a majority of the population and the Indian revolts had not been forgotten). Numerous proclamations and decrees dealt with the "Indian problem," mostly from the

[7] Modesto Basadre y Chocano, *Diez Años de Historia Política del Perú*, p. 166.

[8] Jorge Basadre, *La Promesa de la Vida Peruana*, p. 43.

point of view of the liberal creed of the first half of the last century: freedom and equality were their objectives; but, as José Carlos Mariátegui indicates:

the policy of ignoring agrarian property, imposed by the political bases of the Republic, did not attack the *latifundia*. And, although the new laws ordered in compensation the distribution of land to the Indians, they attacked instead, on behalf of the liberal postulates, the "community." Thus started a system which, whatever were its principles, worsened to a certain extent the situation of the Indians.[9]

Another Peruvian scholar, after studying the legislation carefully, reaches the following sad conclusion:

There exists in all this legislation a frank emancipating tendency, a search for equality, and a strong desire to eliminate the colonial structure. . . . Unfortunately, the principles did not agree with reality, and . . . legislation with such a noble objective contributed not to the Indian's recuperation and to the consolidation of economic freedom in the Fatherland, but to the damaging of the Indian "communities" and to the enlargement of the *latifundia*.[10]

It has become clear that the liberal intellectuals, with their urgent desire—whatever their motivations—to annul the laws the Spaniards had developed to deal with the Indians without taking time to bring the Indians up to the level of the other inhabitants of Peru, played into the hands of the traditional upper class. The Indians had nothing to match the alliance of the landlord, the district judge, the local bureaucrat (who was easily bribed), and the military officer, particularly when the game was played under rules he neither wrote nor understood. Instead of effectively protecting the Indians, the liberal thinkers placed them in a position of legal equality with the whites and mestizos under a "laissez-faire" system designed by the whites, thus ignoring the nearly three centuries of Indian subjection to Spanish rule. This long period, plus the skillful use of religion for political purposes, had brought

[9] *Siete Ensayos de Interpretación de la Realidad Peruana*, p. 58.
[10] Carlos Ferdinand Cuadros y Villena, *Análisis Crítico de la Legislación Peruana Tutelar del Indio*, p. 5.

about a "mentality of subjection" on the part of the Indians, which the wars of independence did not alter. It should be remembered that "independence" in the Peruvian context did not have a great deal of meaning for them, as long as other whites (the Creoles) and some mestizos continued in control of the economic and political structure, which is precisely what happened. Most of the Indians never realized that, at least theoretically, they were equal before the law to the whites and mestizos; and it is evident that the latter were not particularly eager to inform the Indians of their newly acquired rights. In any case, it is unlikely that the knowledge would have helped them. As Emilio Romero points out:

The measures of revolutionary character dictated under Bolívar to individualize the Indian's property, dissolving the community and everything else inspired in the same system, have been contrary to the interest of the Indian. Instead of getting him land, it caused the massive dispossession of many communities. . . . It was believed that it was enough to give freedom, to declare the independence and the political liberty of the Indian as a constitutional principle, granting him ownership of the ayllu and the community. But the Indian, illiterate and miserable, defeated and enslaved, sank into misery, without the guarantees that the colonial legislation gave him. The social equality of the republican democracy was a myth and a punishment for the Indian.[11]

All these legal changes took place in a haphazard manner, as the internal struggle continued. Although no civilian president served a full term until 1872—clear evidence of the paramount role of armed might—it would be erroneous to assume that the country was run by a military stratum. In fact, many of the so-called military men were self-appointed *caudillos* who used military titles to convince their friends and enemies of military expertise which in fact they very often lacked. They were either

---

[11] Emilio Romero, *Perú por los Senderos de América*, pp. 120–21 (emphasis added.) The author refers to the decree issued by Simón Bolívar on April 8, 1824, authorizing the distribution among the Indians of the lands owned by their communities (Articles 2 and 3). Later on, regulations issued by other administrations amended Bolívar's decree, but the end result was the loss of land by the Indian ayllus and the dissolution of many of them; on this point, see MacLean y Estenós, *Sociología*, pp. 278–79.

wealthy enough to finance their own military organization or hired by those who could provide such financial support.

This almost continuous state of civil strife, which has been described in careful detail by some of its participants, had its effect on the economy, particularly with the drop in mineral production and the reduction in the number of heads of cattle.[12] It seems clear that everybody suffered, and the aristocracy, owning more, lost more, although it more than compensated for its losses by enlarging its landholdings at the expense of the Indians. Two events in the 1840's and 1850's helped at least some of the members of the aristocracy to regain and even increase their wealth. In 1841 guano was discovered to be an excellent fertilizer (a fact that had been known to the Indians centuries earlier). Almost at the same time, large nitrate deposits were found in the Tarapacá area of southern Peru. And in 1845 Ramón Castilla, a mestizo military officer from this region, occupied the presidency and remained a dominant figure in national politics until his death in 1867.

In order to develop a rapport with the coastal aristocracy, Castilla established governmental monopolies for the commercialization of guano and nitrates, but then awarded concessions to private individuals, who paid the government a fixed charge per shipment. Through this procedure Castilla (as well as some of his predecessors) reinvigorated the private exchequer of some of the "good families" and made it possible for others to enter the plutocracy. The consolidation and conversion of the public debt, facilitated by the payments being made to the central government's treasury and by Castilla's policy of "fiscal responsibility," further benefited the coastal upper class, who were the principal bondholders. The established families and the new members of the coastal plutocracy rapidly amalgamated and engaged in the exploitation of cotton and sugar plantations. Their center of power was the city of Lima, and with their control of trade and banking, they came to exercise overwhelming influence over whoever was in control of the national government.

[12] A good example of such a description is the information collected by Basadre y Chocano in *Diez Años*.

The mismanagement of national affairs by Castilla's successors, and particularly by Colonel Balta, led members of the coastal elite to organize themselves into a political party whose main aim was to rid the country of government by military men; this organization was called Partido Civilista (literally, pro-civilian party). The election of 1872 gave its candidate Manuel Pardo (from one of the best-known families of Lima) a majority in the electoral college, which, in spite of Balta's pressure and attempts at coercion, ratified the preference for the Civilista candidate expressed by those who could vote. Faced with coups and countercoups, the Civilistas were able to mobilize the populace and defeat the *militaristas* in the street fighting that ensued. Thus Manuel Pardo became the first civilian president in Peru's history.

Although he made some attempts to settle the country's financial difficulties and improved education and administration, Pardo was weakened by the divisions within the Civilista party and by the newly created Democratic party, which Nicolás de Piérola led, as well as by a severe depression. Threatened by plots, revolts, and assassination attempts, Pardo determined to complete his term, which he did. The Civilistas, in an obvious attempt to make a deal with the military, nominated General Mariano Ignacio Prado, who then presided over the internal bankruptcy and the international discrediting of Peru, and led the country, however reluctantly, into the War of the Pacific.

The details of the War of the Pacific (Chile vs. Peru and Bolivia, 1879–84) have been presented in numerous works and are not directly relevant to this study.[13] Suffice it to say that Chile's victory was overwhelming; its forces occupied Lima from 1881 to 1884, disintegrated the armed forces of Peru, imposed its point of view in the Treaty of Ancón (the name of a resort town near Lima, where it was signed), and obtained the Tarapacá nitrate fields, which gave Chile a near-monopoly in the world nitrate market. It is an unquestionable fact that "the national humiliation suffered through the War of the Pacific is still sharply felt in Peru."[14]

[13] The best study is probably that of Jorge Basadre, *Historia de la República del Perú*, V, 2269–481 and VI, 2507–659.

[14] Owens, *Peru*, p. 49.

The war affected the Peruvian aristocracy, both that of Lima and that of the Sierra. Basadre concludes:

The war with Chile, the invasion, and the occupation provoked the collapse of the state machinery, the impoverishment of all social classes, the ruin or reduction of economic activities. This was, then, the fourth great jolt suffered by the traditional society in nineteenth-century Peru. . . . But none of the previous commotions . . . had the importance of the disaster consummated between 1879 and 1883.[15]

Some representatives of the ruling groups of the epoch benefited from the war. The best example may be that of President Prado, who commissioned himself to go to Europe toward the end of 1879; the trip was announced as an attempt to purchase modern weapons, which were badly needed. According to all available evidence, the weapons never came and the money with which they were going to be bought was never returned to the Peruvian treasury. Nor did Prado return to the country. The possibility that this money may have been an important contribution to the Prado family's wealth is widely mentioned in Peru, although not in writing.

Traumatic as the experience of the War of the Pacific had been, it did not alter Peruvian society. The Chilean victors were not reformers, and the defeat showed the incompetence of both the military establishment and the Civilistas. Control of the central government fell into the hands of the military, but in 1895 the popular *caudillo* Piérola took over after bitter fighting during which his mostly civilian followers defeated the army. With the armed forces subject to a professionalization process under the guidance of a French military mission requested by Piérola, the Democratic and Civilista parties shared the presidency until the end of World War I.

Both the Civilista and the Democratic organizations were controlled by elements of the coastal plutocracy; consequently, they improved trade, reorganized the country's finances, and modernized the city of Lima. The increase in trade and in governmental activity at the beginning of this century made possible the development of a middle class, mostly in the capital city. They identi-

[15] *Historia*, X, pp. 4730–31.

fied their interests with that of Augusto Leguía, who had entered the public scene under the Civilista label and had won the presidency in 1908 on that party's ticket. During his term, Leguía split with his party and was not able to influence the choice of his successor. The party was disintegrating, and Leguía returned to the presidency in 1919 by force at the head of a coalition of some members of the coastal plutocracy, the bureaucratic and commercial middle class, and a tiny but well-organized group of urban workers.

Leguía's dictatorship, known in Peruvian history as *el oncenio,* indicated the leader's keen awareness of his constituency. The laws which regulated working conditions of urban white- and blue-collar workers were improved and enforced. Even some plantation workers were able to organize, bargain collectively, and improve their working conditions. During his first term in office, Leguía had "won genuine and widespread popular support not only by his convincingly expressed hopes for the future development of Peru, which aroused patriotic fervor, but because he worked effectively to improve conditions in education and labor." It is not surprising, then, that during the *oncenio*

the middle and traditional upper classes had begun to cooperate in Peru and both seemed to be prospering from and enjoying the experience. . . . [Until] menaced by the effects of the depression, the traditional Peruvian aristocracy ceased its tolerant acceptance of and cooperation with new social elements, thinking only of protecting its own limited interests largely through alliance with the military.[16]

As might have been expected, the once popular dictator was overthrown by a military coup in August, 1930. Since then, military men and members of the traditional upper class have led the government, with the possible exception of José Luis Bustamante y Rivero (1945–48), a Catholic intellectual who was elected with APRA support and overthrown by the military three years later. The elections of 1956 and 1962–63 will be discussed in detail in future chapters.

[16] Fredrick B. Pike, "The Old and the New APRA in Peru: Myth and Reality," pp. 6, 14–15.

The one important event since 1920 that should be mentioned is the appearance of the Alianza Popular Revolucionaria Americana, or APRA, a party created by Víctor Raúl Haya de la Torre while in exile in Mexico City in 1924. This party was unquestionably the majority party in Peru from the 1930's until the late 1950's; during this period it represented the views of the lower classes and some middle groups, and particularly of those who were (and still are) unable to articulate their interests or to participate at all in Peruvian politics. As will be seen in Chapter 5, APRA has given up the reformist zeal expressed in the twenties, thirties, and forties, possibly in order to make itself more palatable to the power elites and to be allowed to take office. This change, coupled with the failure to take over the government, legally or otherwise, has disappointed many of its former followers, a process which will be explored in this study.

A recent observer has summarized the position of Peru in the mid-sixties:

Peru was changing slowly, possibly too slowly. Ownership and wealth were still concentrated in the hands of a small minority. The indigenous problem had never been approached carefully. Living standards were generally low and at the same time a growing percentage of the people were coming to know that there was a better way of life than the one they had. The centers of power were still to be found in the wealthy oligarchy (industrialists and capitalists now in its ranks, along with the great landowners), in the military, and in the Church. Organized labor was still relatively weak. Both the Church and the Army displayed attempts at modernization, albeit belatedly. But would they move rapidly enough to avoid a bloody uprising? [17]

[17] James C. Carey, *Peru and the United States, 1900–1962,* p. 13.

4. The Upper and Middle Classes in Contemporary Peru

The policies pursued by the Spanish Crown and the conquistadors toward the original inhabitants of Peru made inevitable the eventual development of a dichotomous society—a society that can be intuitively perceived by taking a walk around Lima and actually seen by travelling a few miles into the Andes. This white-Indian (or Creole-Indian) duality is not as clear-cut today as it was in colonial times, nor are the lines as rigidly drawn as they were then, but the two racial poles are still there; 400 years of more or less peaceful coexistence, however, have produced a transitional category, the mestizo (although "cholo" is preferred by most Peruvians).[1]

Unfortunately for those interested in studying Peruvian social reality, the latest census did away with racial distinctions on the grounds that the topic was offensive to many Peruvians; consequently, the most recent available figures go back to 1940. At that time, whites and mestizos constituted 52.89 per cent of the population; Indians, 45.86 per cent; Negroes and orientals, 1.25 per cent. The white element constitutes a small minority, perhaps 8 per cent of the population. In any case, these figures can be considered only as estimates inasmuch as there were no universal

[1] It seems that the word "cholo" originally meant "dog," although some have traced it to the name of a hat which the Indians wore. At any rate, the word was employed by the Spaniards to identify the offspring they had with Indian women, and it was soon incorporated into the Indian languages. Today it may have a friendly or derogatory connotation, depending on how it is used. For a long analysis see José Varallanos, *El Cholo y el Perú: Perú Mixto*, ch. 1.

criteria employed in the census (none exists today either, as will be discussed later), and at least one study has demonstrated that individuals who are normally considered Indians call themselves cholos and often become convinced that they in fact belong to the transitional group.[2]

The overwhelming majority of the whites and a large percentage of the cholos live in the Costa; the Indians, on the other hand, have remained in the Sierra, where the Spaniards found them in the sixteenth century. The figures in Table 7 show the concentration of Indians in five of the departments located in the Sierra, as well as the level of illiteracy and monolinguality.

Table 7. Indians, monolinguals, and illiterates in selected departments of the Sierra (in per cent)

Department	Indians	Monolinguals (Non-Spanish-speaking)	Illiterates
Puno	92.36	83.44	85.78
Huancavelica	78.68	78.84	83.18
Ayacucho	75.94	82.39	85.31
Cuzco	71.73	79.44	81.82
Apurímac	70.02	86.22	87.36

Source: Luis E. Valcárcel (ed.), *La Educación del Campesino,* p. 17.

The presence of these two races has, for a long time, divided the intellectuals, mostly in regard to the national identity of Peru and that which is Peruvian. The *indigenistas*, probably led by Luis E. Valcárcel, believe that the Indians and the Inca empire constitute

[2] On this point see Humberto Rotondo, Javier Mariátegui, and Pedro Aliaga, "Areas de Tensión en una Población Urbana Marginal," in Baltazar Caravedo, Rotondo, and Mariátegui, *Estudios de Psiquiatría Social en el Perú,* pp. 138–42. The authors said: "It is evident that a majority of those tested, except those of the Negro race, identify themselves with an ethnic group which they consider the majority: the mestizo. The fact that more than one Indian considers himself a mestizo brings to mind some sort of defense against possible rejection because of his own condition" (p. 141).

the real Peru and that the country's greatness will be achieved by returning to their way of life. Manuel González Prada, one of the most outstanding Peruvian intellectuals, claimed that the Indians constituted the essence of the Peruvian nation and that whatever vices they had acquired had been transmitted by the whites.[3] Valcárcel has restated this view:

> By defending the purity of the Indian communities against any type of white and mestizo involvement it is possible to claim that precious human capital will be saved; capital which neither oppression nor vices nor the diseases introduced by the discovery and conquest of this hemisphere have been able to destroy.[4]

The *hispanistas,* by no means unified in their goals, disagree with this view and feel that the Peruvian nation is, or should be, based on the whites, and to a certain extent on the cholos. They emphasize the vices and weaknesses of the Indians—their backwardness and their lack of initiative, for example—and feel that the best that can happen to Peru is that the Indian as such disappear, that he become a cholo and give up his sociocultural identity. One of the most articulate presentations of this view has been made by the distinguished scholar Francisco García Calderón; referring to the Peruvian Indian, he writes:

> On the one hand, it is necessary to respect his traditions regarding property and the family; on the other hand, it is necessary *to govern this race* through a wise trusteeship, *to make of the Indian* a worker or a soldier, to cause migrations within the country, *to liberate him* from his local traditions, his pet ideas, his monotonous and depressing framework; to extend, through special schools, the Spanish language; and to create an Indian elite which could *assist the government* in its civilizing enterprise. . . . The Spaniards, whose policy was wiser than ours, soon understood that freedom and individuality given suddenly to the Indians were dangerous and useless, and that the habit of living in an ordered and inflexible environment, under a well-meant trusteeship, was too deep-seated in them to destroy it by a legal gesture.[5]

---

[3] *Horas de Lucha,* pp. 311 ff. and *Páginas Libres,* p. 177. See also Eugenio Chang-Rodríguez, "Cosas y Gentes."

[4] Luis E. Valcárcel, *Mirador Indio,* p. 52.

[5] *En Torno al Perú y América,* p. 143 (emphasis added).

Another widely known Peruvian thinker, member of one of the most aristocratic families, descendant of those who led Peru at the beginning of its existence as a state, devout Catholic and prime contributor to the creation of the Catholic University of Peru, wrote in 1939:

I arrive in a triumphant and pacified Spain, which represents my ideals. . . . Today, we have not only the rational possibility, but the well-based probability of continuing the great and interrupted work of our common predecessors, to rebuild the spiritual and moral empire which, while respecting our intangible political sovereignty, our respective state independences, will realize the supreme unity of culture and sentiments, the *hispanidad,* not less effective and powerful because it has to be federative.

And reacting against the *indigenista* point of view, he said

The exclusive and frenetic *indigenismo,* the delirious and stubborn anti-Spaniard attitude, is no longer a licit error, after the careful historical rehabilitations produced and documented in the last decades: it is a combat weapon wielded by disloyal hands not subject or committed to the truth; it is the gesticulating, fraudulent, and ominous mask of the Bolshevik revolution, which is bent on stirring up and using the lowest racial rancors.[6]

The *indigenista* group has provoked reactions which, though probably in the minority, are heard among some whites and mestizos. A strictly racial approach is often found, with the explicit or implied suggestion that the Indians should be transformed and acculturated forcibly or eliminated. Other Latin American countries, and particularly Argentina, are cited as successful examples of this policy, either for their military actions against the Indians or for their encouragement of white European immigration. A representative of the anti-*indigenista* position writes:

I am quite sure of the future benefits of immigration for Peru: so that the future modern society, purified and reformed, may bring us generations inclined toward the truth and not to falsehood, to a good reputation and not to slander, to praising merit and work and not to libel, to

[6] José de la Riva Agüero, *Afirmación del Perú,* II, 38, 27.

virtue and not to pornography, to morality and not to immorality, and then, and only then, agitators and fanatics, the perverted and the ambitious, will cease to exist, for the good of all Peruvians.

And he feels that immigration, by which he obviously means European immigration, is the only possible solution to the racial problem.

Let us contemplate our demographic panorama and, humanely, let the 300,000 whites, with immigration, assist the more than 4,000,000 Indians. Let us contemplate our demographic panorama, and let the same 300,000 whites assist the more than 3,000,000 of mixed blood, with the same recourse to immigration. . . . Let us transform the vices of the Indian—cocaine and promiscuity—by the healthy customs of immigration.[7]

Regardless of this minority view, most Latin American scholars emphasize that the racial distinctions made in Peru, either by *indigenistas* or by *hispanistas*, refer mainly to the sociocultural characteristics of the individual and not to his ethnic background. They would agree with Valcárcel that, "it is justified to conclude that the word 'race' does not correspond only to a biological entity, but that it includes a certain economic and social status, as well as cultural participation."[8]

This view has been generally accepted by American and European writers. Frank Tannenbaum, writing about racial prejudice in the Latin American countries, observes:

It is social and economic and cultural. It is determined more by social status than by a sense that people of color are inferior in nature. . . . Any Indian, any mulatto, if he can escape from his poverty, if he can acquire the graces, the language, the manners, the dress, the schooling, and the associations that will admit him into the best society, will have no insuperable difficulties socially, especially if he is wealthy, and can,

[7] Leónidas A. Marquina, *¿A Dónde Vamos Nosotros? Pensamientos Peruanos*, pp. 39, 73, 75–76. For a comparison of these schools of thought, see also Harold E. Davis, "Trends in Social Thought in Twentieth Century Latin America," in John D. Martz (ed.), *The Dynamics of Change in Latin American Politics*, pp. 56–66.

[8] *Ruta Cultural del Perú*, p. 94.

if he has it in him, be elected to Congress, be a member of the cabinet, or become president of the country.[9]

But this point may be overemphasized or exaggerated, particularly when the purpose is to stress differences between Peru and other countries. It does not seem fruitful to consider this question in terms of what the Indian and the cholo should be, can be, or even will be, in Peruvian society. It would seem more useful, at least from the standpoint of political inquiry, to begin by dealing with what the relationship between the various groups has been and is. When that is done, the ability of a few mestizos or Indians to crash political, social, or economic barriers and perhaps enter the Peruvian upper class, or the discovery of a few whites in the ranks of the lower middle class, should not distract anyone from the fact that the majority of the upper class and upper middle class is overwhelmingly white and the lower class seems to be reserved for the Indians and some cholos. Ozzie G. Simmons, who perceived this situation some years ago, wrote:

It is apparent that the Creoles, as a group, occupy a dominant status with respect to the Indian, that this control reaches the economic, occupational, social, and political fields, and that the Indians, as a group, are subject to all the incapacities which commonly accompany a subordinate status, incapacities which consist in receiving a relatively small share of the rewards and privileges available in the society which includes both the Creole and the Indian. . . . Indians and Creoles seem to be living in widely separated worlds, mainly at the cultural and social levels, but also in many ways at the physical level. Regarding their activities, there seems to be a tendency on the part of the Creole to assess the Indian unfavorably, to underestimate him, to ridicule him, and sometimes to show an active hostility toward the Indian way of life, to consider him inferior and, as a result, the contacts with the Indian group are reduced to a minimum.[10]

In considering Peruvian society, then, the student cannot ignore the direct relationship between the social structure and the racial

[9] *Ten Keys to Latin America,* p. 50.

[10] "El Uso de los Conceptos de Aculturación y Asimilación en el Estudio del Cambio Cultural en el Perú," p. 3.

make-up of the population. That class, according to available evidence, seems to be more important than race should also be recognized. It is on this basis that the social, economic, and political status of the whites, the Indians, and the transitional group (cholos) will be studied.

The Creole Upper Class

The word Creole (*criollo*) is being used here and throughout this study to identify the heirs of Spanish power. The expression has numerous connotations, depending on how and under what circumstances it is used.[11] While these subtle interpretations may warrant a discussion in an anthropological or linguistic study, the more traditional meaning is assumed for the purpose of this analysis.

Unlike other Latin American countries and the United States, Peru never really tried to attract immigrants from those European countries that have had population surpluses. The latest available figures indicate that a total of 66,723 residents of Peru were born elsewhere; of these 22,131 came from other Latin American countries (the majority from Peru's neighbors), 15,008 from Asia, 5,843 from the United States and Canada, and 22,970 from Europe.[12] The limited data available indicates that this low proportion of foreigners has existed since independence. It seems to be rather apparent that those in power have not considered it advantageous to facilitate the immigration of European settlers. Obviously, this policy runs counter to the one followed by countries such as Argentina and Brazil (particularly the State of São Paulo), where it had important political consequences.[13]

The first and most obvious characteristic of the Creole minority is that they were and are located in the urban areas and mostly in the Costa. They are concentrated primarily in the Lima-Callao

[11] Some of the meanings of the word *criollo* in Peru are explored by Richard W. Patch, in his three-part report, "La Parada, Lima's Market."

[12] Computed by the author from *Sexto Censo Nacional de Población*, vol. I.

[13] On the political consequences of significant European immigration to Argentina see Gino Germani, *Política y Sociedad en una Época de Transición* . . . .

area, in Arequipa, Trujillo, and a few other coastal towns. Those whites found outside the coastal urban centers, and particularly in the highlands, are usually government officials sent from the capital, military officers, or owners of large landholdings who are inspecting their properties. But the descendants of the Spanish conquistadors and the small number of immigrants who came from other European countries after independence inherited the Spanish predominance in the coastal towns and valleys. In most cases they left the highlands to their mestizo counterparts, the offspring of white *encomenderos* and Indian women, who became the ruling class of the Sierra.[14]

This situation led to the development of two distinguishable segments within the traditional upper class: the "coastal plutocracy" and the Sierra landlords. In view of this division (which will be discussed later), it may be surprising to many that a unitary form of government was chosen, since this constitutional framework provided for a very high degree of concentration of power in Lima. In fact, there seems to have been an understanding, which can be traced back to the period immediately following independence, between the coastal plutocracy and the landlords of the highlands: the Creole heirs of the Spanish leadership became the liaison between the rest of the country and the outside world. The bankers and businessmen located in the Lima-Callao area maintained and increased their financial and commercial quasi monopolies and dominated the sources of capital.

The Sierra landowners, on the other hand, received a *de facto* veto power on appointments of local officials and magistrates (constitutionally reserved to the national government). Furthermore, they were able to block the enactment and enforcement of measures they opposed because of the region's legislative overrepresentation in relation to the voting population (See Tables 8 and 9). This overrepresentation of the Sierra has been the product of a vague constitutional provision (Article 88 in the present constitution) which states that the electoral system

---

[14] For a first-hand report on the landowners of the southern part of the Peruvian Sierra see Hugo Neira, *Cuzco: Tierra y Muerte,* especially pp. 21–24.

for legislators should show a "tendency to proportional representation," but leaves the allocation of seats and the selection of electoral procedures to an act of the legislature (Articles 90 and 91). Thus, the total number of Senate and House seats and their allocation among the departments is decided by the legislative majority and by executive approval and can be modified by the same procedure.

Table 8. Electoral participation in selected departments, 1963 election

Department *	A Estimated total population	B Estimated voting-age population	C Qualified voters	D Total number of votes	E D:A as %	F D:B as %	G C:B as %
Arequipa	428,900	208,350	105,659	100,337	23.4	48.2	50.7
La Libertad	643,500	343,564	117,390	112,568	17.5	32.8	34.2
Lima	2,301,200	966,504	802,910	757,403	32.9	78.4	83.1
Cuzco	667,000	320,155	59,506	53,844	8.1	16.8	18.6
Huánuco	362,700	163,295	37,767	35,608	9.8	21.8	23.1
Puno	750,300	383,758	60,467	58,411	7.8	15.2	15.8

Source: Prepared by the author with data from *Sexto Censo Nacional de Población,* vol. I, and from César Martín Saunders, *Dichos y Hechos de la Política Peruana.*

* The first three departments are in the Costa, the last three in the Sierra.

The constitution also provides that literacy is a voting requirement (Article 86); this qualification limits considerably the number of voters in most departments of the Sierra, as Tables 7 and 8 indicate. Consequently, the political importance of these departments at election time is limited, although a majority of the population lives there. However, in allocating Senate and House seats, a compromise is in effect, and the departments of the interior are awarded more seats than they are entitled to according to the voting population. These arrangements give the ballots of those who actually elect the senators and representatives much more weight than ballots of voters in the Costa, and particularly in the city of Lima. If we examine the figures of the latest congressional elections and compare urban coastal and highland

Table 9. Qualified voters and congressional representation in selected departments, 1963 election

Department *	Qualified voters	Representation		Ratio of votes per	
		Senate	House	Senator	Representative
Arequipa	105,659	3	9	35,220	11,740
La Libertad	117,390	3	8	39,130	14,674
Lima	802,910	9	20	89,212	40,146
Cuzco	59,506	3	15	19,835	3,967
Huánuco	37,767	2	8	18,884	4,721
Puno	60,467	3	11	20,156	5,497

Source: Prepared by the author from data reproduced in César Martín Saunders, *Dichos y Hechos de la Política Peruana.*

* The first three departments are in the Costa, the last three in the Sierra.

departments, it becomes clear that the votes of the Sierra voters count more; in other words, a smaller number of votes is needed to elect a Sierra senator or representative than to elect his coastal counterpart (see Table 9).

In order to complete the picture, it should be said that the percentage of those voting is substantially lower in the Sierra than in the Costa. Perhaps the most important reason for this difference is the literacy requirement, which excludes the great majority of the highland population (see Table 8). For all practical purposes, the legislators representing most departments in the Sierra are elected by a small minority of the local population—landlords, professionals, and merchants—either Creole or, in most cases, mestizo.

This overrepresentation of the votes of the Sierra serves the political purpose of the landowners only as long as a constitutional government is in office and they can have their own candidates elected (the question of governments outside the constitution will be considered later). In regard to the duly elected authorities, it should be sufficient to say that, because of the obvious correlation between education, class, and race in the highlands, the franchise is largely limited to the landowners, public officials, small-town merchants, teachers, and a few who, for lack of a more precise word, could be called "intellectuals." The illiterates, who also happen to be peasants and mostly Indians, play no electoral role, can do nothing for the candidates, and consequently cannot exercise any leverage over those who represent their department; this situation does not differ substantially from that existing in the American South, at least until recently. In fact, it is surprising that at times senators and representatives who attempt to articulate the interest of the rural lower class appear, but these congressmen usually are elected through the system of proportional representation, which guarantees certain seats to the minority. The minority has not had any influence in the legislative process.

Furthermore, it is as true in Peru as anywhere else that the campaign for office requires money. Consequently, either the candidate for a legislative post has wealth, which in the Sierra can only come from the ownership of land, or he has to appeal to the only source of help, the landowners' organizations. On occasions national parties such as APRA have subsidized the campaigns of some of their candidates running in the rural areas, but such candidates have seldom been successful when running against the departmental political "boss"—who serves as the bridge between the central administration and the region—and his backers, the power structure. Patronage and campaign expenses, plus the limited number of voters, tend to contribute to the perpetuation of the *status quo*, even when the electoral road is followed.

It has already been suggested that the upper class of the coastal area—many Peruvians prefer to call it the "plutocracy"—is quite different from the upper class of the Sierra. And cleavages are beginning to appear even among the "plutocrats." An accurate observer writes, "The traditional oligarchy, which derives its income from sugar, cotton, or metals sold in New York, Hamburg, or London, looks with mistrust upon the *nouveaux riches* who favor rapid industrialization, a source of dangers for many old-line oligarchs." [15]

In contrasting the upper class of the Costa with that of the

[15] François Bourricaud, *Poder y Sociedad en el Perú Contemporáneo*, p. 353.

Sierra, the first point that ought to be mentioned is their composition. To put it briefly, the upper class of the interior is more closed, drawn from a small number of families, more "aristocratic"; its coastal counterpart is a conglomeration of landowners, real estate developers, financiers, owners of small mining corporations, guano profiteers, people who benefited from renegotiations of Peru's foreign loans, producers of fish meal, and the like. In fact, it could be said that the coastal upper class has been flexible enough to co-opt almost every group or individual who could threaten its power, including ambitious military officers and enterprising foreigners, while at the same time doing its utmost to block or discourage attempts by them to threaten the established (if flexible) order. The exploitation of the guano, consolidation and conversion of the public debt, the development of financial institutions, the exporting of cotton and sugar, the War of the Pacific, and other economic ups and downs, have led a distinguished historian to write:

The aristocracy of the viceroyal era has been slowly disintegrating, although a few families are left, powerful from the economic standpoint because of their ties with urban property, the coastal plantations, and business. Peru's ten wealthiest families in 1899 were not the same as in 1879; by the same token, they differ from the ones of 1850 or 1800; but society has continued to be characterized by a patrician structure.

And after describing in detail the relative failure of the steps taken by the coastal upper class at various times to make it more difficult to "belong," the same author concludes:

The heterogeneous and mobile plutocracy which began to predominate at the economic level carried the peaceful injection of new blood (sometimes of other than Spanish origin) to the highest echelons. This implied a revolutionary phenomenon which, although it has shown certain aspects lacking in elegance, presents, on the whole, an encouraging picture. The frivolous records of this transcendental revolution can be found in the social pages of newspapers and magazines, unwillling to include the new names until 1919, and, in a certain way, until 1930, but later on open, in fact, to all those who wanted to apppear in print.[16]

[16] Jorge Basadre, *Historia de la República del Perú*, X, 4732–35.

This view is confirmed by former President José Luis Bustamante y Rivero, a scholar and careful observer of Peruvian society and a product of Arequipa's upper class, who emphasized that many members of the "plutocracy," regardless of their claims, were often in difficulty when asked to provide specific evidence of their status and even of their "authentic Peruvian origin." On another occasion, Mr. Bustamante y Rivero identified the members of Peru's coastal upper class as follows:

there are aristocrats of agrarian background; middle-class Peruvians who, through hard work, have moved up into fortune; immigrants who, with their effort, have reached an outstanding economic situation; and foreign investors who, by themselves or through their representatives, direct in the country the development of their abundant resources.[17]

Who are these plutocrats? A few examples will provide an idea of the configuration of the coastal upper-class "clans," an expression that comes readily to mind to describe them. The Aspillaga Anderson brothers own six sugar plantations in the Zaña valley, which occupy a total area of 18,962 acres; they also own or are major stockholders of four insurance companies, three banks, an airline, two building concerns, a brewery, two glass factories, and two electric companies. The Izaga family owns five sugar and rice plantations and leases another 16,505 acres, for a total of 27,907 acres; they also own or are major stockholders of two urban land development enterprises, two building concerns, a bank, and three financial and industrial corporations. The Gildemeister family, of German origin, are the largest producers of sugar and rice in the country; they own, through various corporations, 114 landholdings, which occupy 343,360 acres. This family has moved into the Sierra, where they have purchased approximately 1,050,000 acres, part of which is currently engaged in cattle raising and exploitation of timber; in addition, they have sizable investments in two fish-meal producing enterprises, two oil companies, a shipping concern, an insurance company, and a newspaper; there is evidence

[17] *Tres Años de Lucha por la Democracia en el Perú,* p. 75 (surprisingly, Mr. Bustamante y Rivero places himself in the middle class), and *Mensaje al Perú y Perú, Estructura Social,* p. 117.

that they also have investments in other countries, in some cases with the purpose of supplementing their activities in Peru, such as a sugar refinery in Chile. Finally, the de la Piedra family (one of the brothers, Julio de la Piedra, has presided over the Senate and is a ranking member of the Odriista party) owns twenty-two land-holdings in the northern coastal region, producing sugar, coffee, and rice, with a total area of 26,767 acres; they have also moved into the northern highlands, where they own four landholdings with a total area of approximately 380,000 acres, mostly used for cattle raising; outside agriculture, they either own or are major stockholders of one investment corporation, three importing companies, a cement enterprise, two land development concerns, and two general corporations.[18]

When compared with these examples, which are not unique but as representative as individual cases can possibly be, the upper class of the interior shows important differences. The most obvious one is the reliance on agriculture and the production of foodstuffs and other items directed toward domestic consumption; for various reasons, their share has shrunk to no more than 10 per cent of the total value of agricultural production.[19] Imports from neighboring countries and the extremely low purchasing power of the majority of the country's population tend to maintain low prices compared to the export commodities of the coastal plantations. Table 10 provides some indication of the constant and significant decrease of domestic agriculture's share of Peru's gross national product to only 13 per cent in 1964. If we remember that not all domestic agricultural products are grown in the Sierra (rice, one of the key foodstuffs, is cultivated in the Costa) and that the overwhelming majority of the 51.8 per cent of the country's population who live in the highlands derive their livelihood from agriculture, we can see that the economic power of the Sierra's upper class is constantly decreasing, at least in relative terms.

[18] This information has been compiled by the author from various sources, among which can be mentioned Carlos Malpica, *Guerra a Muerte al Latifundio* and *Los Dueños del Perú;* Banco de Crédito del Perú, *Vademecum del Inversionista;* and numerous newspapers and magazines.

[19] Bourricaud, "Remarques sur l'Oligarchie Peruvienne," p. 680.

Table 10. Distribution of the gross national product of Peru, by economic activity (constant 1960 prices)

Activity	Percentage of GNP		
	1950	1960	1964
Agriculture	29.0	23.0	19.6
Export	5.9	6.8	6.6
Domestic	23.1	16.2	13.0
Mining	7.1	10.4	7.6
Industry	15.8	16.5	19.6
Manufacturing	12.0	13.1	16.5
Small-scale	3.8	3.4	3.1
Services	5.2	5.6	5.3
Transportation and communication	1.7	1.6	1.4
Other	3.5	4.0	3.9
Energy	6.7	5.8	6.5
Electricity	1.8	1.7	1.6
Oil	4.9	4.1	4.9
Commerce	18.4	17.2	17.6
Finance	1.9	3.4	3.7
Government	12.1	12.9	7.8
Others	3.8	5.2	12.3

Source: Prepared by the author from data published in Fernando Romero, *Educación y Desarrollo Económico,* and Perú, Instituto Nacional de Promoción Industrial and Banco Industrial del Perú, *Situación de la Industria Peruana en 1964.*

The erosion of economic and political power in the provincial upper class began a century ago, when the fiscal reorganization of the country concentrated the government revenue in Lima. Without their own resources, the departments and municipalities became completely dependent on the central government, perhaps increasing the power of the regional "boss" and his backers in the area at everybody else's expense but decreasing the region's influence vis-à-vis the central government, controlled by the coastal plutocracy.[20] Slowly, the "good families" of the towns of the interior were separated from the "great families" of Peru. A member of

[20] Emilio Romero, *Perú por los Senderos de América,* ch. 16.

one of the former, saddened by this gap, has an idealistic view of the provincial upper class: "heads of model households, exemplary citizens, vigorous in their work, courteous in their manners, and dignified in every aspect of their lives. One word could outline all these qualities: lordliness." [21]

This erosion of power was compounded by the appearance in the Sierra of coastal and foreign investors, who began to compete with the provincial upper class for regional influence. The ancestors of the APRA leader Haya de la Torre have belonged to the provincial aristocracy since colonial times; they, together with the Cárdenas, Valdemar, Herrera, Urdapilleta y Portalanzas Bracamonte and a few other families, have provided regional leadership. One of Haya de la Torre's biographers writes:

Suddenly there appear the great corporations, the banks, and the powerful export houses, which sell abroad the sugar grown in the Chicama Valley. The foreign enterprises, lacking national control, begin to take over the landholdings, mines, and business enterprises. The downfall of the prestigious families deepens by the day. The old now-deprived owners, withdrawing, take refuge in administrative positions of little significance, but in accordance with their pride and social rank.[22]

This apparent alteration of the economic rules of the game is confirmed by another observer of Peruvian reality, who, after pointing out that the provincial aristocracy does not have a great deal of direct influence at the national level and limits itself to the exercise of power within its immediate area, warns that "in the last few years powerful business enterprises from the capital city have extended their activities to other parts of the country and have founded there branches which compete advantageously with the local government." [23] In other words, the coastal upper class seems to be taking the form of a national corporate elite, at the expense of local agrarian capital.

Who are these counterparts of the coastal plutocracy? Their

[21] Víctor Andrés Belaúnde, *Arequipa de mi Infancia*, p. 237.
[22] Felipe Cossio del Pomar, *Víctor Raúl: Biografía de Haya de la Torre*, p. 22.
[23] Bustamante y Rivero, *Perú, Estructura Social*, p. 119.

background can be easily traced to the Spanish *encomenderos* and *corregidores,* people who were granted control over the Indians. This does not mean that they are all white; in many cases the Spaniards, particularly in the highlands, either legalized their relations with Indian women or recognized their offspring. Some are white, most are dark-skinned mestizos, but there does not seem to be a difference because of this; if anything, the mestizos appear to be more conservative, less compromising than the whites.[24] To understand their position it is important to remember that the ownership of land constitutes evidence of a solid economic position and places the owner, *ipso facto,* in the category of the *gente decente* (literally "decent people" or "gentlemen," those who are entitled to deferential treatment). Landowners, because they are landowners, receive special consideration and are addressed in a certain way—only with certain words which indicate their status—and this treatment is extended to their immediate families; this social code is rigidly enforced by landlords and particularly by mestizos, who realize that the only difference between them and the rest of the population is their right of ownership.[25]

Comprehensive and reliable data regarding land ownership in Peru has been quite difficult to obtain, particularly in the Sierra, inasmuch as there is no nationwide registry of landholdings, and the Real Estate Registry (Registro de la Propiedad de Inmuebles) does not carry out its duties properly. Therefore, contradictory estimates abound, and it is necessary to rely on area surveys. Table 11 contains a list of the large landowners of the department of Puno, which has one of the highest percentages of Indians in the country (See Table 7, p. 43). The total area of the department is 1,799,560 acres, including its share of the 124,905 acres covered by Lake Titicaca (approximately half).

[24] See the description of the landowners' attitude toward land invasions in Neira, *Cuzco,* pp. 11–12, 21–23, and 78–79.

[25] For a discussion of this matter see Mario C. Vásquez, *Hacienda, Peonaje y Servidumbre en los Andes Peruanos,* ch. 6. A more comprehensive treatment of the subject can be found in Javier Sologuren, "Fórmulas de Tratamiento en el Perú;" Sologuren writes: "respectful treatment has become in the idiomatic usage of a large part of the Peruvian population—because of certain social and historic conditions—true submission formulae" (p. 256).

Table 11. Landholdings and landowners in the department of Puno, 1962

Name of land-holding	Registered owner	Total area including nonagricultural land (in acres)	No. of families living within property
"Asiruni"	Muñoz Najar	6,250	20
"Brenguela"	Emilio Vere	5,000	22
"Carumas"	Heirs of Arroyo	40,000	39
"Chasamaya"	Giraldo Mosodias	50,000	30
"Chincheros"	Valerio Sala	5,000	20
"Collacachi"	Muñoz Najar	75,000	200
"Conivires"	Giraldo Mosodias	11,875	23
"Curi"	Juan José Z.	10,000	40
"Haquechina"	L. Zavillanos	7,500	5
"Illpa Stud Farm"	John Rivie	3,500	5
"Llurigo"	Giraldo Mosodias	17,500	25
"Molina"	Heirs of Arroyo	16,250	26
"Moro"	Molina Brothers	22,500	5
"San Carlos"	Heirs of Arroyo	12,500	10
"San Fernando"	Heirs of Arroyo	13,900	19
"San José y Platería"	Heirs of Arce	3,875	16
"Sutuca"	J. Carrión	3,125	4
"Tanca Marca"	Heirs of Arce	7,500	27
"Tiritiri"	A. de Macedo	30,000	12
"Totorani"	Heirs of Arce	9,558	30
"Viluya" (including additions)	Muñoz Najar	750,000	250
"Viscachani"	C. Sánchez	2,500	5

Source: Hilda C. Sosa Secchi, "Estudio Socio-económico del Departamento de Puno," p. 49.

Further data on the concentration of landownership throughout Peru from a different perspective has been provided in Table 4 in Chapter 1. The apparent disparity between these two tables results because Table 11 includes all types of land while Table 4 includes only agricultural land. Only agricultural land is valuable for income, but total area is important, particularly in the Sierra, for reasons of prestige, possible mineral rights, and future agricultural use.

Some of the wealthiest landowners maintain residences in Lima and even abroad, but most reside in the downtown districts of departmental capitals or other nearby cities. The day-to-day administration of the haciendas is left to supervisors (*mayordomos*), almost always mestizos, who usually receive a share of the profits; these supervisors are often directly associated, at least in the peasants' minds, with the abuses to which the latter are subject. Consequently, the landlords manage to appear as providers and protectors of the peasants against civil authorities, need, and particularly the constant insecurity that the peasants experience.[26] This relationship is reinforced by social and religious customs, such as the *compadrazgo*.

The *de facto* psychological leadership of the landlords is reinforced by their actual control over the careers of central government officials serving in the area. This situation gives landowners in the Sierra ample opportunity to engage in partisan politics at the local level, to become regional "bosses," and sometimes to run for office. Most of them, however, utilize their power to try to extend their holdings, usually at the expense of small owners or of Indian communities.

Extremely conservative, not only in politics but also in the technical field, this Sierra upper class resembles Fred Riggs' description of that mythical society, "Agraria," which is supposed to have existed centuries ago.[27] Their system is based on quasi-feudal personal service, is underproductive, and is unwilling—to a certain extent unable—to modernize. Many writers have maintained that time is working against the system, and to a certain extent it has. François Bourricaud quite accurately presented the view held by most Peruvians when he wrote: "The lords of the capital are not

[26] On this point, see Julio Cotler, "La Mecánica de la Dominación Interna y del Cambio Social en el Perú," pp. 14–20.

[27] See "Agraria and Industria: Toward a Typology of Comparative Administration," in William J. Siffin (ed.), *Toward the Comparative Study of Public Administration*, pp. 23–116.

prepared to fight for the *gamonales* of the interior; too bad, but, after all, these backward landowners—and it can be said softly—will get only what they deserve." [28]

The fact that the redistribution of Sierra landholdings has not taken place yet can be explained essentially in terms of the over-representation of the landowners in Congress; a contributing factor is the relationship which seems to exist between the officer corps of the armed forces, particularly the Army, and the upper and middle classes of the interior, a point which will be discussed at length in Chapter 7. Some members of the coastal plutocracy sympathize with the Sierra's upper class, particularly in their desire to see "the sanctity of private property" respected and the principle of coercive land redistribution blocked. It is not too daring to assume that the coastal upper class finds it easier to identify with the Sierra landlords than with the peasants, although it may be willing to sacrifice the former, *if need be,* to protect itself.

The Industrial Upper Class

In some countries of Latin America the existence of a segment of the upper class which does not derive its resources from the ownership of land or related commercial activities cannot be denied. Both Argentina and Mexico (and perhaps southern Brazil) have developed industrial sectors clearly distinguishable from the traditional upper class, and often competing effectively with it.[29] As the name clearly indicates, the main source of wealth of this group is the control of the nation's industries, although some mem-

[28] *Poder y Sociedad,* p. 337.

[29] For evidence of the existence of an industrial upper class in Argentina see José Luis de Imaz, *Los que Mandan,* ch. 7 and 8; and Dardo Cúneo, *Comportamiento y Crisis de la Clase Empresarial,* pp. 43–65, 73–93, 129–36, 167–90, and 267–76. On Mexico see Pablo González Casanova, *La Democracia en México, passim.* On Brazil consult Helio Jaguaribe, *Desenvolvimento Económico e Desenvolvimento Político,* ch. 4. A different point of view in regard to Argentina is expressed by Gustavo Polit, "The Industrialists of Argentina," in James Petras and Maurice Zeitlin (eds.), *Latin America: Reform or Revolution?*, pp. 399–430; unfortunately, Mr. Polit relies on old sources for much of his documentation and does not provide sufficient evidence to refute the well-researched studies of Imaz and Cúneo.

bers may turn to land ownership for prestige or insurance. A condition for the existence of such a group is that industries be significant and independent enough to provide the resources necessary to compete. This implies a substantial percentage of economically active inhabitants deriving their livelihood from industry and their being responsible for a sizable share of the gross national product. Furthermore, this requires that the industrial upper class be willing to take its disagreements with the other groups into the national political arena.

Table 12. Size of Peru's manufacturing establishments, by number of workers, 1962

Size	Factories		Workers		Workers per factory
	Number	%	Number	%	
Less than 5 workers	1,037	25	2,963	2	3
5 to 20 workers	1,842	44	20,077	13	11
More than 20 workers	1,272	31	128,634	85	101
Total	4,151	100	151,674	100	

Source: Fernando Romero, *Educación y Desarrollo Económico*, p. 110.

A superficial review of the statistical data available shows that Peru does not fit this description. Table 12 shows a total of slightly more than 150,000 workers employed in manufacturing establishments, 85 per cent of whom work in factories employing more than 20 workers. This is approximately 4 per cent of the economically active population. (Although Table 13 indicates that 19.1 per cent work in "industry," this category unquestionably includes a very large number of artisans, repairmen, and others who do not "manufacture.") The industrial sector accounts for 19.6 per cent of Peru's gross national product (see Table 10, p. 56). But a substantial portion of this total—59 per cent in 1963—comes from the production of light consumer goods such as clothing, foodstuffs, beverages, and the like. An intermediate sector which includes chemicals, woods, construction materials, and metals seems to be gaining in importance; it accounted for 40 per cent of total manufacturing in 1963. However, most of this intermediate sector and of whatever heavy industry exists is controlled by foreign investors, and even managed by foreigners on temporary assignments who cannot be said to constitute a Peruvian industrial upper class. In the field of extractive industries, more than 90 per cent of the oil production is handled by foreign firms, mostly by the International Petroleum Company, a subsidiary of Standard Oil of New Jersey. The large mining enterprises are in the hands of Cerro de Pasco Corporation, Southern Peru Mining Corporation, and Marcona Mining Company, all foreign firms. Even in textiles, the most important firm is Duncan Fox & Company, Ltd., controlled by British capital. Management and supervisory personnel in the textile industry are overwhelmingly non-Peruvian and are usually individuals with very little formal training.[30] As William F. Whyte concluded, "in any gathering of industrialists in Peru today, you will find a large proportion of immigrants and sons of immigrants." [31]

Table 13. Distribution of the economically active
population of Peru, 1960

Activity	Economically active persons	Percentage of total economically active population
Agriculture	2,352,000	57.6
Mining	74,000	1.8
Industry	774,000	19.1
Services	204,000	4.9
Commerce	231,000	5.7
Finance	17,000	.4
Government	138,000	3.4
Others	290,000	7.1
Total	4,080,000	100.0

Source: Oficina de Estudios para la Colaboración Económica Internacional, *Perú: Síntesis Económica y Financiera,* part 2, p. 2.

[30] David Chaplin, "Industrial Labor Recruitment in Peru," p. 30.

[31] "Culture, Industrial Relations, and Economic Development: The Case of Peru," p. 585.

When the researcher investigates the ties of the industrialists, such as Luis Banchero and Oscar Ferrand, he finds that they and their families have joined the Jockey Club and other exclusive organizations (see Chapter 9), that they own land and have become closely associated socially and commercially with the traditional upper class, and that it would be difficult to find a conflict of interests with the coastal sector of the traditional upper class which the industrialists have taken to the political arena. The fact that Eduardo Dibos Dammert, from one of the largest landowning families in the Costa, was recently acting president of the National Industrial Society while Enrique Dibos Dammert, his brother, is a member of the board of the National Agrarian Society is highly illustrative. In the words of David Chaplin:

All too often we find owners and managers more mercantilist than industrial in their actions and beliefs. One of the major obstacles to industrial progress in Peru is that there does not yet exist a powerful, cohesive group of "industrialists," that is, men whose primary economic concern is a manufacturing operation. In many cases Peruvian textile mills are peripheral activities of men whose major interest is more apt to be commerce and real estate speculation.[32]

The mercantilist beliefs mentioned by Mr. Chaplin can be traced back to the traditional Spanish preference for dignified "country-gentleman" and income-producing activities which are in no way related to manual labor. But there are economic reasons too: with a deficient transportation system, lack of skilled labor, and an extremely limited market, industry often appears as a risky enterprise, particularly when there have been periods of significant inflation. Furthermore, a degree in law or medicine is usually not sufficient to manage or supervise an industrial enterprise, and specialists from outside the family circle tend to be distrusted. Commerce and real estate speculation appear to be simpler activities which can be performed from a pleasant office and do not require highly specialized knowledge, particularly when capital is concentrated in relatively few hands.

[32] "A Discussion of Major Issues arising in the Recruitment of Industrial Labor in Peru," p. 18.

The possibility of an independent, counterbalancing industrial sector in the future will be discussed in Chapter 11. But it may very well be that the significant facilities given by the successive administrations to foreign investors, plus the control of banking and the rapid co-optation of creative industrialists, will provide a way acceptable to the traditional upper class to have industries without developing a strong native industrial upper class.

The Middle Classes

It has been said too often that Peru—like most, if not all, Latin American countries—does not have a middle class or that, having it, the middle class does not fulfill the expectations of those studying it. These expectations usually are based on the experiences and background of the researchers who, explicitly or implicitly, have developed a conception of an ideal middle class not too different from that of the most advanced Western countries. When the ideal is nowhere to be found, they conclude that there is no middle class or that it is not performing its role. In many cases, the middle class rates only a passing reference.[33]

If the middle class is accepted as that social grouping which separates two extremes in a hierarchical conception of society and if it is recognized that certain occupations and income levels carry with them membership in this segment of society, then Peru has had a middle class for a long time. It can be added, with the understanding that it will be discussed later, that the Peruvian middle class has not behaved the way many observers had said it should.

Because this class is in the middle, it is not surprising that it should be extremely interested in its relationship with those above and below it. In Peru, where the upper class can be identified easily:

the middle class can very well be defined by its exclusion from the elite, either because it has been excluded against its will or because it refuses

[33] Examples can be found in William L. Schurz, *Latin America: A Descriptive Survey,* pp. 303–09; Martin C. Needler, *Latin American Politics in Perspective, passim.;* James L. Busey, *Latin America: Political Institutions and Processes,* pp. 7–9; and Ronald J. Owens, *Peru,* ch. 4.

to enter. Since, on the other hand, the country has a high percentage of illiterate Indians, the middle class will perceive everything that distinguishes it from them, particularly when the hierarchical distinction between the high and the low is symbolically reinforced by the qualitative, racial, and cultural distinction between Indians and non-Indians.[34]

Since independence Peru has had its physicians, pharmacists, dentists, lawyers, teachers, professors, small businessmen and shop owners, public employees, and military officers; all these occupations carry with them middle-class status. But what many observers are searching for is the relationship of these members of society to the upper class. Students of Peruvian society see its middle class acting as an appendage or extension of the upper class. When they compare this position with the often unrealistically idealized situation in the highly developed Western countries, they become unwilling or reluctant to award the Peruvian middle class the "brand name." [35]

It is possible to ascertain that the middle class of Peru constitutes between 18 and 20 per cent of the economically active population and receives between 40 and 45 per cent of the national income. The figures presented in Table 14 tend to confirm this assertion, although they do not provide a neat class breakdown (the skilled blue-collar workers would not be members of the middle class regardless of their income).

But the middle class that has existed and to a large extent continues to exist in Peru has not been politically, socially, or economically independent. Spanish colonial tradition and institutions led to the formation of a state bureaucracy tightly controlled by a centralized government within each viceroyalty. Its members, plus the liberal professions, provided the foundation of the middle class, a stratum which had a stake in the system from the very beginning. This middle class was, and is, urban, and it has developed with the constant growth of the urban areas (indicated in Table 5 in

[34] Bourricaud, *Poder y Sociedad,* p. 54.

[35] An example in regard to the Latin American middle class in general, is William S. Stokes, *Latin American Politics,* pp. 22–24.

Table 14. Distribution of income in Peru, 1960

Social Group	% of economically active population	Average monthly income (in sols)	% of national income
Large landowners and investors	.1	100,794	19.9
Highly-paid professionals, executives, small investors	.4	8,000	6.3
White-collar and skilled workers	20.0	1,500	46.7
Unionized urban and coastal rural workers	22.8	681	14.2
Nonunionized Sierra and Selva peasants	56.7	117	12.9

Source: Prepared by the author from data provided by Edgardo Seoane, *Surcos de Paz,* pp. 31–40 and partially reproduced in Claudio Véliz (ed.), *Obstacles to Change in Latin America,* p. 86.

Chapter 1). The officer corps of the armed forces, particularly when they acquired a professionalized appearance, contributed new members.

Peruvian urban growth has preceded industrial development (as in other Latin American countries and contrary to most advanced Western countries) and has led to the formation of a middle class of limited usefulness, with an indefinite role in the type of society which still exists in the country; nevertheless, it provided occupation for a somewhat educated segment of the population, which constituted the articulated public opinion of the urban areas and developed a loud political voice, particularly under the Leguía dictatorship.

But the Peruvian upper class has been providing a solution to what may have become a difficult problem. It has provided for the absorption of the old middle-class segment into the civil and military bureaucracy and even into private organizations such as corporations and banks, thus subsidizing the middle class and giving it a clear stake in the *status quo.* Naturally, there is a built-in limitation in this type of subsidy, since its uncontrolled growth would place a heavy financial burden on the upper class. The limit has been maintained in part, at least until recently, by a deficient educational system: most secondary schools are privately owned and quite expensive, and the few universities have complex admission requirements and practically no scholarships.[36]

The procedure has been identified in Brazilian politics by Helio Jaguaribe as *o estado cartorial* (literally, "the notarial state") and can best be conveyed by the expression "politics of clientele."[37] It consists in a *quid pro quo* of at least passive acceptance of the system in exchange for stable employment and a dignified role in society. This "politics of clientele" provided the Peruvian middle class with a tolerable way of living, which could have been justified by the apparent aim of increasing services but which was actually intended to make available positions of varying usefulness in the economic survival of this urban stratum. This was particularly true of the armed forces, whose size and equipment were, and are, almost universally justified at all social levels by real or imaginary dangers posed by the country's neighbors.

Upon perceiving the different outlook of this middle class, writers denounce it for slavishly aping the aristocracy and for imitating its habits, such as those of conspicuous consumption and of not carrying packages in public.[38] Evidence from various sources and personal observation indicate that these charges are often true: it is unquestionable that most members of the middle class

[36] The best analysis of Peruvian education can be found in Fernando Romero, *Educación y Desarrollo Económico*. Other writings which deal with this problem are: José Jiménez Borja, "La Universidad Peruana en el Siglo XX," in *La Universidad y el Pueblo*, I, 90–108; F. M. Arriola Grande, *Discurso a la Nación Peruana*, pp. 215–25; Víctor Andrés Belaúnde, *La Realidad Nacional*, pp. 37–53, 195–96, and 199–206; and Luis Alberto Sánchez, *El Perú: Retrato de un País Adolescente*, ch. 6.

[37] The concept of *o estado cartorial* has been developed by Helio Jaguaribe in "Política de Clientela e Política Ideológica." The concept also appears in his *O Nacionalismo na Atualidade Brasileira*, p. 40, and "The Dynamics of Brazilian Nationalism," in Claudio Veliz (ed.), *Obstacles to Change in Latin America*, pp. 168–69.

[38] Stokes, *Latin American Politics*, p. 23.

on the whole accept and adopt the social, economic, and political values handed down to them by the upper class, more so perhaps in the Sierra than in the Costa, but not by a significant margin. On those issues where there is disagreement between the two sectors of the upper class, they tend to show agreement with their immediate leaders; in most instances, both social groups share their concern about attempts to alter the *status quo,* even though the alteration would only threaten (at least directly) the interest of the upper class—as in the case of the occupation of landholdings by peasants in the Cuzco area a few years ago.[39] Thus, Peru appears to be a country in which

the existence of a middle class in cities not yet industrialized is in no way incompatible with the fact that its conduct conforms to certain traditional types. The middle classes may thus, in some circumstances, represent a force committed to maintaining the traditional social system, despite the fact that they appear to favor the introduction of various symbols of modernity.[40]

When the individual member of the Peruvian middle class feels that the present system offers him sufficient opportunities for upward mobility, or when he is satisfied with the rewards which society is presently bestowing upon him and confident that they will continue, he will support the *status quo.* If he comes to believe that he can "do better" through primary connections and personal relations than through a system which accepts efficient performance and merit as the criteria for recruitment and improvement, then he will tend to model his behavior and standards after those of the upper class. This is exactly what has been happening, and to a certain extent is continuing to happen, in the country: with its minimum requirements apparently met by the existing sociopolitical system, the dependent middle class "seeks alliance with the powerful and privileged groups in the community, and . . . thus contributes to the maintenance of the existing order." [41]

[39] This is reported in Neira, *Cuzco, passim.*

[40] Luis Ratinoff, "The New Urban Groups: The Middle Classes," in Véliz, *Obstacles to Change,* pp. 67–68. A difference between modernization and development is implied by Ratinoff.

[41] *Ibid.,* p. 69.

The above paragraphs, of course, imply the existence of another sector of the middle class, a sector whose interests are not tied to the traditional upper class engaged in the production of foodstuffs or raw materials for export. This "new middle class" or "modernizing middle class" is usually identified with the by-products of industrial development (engineers, scientists, and technicians, for example), but there is no reason why white-collar workers, physicians, and lawyers canot be included as long as they do not rely on the traditional system for employment.[42] Because of the limited significance of the industrial sector in Peru and the overwhelming control exercised by the traditional upper class, however, the political weight of the "new middle class" is presently insignificant. Nevertheless, all available evidence tends to indicate that this sector of the middle class will grow as industrial development and independent professional activities multiply; the evidence of countries not too different from Peru, such as Mexico, warrant this belief.[43]

It would be a mistake, though, to confuse the "new middle class" with the urban population, even in Lima. The fact that this sector of the middle class is found exclusively in the urban areas does not mean that most residents of the urban areas should be considered as belonging to it. As we shall see, a substantial proportion of the urban population can be considered urban only in terms of physical location, but not in terms of enjoying the benefits normally associated with urban living.

[42] In regard to the concept of the "new middle class" in Peru see Bourricaud, "Remarques"; José Matos Mar, "Consideraciones sobre la Situación Social del Perú". Elsewhere in Latin America see Jorge Graciarena, *Poder y Clases Sociales en el Desarrollo de América Latina,* pp. 155–68; Carlos M. Rama, *Sociología del Uruguay,* p. 88; Francisco C. Weffort, "Estado y Masas en Brasil," *Revista Latinoamericana de Sociología,* 1:53–71 (March, 1965); and Celso Furtado, "Political Obstacles to Economic Growth in Brazil," in Véliz, *Obstacles to Change* pp. 145–61.

[43] See González Casanova, *La Democracia,* ch. 6.

5. The Lower Class in Contemporary Peru

Students of the social reality of the Latin American countries have issued warnings against the indiscriminate use of the term "class," its economic and noneconomic meaning, its perception by the subjects, and particularly the confusion of social class and subculture. Alfonso Trujillo Ferrari goes so far as to write, in reference to Latin America:

Any attempt to utilize this scheme of subcultures to prove the social classes in Latin America will be inoperative, since by trying to verify the processes of social sedimentation or to develop structures of social stratification, by pointing out the strata in which each of the subcultures would be located, only subcultural stratified contents and not social classes will be englobed.

And yet he recognizes that it is possible "for a social class to be contained within one characteristic subculture which could be perfectly defined as a social class." [1]

Direct observation and all available evidence indicate that subcultures provide the bulk of social classes in Peru, as we have seen in dealing with upper and middle classes. This situation is reinforced at the bottom of Peruvian society: the various sectors of the lower class are cholos in various stages of transition (mostly in the urban areas and coastal plantations) and Indians (the majority, mostly in the highlands). The information in Table 14 indicates that 79.5 per cent of the population of Peru, if not more, can be placed in this social layer.

[1] "Incidencias Teóricas en el Estudio de las Clases Sociales en Latinoamérica," pp. 552–53.

The Cholo

There is no agreement among sociologists and anthropologists re-garding the moment when an Indian becomes a cholo since, as in-dicated earlier, the difference is sociocultural and economic rather than racial. This disagreement becomes more pronounced among laymen, and a person who is considered an Indian in one commu-nity may be judged a cholo in another. Nor would self-awareness help us in solving the problem, since persons normally considered Indians (at least by those who conducted the studies) often iden-tified themselves as mestizos, particularly in their dealings with non-Indians. There is agreement on one point, however: the major-ity of the population at all levels considers it more advanced to be a cholo than an Indian. There is the temptation to use the word "better" here, but this may not be true of the landlords and of some *indigenista* thinkers, who claim that the Indian possesses a natural goodness, which he loses when he becomes a transitional cholo. A study of an Andean community found it impossible to de-termine for 36 per cent of the families whether they belonged to the Indian or the cholo group; the study concluded:

Through the years the observable criteria by which one could distin-guish an Indian from a *mestizo* have become modified, disappeared, or become common to both groups. The greatest difference now lies in social participation and the attitudes which the people hold with respect to the members of the other class. On the surface, differences seem to be greater between rich and poor, educated and uneducated, more cosmopolitan and less cosmopolitan, than between classes on the basis of specific cultural traits. Social participation itself, while provid-ing the most important difference, is subject to variation, and with con-stant mobility new class members are little by little accepted into the *mestizo* group.[2]

[2] Richard N. Adams, *A Community in the Andes: Problems and Progress in Muquiyauyo*, p. 88. For evidence of the superior prestige of the cholo over the Indian see Mario C. Vásquez, "Changes in the Social Stratification of an Andean Hacienda" in Dwight B. Heath and Richard N. Adams (eds.), *Contemporary Cultures and Societies of Latin America*, pp. 405–23; and Paul L. Doughty, "Pitfalls and Progress in the Peruvian Sierra," in Robert B.

In fact, the cholo can be best described as a transitional element who has given up, at least temporarily, his Indian group and its characteristic cultural patterns in order to seek an improvement in his economic situation. The decision as to whether he constitutes the "new Peruvian race," as some writers claim, should be left to the anthropologists. While it is possible to find people of mixed racial origin at all socioeconomic levels, it is clear that the great majority of the cholos, as defined above, are found in the upper echelons of the lower class: organized blue-collar and plantation workers, small-town shopkeepers, noncommissioned officers in the armed forces, policemen, and the like.[3]

What is perhaps more important is that the cholo appears to be much more ambitious than the Indian in the political and economic arena. It is true that one with sufficiently powerful political and economic ambitions becomes, almost by definition, a cholo; in no other way can the migration from the Sierra towns and villages, where the cholos enjoy a relatively high status, be explained.[4] When they move to the large urban centers and plantations of the Costa, they find themselves at the bottom of the social pyramid but with a better opportunity to improve their economic situation and to participate in politics at a higher level than before. Studies

---

Textor (ed.) *Cultural Frontiers of the Peace Corps,* pp. 229–31. Regarding the problem of self-identification see Humberto Rotondo, Javier Mariátegui, and Pedro Aliaga, "Áreas de Tensión en una Población Urbana Marginal: Los Prejuicios Raciales," in Baltazar Caravedo, Rotondo, and Mariátegui, *Estudios de Psiquiatría Social en el Perú,* pp. 138–42.

[3] The identification of the mestizo as the "new Peruvian race" is found in José Varallanos, *El Cholo y el Perú: Perú Mixto,* particularly ch. 2, where he indicates that cholos can be found at all socioeconomic levels. This is racially true, but it has already been pointed out that the racial aspect has little relevancy; a general, a banker, and a large landowner are not called "cholos" by the general population, no matter what the color of their skin is. See Emilio Romero, *Perú por los Senderos de América,* particularly ch. 13.

[4] At the risk of belaboring the point, it may be useful to consider the conclusion of William F. Whyte and Lawrence K. Williams that "there is an expectation on the part of both groups that the mestizos will manage and finance village affairs and that the Indians will supply the muscle needed for whatever improvements are undertaken ("Structural Dimensions of Rural Development and Change in Peru," p. 16.)

of shantytowns (called *barriadas* in Peru) have demonstrated that the migrants from the highlands included a high percentage of mestizos who were considered members of the middle or even of the upper class (the latter term may be of relative validity) in their native villages.[5] But, as the cholos have accurately perceived, this loss in terms of relative social status will in all likelihood be compensated by an improvement in the scale of living, a change to the money economy, and a greater possibility for their children to obtain a better education.[6] They are willing to subject themselves to greater insecurity, more impersonal relationships, and an acute housing problem in order to obtain these benefits.

The political role of the cholo should be considered in two contexts. In the rural areas, small towns, and villages of the highlands, he is in effect the intermediary between the regional upper class and the Indians. One of the important reasons for this is his ability to speak both Spanish and Indian dialects; another is his familiarity with the customs and the way of life of those who occupy the bottom of the socioeconomic structure. It is in this capacity of middleman that he becomes rural policeman, minor official, or retail storekeeper. In these positions he benefits sometimes one side, sometimes the other, and mostly himself, *when he has a choice.* But more often he does not have a choice and performs as the extension of the local traditional upper class.

There are other alternatives in the urban areas, but there is no need for the role of go-between. Some cholos become semimigrants by traveling constantly between the cities and their native towns, taking local products to the city market and city goods to their neighbors. In the process they may perform minor administrative chores, particularly if the city is Lima and if the representatives of the central government in their localities are unsympathetic to the requests of the inhabitants. The cholo who has migrated permanently can, and usually does, join the organization of

[5] See Vásquez, "Changes," pp. 408 and 414–16; and Adams, *A Community in the Andes, passim.*

[6] José Matos Mar, "Migration and Urbanization—The 'Barriadas' of Lima: An Example of Integration into Urban Life," in Phillip M. Hauser (ed.) *Urbanization in Latin America,* pp. 170–90.

natives of his region which is likely to exist in the city. If he achieves a position of leadership he may become his region's unofficial and unpaid ambassador before the authorities. But competition is keen, and university students and white-collar workers seem to have the upper hand in holding office.

The only alternative is for the lower-class cholo to enter the political arena in his new environment, either as a member of his shantytown's association, of his labor union (if his line of work is organized), or of a political party. Obviously, his best opportunities lie in the first two, but even there competition is keen, and long residence in the city is an essential, although unwritten, requirement. His vote, if he is literate, diminishes in value because the district is larger and a higher percentage of the population is likely to enjoy the franchise. In brief, his political significance drops as he moves to an urban area. The situation of those who migrate to the modern, unionized plantations of the Costa or to the large mines or oil fields does not vary substantially from that of the new urban dwellers.

Not every cholo who migrates to the urban areas or to the coastal plantations obtains the type of employment he was hoping for when he decided to move. It is clear from the figures on urban growth and on the growth of the industrial sector in Peru—most of which is located in Lima—that the process of urbanization is progressing faster than the country's industrial base (see Tables 5, 10, and 12).

Hard data is particularly difficult to obtain, but it has been estimated that the physical volume of industrial production grew 101.2 per cent between 1952 and 1961, or at an average yearly rate of approximately 10 per cent.[7] Even if we assume that this growth rate is reflected in the number of industrial positions (it need not be that way, and it probably was not), the size of the base is so small, as indicated in Table 12, that the total number of new industrial jobs throughout the nation in any one year will not suffice to provide employment for those who enter the job market in the city of Lima alone (see Table 5). And it must be remembered that

[7] David A. Robinson, *Peru in Four Dimensions,* p. 359.

not all industrial jobs are unionized and thus equally attractive and rewarding.[8]

An estimate for the period 1950–60 indicates that, of approximately 1,300,000 who entered the labor market, only 38,000 found employment in manufacturing and 20,600 in mining and petroleum activities.[9] Thus, it is logical to expect that a substantial percentage of those who migrate to the urban areas are forced to engage in menial occupations or in services that do not represent a meaningful improvement over what many of them knew in the Sierra. On the other hand, these occupations may constitute a steppingstone to more rewarding activities, as some recent case studies of the inner slums of Lima indicate.[10] The universality of these case studies, however, should be considered in relation to the above data.

The general conclusion is that the cholo loses individual sociopolitical significance as he migrates to the urban areas and, on the whole, becomes more alienated from the political process. One report says that in one of Lima's inner slums: "there is a general lack of political feeling. Political organizers have little success in organizing movements, even those which profess to seek the betterment of the slum-dwellers' conditions." [11] A similar situation is found in the shantytowns that surround all urban areas, as Table 15 shows in reference to two of them in Lima's metropolitan area. These findings contradict studies carried out in other countries, where a higher level of participation existed; this disparity seems to be a reflection of the differences between the countries involved.[12]

The limited political involvement of the urban lower class prob-

[8] James L. Payne, *Labor and Politics in Peru: The System of Political Bargaining*, pp. 15–16, 23.

[9] Jorge Grieve, *Análisis de la Economía Peruana, 1950–62*, cited in Fernando Romero, *Educación y Desarrollo Económico*, p. 12.

[10] Richard W. Patch, "La Parada, Lima's Market."

[11] *Ibid.*, part III, p. 12.

[12] See Gino Germani, "Inquiry into the Social Effects of Urbanization in a Working Class Sector of Greater Buenos Aires," in Hauser (ed.), *Urbanization*, also by the same author, *Política y Sociedad en una Época de Transición . . .* , *passim;* and Carlos A. de Medina, *A Favela e o Demagogo*, *passim.*

Table 15. Responses to questions concerning political involvement in two shantytowns near Lima, 1965

	Responses	
Position	Pampa Seca (%)	El Espíritu (%)
Have little or no interest in national government activities	64	72
Have little or no interest in city government activities	71	75
Seldom or never discuss politics with family	80	91
Seldom or never discuss politics with friends and neighbors	82	91
Seldom or never discuss politics with co-workers	87	90
Do not participate in meetings and demonstrations	72	75
Partially or totally agree that political activity produces nothing	64	68
Have no political party affiliation	54	53

Source: Prepared by the author from data provided by Daniel Goldrich, Raymond B. Pratt, and C. R. Schuller in "The Political Integration of Lower Class Urban Settlements in Chile and Peru: A Provisional Inquiry."

ably reflects its marginal socioeconomic situation. The physical location of these cholos in the city does not make them city dwellers, if that status is defined in terms of the availability of facilities associated with urban living. Their housing is often temporary and mostly inadequate. There are no sanitary facilities, and drinking water is difficult to obtain; usually one or two pumps are found in the *barriada,* and the residents wait in line with huge containers which they use to take the water to the houses. The increasing number of migrants coming mostly from the Sierra swells the supply of unskilled and semiskilled labor. Consequently, wages remain relatively low and a large number of newcomers are forced to go into activities such as personal service, street peddling, sale of lottery tickets, shoe-shining, and "protection" of parked cars, which produce little for the individuals who are forced to engage in them and contribute nothing to the nation's economy. This underemployment, together with the unemployment (for which there are no reliable figures in Peru), has already been sufficiently described elsewhere.[13] Yet, the indications are that the cholos are better off in the tenements and shantytowns of Lima, Chimbote, or Arequipa—where they have access to some health and social services—than in their home towns and villages; it would seem that relatively few go back, although here, again, adequate data is lacking.

The Rural Lower Class

From what are these mestizos escaping? To perceive their view of society and share their thinking it is necessary to look directly at the rural areas of Peru, and more specifically of the Sierra, where the great majority of its rural population lives. Table 3 (p. 8) and Table 16 provide an insight into the income distribution by region and within the highlands; these tables indicate that the economic significance of the Costa has increased at the ex-

Table 16. Yearly gross national and per capita
income, by region (constant 1960 prices)

Region	% of G.N.P.		Sols per capita	
	1950	1960	1950	1960
Costa	51.6	55.2	6,772	6,908
Sierra	43.0	40.6	2,564	2,523
Selva	5.4	4.2	1,536	1,168

Source: Fernando Romero, *Educación y Desarrollo Económico,* pp. 184–85.

pense of the other two regions and that the per capita income of both the Sierra and the Selva has decreased (in the first case slightly) in the ten-year period under consideration. And the brunt of this decrease has been borne by the owners of *minifundia* and

[13] See, for instance, Secretariat of the United Nations Economic Commission for Latin America, "Creation of Employment Opportunities in Relation to Labour Supply," in Hauser (ed.), *Urbanization,* pp. 118–48.

the landless peasants, whose income is equivalent to 35 to 40 United States dollars a year.

It is not necessary to determine whether the purchasing power of the Peruvian peasants' yearly income is greater than elsewhere in the world. Even if it were to buy two or three times as much as it does, it would still be miserably low. What is perhaps more relevant is to compare it with the salaries paid in industry and with the yearly per capita income for the coastal region. Table 16 shows the disparity between the Costa and the Sierra, and a recent study indicates that salaries in industry run from 40 to 89 sols a day in organized factories (it is lower in nonunion establishments), while one American company was reported to be paying 60 sols a day to beginners with no special skills[14] This should be compared with a *legal* wage (seldom paid) of 12 to 15 sols in the rural areas. If fringe benefits are added to the salary figures cited for industrial workers, it is even easier to see the disparity between the lower class of the Costa and that of the Sierra. And yet, the people of the Costa live miserably, as any impartial observer who has been in Peru knows; so the economic plight of 98.4 per cent of those who live in the rural areas of the Sierra can be easily imagined.

Since practically all these "forgotten ones," or perhaps "excluded ones," [15] are Indians, it is necessary to look at them, not in archeological or anthropological terms (it has been done many times, and quite well), but in political terms. This ought to be done in regard to their role within that nation-state called Peru, and as an identifiable group which encompasses 50 per cent of the population, and who, according to at least one study, are not members of the Peruvian nation.[16]

The Indian of Peru has been variously described as submissive, passive, fatalistic about his lot, unaware of his proper role in so-

[14] Payne, *Labor and Politics,* pp. 15–17, 23; the American investor was General Motors, according to *Oiga* (Lima), July 16, 1965, p. 15.

[15] These terms are used by François Bourricaud, *Poder y Sociedad en el Perú Contemporáneo,* ch. 3.

[16] John Nathan Plank, "Peru: A Study in the Problems of Nation-Forming," pp. 248–49.

ciety, indifferent to the political system, pessimistic; it has been said that he accepts his life as a sad reality, which should not be taken seriously, and that he is still victimized by the feudal system developed in colonial times and which continued in disguise after independence; finally, the Indian problem in the country is tied to the question of landownership.[17]

The concentration of land has been discussed elsewhere, and there is no question about its being a source of power and in the hands of a small number of large landowners. The large landholdings of the Sierra concentrate on the production of foodstuffs, not because they really prefer to do so, but because the type of soil and climate make it impossible for them to produce for export, as do the coastal plantations. Consequently, they produce the majority of the foodstuffs grown in Peru, usually with obsolete methods and practically unpaid labor. The total value of the foodstuffs is only 10 per cent of what the agricultural sector produces, and this is confirmed by the quantity of food bought abroad and the low average daily caloric consumption throughout the country, and particularly in the highlands.[18] After surveying more than 1,000 families, a study somewhat reluctantly concluded:

Regarding calories and proteins, the best situation was found in the urban coastal zone, and the worst in the rural highlands. In the rural areas of the Sierra the diets, which have already been presented and discussed, indicated that the existing amount of usable foodstuffs was not adequate to cover the needs of the people. The evident solution of this problem is an increase in production. It should not be believed that

[17] Cirilo A. Cornejo, *Visión Objetiva del Problema Indígena: Planteamiento y Solución Inmediata,* ch. 1; Abraham Arias Larreta, "Indios y Cholos"; Manuel González Prada, "Nuestros Indios," in Adriana de González Prada (ed.), *Horas de Lucha,* pp. 311–38; José Carlos Mariátegui, *Siete Ensayos de Interpretación de la Realidad Peruana,* pp. 29–89.

[18] See Bourricaud, *Poder y Sociedad,* pp. 33–34; Virgilio Roel Pineda, "La Agricultura en la Economía Peruana" in Augusto Salazar Bondy and others, *La Encrucijada del Perú,* pp. 29–53; Virgilio Roel Pineda, *La Economía Agraria Peruana,* vol. I, ch. 1; and Ricardo Letts Colmenares, *Reforma Agraria Peruana: Justificación Económica y Política,* ch. 2. See also "Forum sobre Economía Nacional," in *Anales de la Universidad de San Marcos,* 1962, pp. 84–166.

maximum production is being obtained with the primitive methods of cultivation now being employed. The introduction of more modern techniques and the fertilization of the fields would probably increase it. *Nevertheless, these changes would be faced with social and economic difficulties.*[19]

Approximately five million Indians subsist in this environment. We cannot have a complete view of their role in Peruvian politics without exploring two different but complementary aspects: politics within the Indian communities and the relationship between Indian and white politics.

Politics within the Indian Communities

The Indian can be found in three different situations: he can be a member of an Indian community which has arable land; he can live within the boundaries of a large hacienda, most likely under some kind of tenancy arrangement; or he can be a small independent farmer. Needless to say, these alternatives do not present themselves neatly to please the student; Indians may engage in more than one of the alternatives listed above or may combine one of them with seasonal work in small mines, usually owned and operated by Peruvians. Yet in most cases the Indian's life and behavior will be dominated by one of these three situations.

The Indian communities are descendants of the basic politico-administrative unit of the Inca empire, the ayllu. Many people hasten to point out that there are substantial differences between the old ayllu, where the land and products were collectively owned, and the present community, where in many cases each adult male member owns a lot and keeps its products, but it is admirable to see how much has been maintained in spite of almost 400 years of servitude and forced cultural mixture. According to recent figures, there are 1,472 legally recognized Indian communities (a national registry was created under President Leguía in 1925), although 4,514 are said to exist throughout the country. The departments of

[19] Ministerio de Salud Pública, "La Alimentación y el Estado de Nutrición en el Perú," reprinted in *Anales de la Facultad de Medicina,* 1960, pp. 284–85 (emphasis added).

Cuzco and Puno appear to contain approximately two-thirds of the total number, 1,691 and 1,366 respectively, with only 204 and 30 registered.[20]

The communities are related to the national government through the local officials appointed by the central government or its departmental representatives; this relationship will be explored later, but it should be understood at this time that, with the exception noted below, they are imposed by a government in which the Indians have neither legal nor actual voice. Against this set of officials imposed from the outside the communities contrapose their own authorities, generally elected once a year—usually on the first of January—by the vote of all heads of household, men and women; every voter is required to serve, if elected. The number of officials elected varies with the size of the community, but there is always a chief executive officer (*varayoc*), and in many cases a Council of Elders, which administers justice and advises the community officials. In a few cases Indian communities have been allowed to express a preference for local representatives of the central government, and those who received a majority of the popular vote were then officially appointed to their posts. But this procedure seems to be exceptionally rare and appears to have taken place only in powerful and wealthy communities, where many Indians could read and write and had their own lawyers, teachers, physicians, and engineers—in brief, where they constituted the most powerful economic and political force in the area.[21]

There appears to be no difficulty in enforcing the laws and regulations of the community, which include the collection of local taxes and the contribution of physical labor for community projects. And while the plots and their products are individually owned, the tradition of mutual aid in tasks whose requirements go beyond the immediate family has continued. In contrast, the diffi-

[20] Roberto MacLean y Estenós, "El Trabajo en las Comunidades Indígenas del Perú," p. 808; see also, Luis E. Valcárcel, "La Vida Rural en el Perú."

[21] For a description of one of these cases, the community of Muquiyauyo, see Roberto MacLean y Estenós, *Sociología del Perú,* pp. 259–61.

culty in enforcing national laws and regulations, such as the military draft, among Indians is obvious and appears to create strong doubts about the Indian character in the minds of large landlords and government officials. The high level of participation and the high degree of legitimacy found in the communities also seem to contradict some of the generalizations made regarding the political behavior of the Indian, valid as these generalizations may be in regard to white-mestizo politics or upper class–middle class politics.[22]

Generally, Indian political action has been limited to the Indian community and, as implied above, the more powerful the community, the stronger its domestic political life. It should come as no surprise, then, that the political activity in communities located within a hacienda, or which are economically dependent on a hacienda, has been minimal or nonexistent.[23] The reasons are to be found in the economic and social organizations found even today in most parts of the Sierra. The specific arrangements between landlord and peasant are countless, and it would serve no purpose to provide a detailed explanation of even the most widely-employed ones here. However, some of the most important common features are worth noting. Practically all arrangements include the performance of services on the part of the peasants, either without monetary compensation or, in a minority of cases, for what amounts to a nominal salary even in Peru. The landlords pay the peasants with plots on which to build a shack and to farm, or grazing rights, or irrigation rights, or any combination thereof. The services provided by the peasants include serving in the house (*pongo, tapaco, mita,* or *mittani*), cooking, carrying messages

[22] These views usually come from those who are disappointed by the reluctance of the Indians to embark upon a unified attempt to alter the *status quo* by violent means; see, for instance, Cornejo, *Visión Objectiva, passim.*

[23] The land-occupation campaign led by Hugo Blanco in La Convención Valley in the early 1960's is a short-lived exception; it was brought under control by the political system through a combination of minor concessions and selective use of force. More optimistic appraisals of this movement appear to have been wishful thinking; Blanco and his lieutenants are now serving long jail sentences. On this subject see Víctor Villanueva, *Hugo Blanco y la Rebelión Campesina.*

(*propio, chasqui,* or *cacha*), caring for the landlords' plots, cattle, and irrigation works, and providing fresh vegetables and poultry products for the landlords' consumption. An added obligation in most of the Sierra is the transportation of the landlords' products to the market, usually at the peasants' expense. More modern share-cropping arrangements, with compensation paid to the landowners with animals or currency, are occasionally found.[24]

The landowner is called upon to provide land, water, sometimes materials and/or equipment, salary payments when the particular arrangement requires them, and protection from outsiders and even from fellow workers; thus, the *patrón* is expected to help his men solve whatever problems they may have with local officials and to act as the court of last resort in all disagreements which develop within his domain. No important event within the hacienda is complete without the landlord's blessing and his presence. It is only natural that those Indian officials who may exist in this situation are subordinated to the *patrón* and serve at his pleasure. Frank Tannenbaum has written:

Perhaps the most serious [effect] of all is that the hacienda fostered and maintained the *hacendado* as a social ideal—a superior being possessed of broad acres and numerous servants, dominant, domineering, patronizing, and paternal, with no restrictions between himself and the peon on the plantation. . . . The *hacendado* was the master of all he surveyed.[25]

Little can be said of the Indian who owns his plot and does not depend on the landlord for anything. The data already provided indicate that there are very few who can be considered free from any sort of economic pressure; depending on the issue they sometimes side with the landlords, sometimes with the peasants, but often prefer to remain aloof from controversial matters, unless

[24] Individual cases of arrangements of this type have been described by H. Gustavo Palacio Pimentel in "Relaciones de Trabajo entre el Patrón y los Colonos de los Fundos de la Provincia de Paucartambo"; Mario C. Vásquez in *Hacienda, Peonaje y Servidumbre en los Andes Peruanos;* and Oscar Nuñez del Prado's "Aspects of Andean Native Life," in Heath and Adams, *Contemporary Cultures* pp. 102–23.

[25] *Ten Keys to Latin America,* p. 90.

their interests are directly and clearly at stake. Naturally, many of the small Indian landowners occupy the higher lands and the sides of the mountains that surround the haciendas; very often they are as dependent on the *patrón* as those who live within and should be considered as belonging to the previous category.

The history of the Peruvian Sierra can best be described as the struggle for land between the landowner and the Indian community, a struggle that the landowner has been consistently winning. Both under the Spaniards and after independence, many landowners have increased their holdings and their power at the expense of the Indians, either by incorporating whole ayllus into their haciendas or by converting the nearby ayllus into satellites. Laws which directly or indirectly favored the landowners, and the favoritism of the local representatives of the central government (judges, petty officials, police) as well as of most of the professionally trained elements, constituted a combination which the Indians found almost impossible to defeat. The same methods have been employed through the years to enlarge the landlords' holdings. Violent upheavals, which took place from time to time but more sporadically as time went by, were crushed with utmost cruelty, and the net result was greater suffering and abuse.

There is no reason to be surprised, then, that the Indians, particularly those who live in communities, are distrustful of and detached from the white-mestizo political and administrative system. The Indians obviously understand that they have no stake in it, be the authorities "constitutional" (which means chosen in elections of varying validity and acting in accordance with the constitution in effect at the time) or the product of a military coup. It is in their relationship with the rest of the Peruvian population that the Indians act as if they were politically inferior (which they are, *de jure* and, even more, *de facto*) not because they ignore their own role, or feel that political activity is unnecessary,[26] but for exactly the opposite reasons. Four hundred years of white and white-mestizo domination have conditioned the Indians toward the "national society." The signing away of essential rights in contracts the In-

[26] As maintained by Cornejo (*Visión Objectiva,* pp. 17–18).

dians could not read and the innumerable losses in legal actions, often because of close ties between the landowners and those who sit on the bench, have surely taught them something regarding the usefulness of "going through legal channels." The killings, jailings, and beatings not only for trying to resolve their problems violently, but also for trying to organize and seek a peaceful solution, have had the effect of developing in the Indians an apparently submissive attitude.[27] The political history of the country seems to have taught them that the only solution is to withdraw, to "stay away," to postpone obedience until the last minute, but to avoid open conflict with the landlord, the police officer, the tax collector, and all other local agents of the national government they are forced to deal with. A keen student of the Peruvian Indian has indicated that in his dealings with outsiders the Indian is

suspicious, silent, withdrawn, and nearly inaccessible; he offers a passive and systematic resistance. He is humble, fearful, and inattentive; reticent and evasive in his answers, indecisive in his attitudes. He suppresses and hides his emotions and rarely reveals his disagreement even when he finds himself in fundamental opposition [to what is being done].[28]

This background has slowly developed in the Indians an extremely fatalistic attitude, the realization that there is nothing they can do to improve their situation; it is easy, therefore, for outside observers to conclude that they are not even looking for a better way of life.[29] And this may very well be the case because the changes which have taken place since the Spaniards arrived have brought them no benefits and much suffering, it is logical for them not to want any more changes. Consequently the Indian peasant has become an extremely conservative individual; in the words of Nuñez del Prado:

he allows no sudden changes and is openly resistive to traits, techniques, and practices different from those to which he is accustomed, at

[27] Specific instances are listed in Vásquez, *Hacienda, Peonaje y Servidumbre,* chs. 6, 7, and 8.

[28] Nuñez del Prado, "Aspects," in Heath and Adams, *Contemporary Cultures,* p. 106.

[29] Cornejo, *Visión Objectiva,* p. 23.

least until he has a chance to convince himself personally and objectively of the advantages he might gain from an innovation. Even so, he vacillates for a long time before deciding to accept the new practice.[30]

The inescapable conclusion is that there have been no basic improvements for the majority of the Peruvian peasants since independence, and perhaps since the Europeans arrived in Peru. The arithmetical improvements which various economic indicators have shown from time to time actually reflect improvements in the scale of living of the upper and middle classes, but, as a recent report puts it, "the increase of the gross national product has not been translated . . . into a substantial improvement of the level of living of the populations, *particularly of the lower income strata.*"[31]

The nearly unbelievable economic situation, the measures taken by most landlords, and the arbitrary and often unjust treatment to which the peasants are subjected have caused the Indian peasantry, in one observer's opinion, to lack political will and an "ideology of power."[32] In this regard it is interesting to point out that recent claims to land by the peasants were based on old rights and titles rather than on the desirability of structural changes, although the final result would have been the same; it is also necessary to indicate that the objective of recent actions by the peasants has been limited to gaining possession of more and better land, although the political implications of such actions, particularly if they succeed, are obvious. Whether these moves evidence the acquisition of political will and an "ideology of power" will be discussed in the following chapters.

[30] "Aspects," in Heath and Adams *Contemporary Cultures,* p. 106.

[31] Perú, Instituto Nacional de Promoción Industrial and Banco Industrial del Perú, *Situación de la Industria Peruana en 1964,* p. 25 (emphasis added).

[32] Claudio Esteva Fabregat, "El Indigenismo en la Política Hispanoamericana," p. 55. On occasions landlords have forced sharecroppers to move periodically from one lot to another in order to discourage a feeling of ownership; see José Luis Bustamante y Rivero, *Mensaje al Perú y Perú, Estructura Social,* p. 129. The unjust treatment of the peasants is part of what Jorge Basadre has called "illegality coefficient" (*La Multitud, la Ciudad y el Campo en la Historia del Perú,* p. 268).

6. Political Parties

Numerous attempts have been made by political scientists to classify or to develop a typology of political parties in Latin America. The natural consequence of trying to deal with twenty countries at once has been confusion and ambiguity of criteria, which seem to have rendered these attempts nearly valueless. Thus, some writers group parties as traditional, personalistic, proreform (with various subcategories), and radical-revolutionary, while others prefer to classify the nations themselves in accordance with the number of parties, and thus the one-party, two-party, and multiparty systems come to the fore. Finally, age becomes of paramount importance, and parties are either "old" or "new."[1]

While all these classifications could presumably be applied to

[1] The first approach has been used by Karl M. Schmitt and David D. Burks in *Evolution or Chaos: Dynamics of Latin American Governments and Politics* (pp. 158–74); it is also found, somewhat modified, in Martin C. Needler's *Latin American Politics in Perspective* (pp. 88–111). The second classification is presented by Alexander T. Edelmann in *Latin American Government and Politics* (pp. 340–50), and, with some differences, by George I. Blanksten in "The Politics of Latin America" (in Gabriel A. Almond and James S. Coleman [eds.], *The Politics of the Developing Areas*, pp. 479–86). The "old vs. new" typology seems to be quite popular, perhaps because of its apparently precise chronological criterion: It is adopted by William W. Pierson and Federico G. Gil in *Governments of Latin America* (pp. 314–36), and, with some variations, by Jacques Lambert in *América Latina: Estructuras Sociales e Instituciones Políticas* (pp. 273–328), and is applied specifically to Peru by Alfredo Hernández Urbina in *Nueva Política Nacional* (pp. 55–130). This approach has also been adopted by Robert J. Alexander in "The Emergence of Modern Political Parties in Latin America" (in Joseph Maier and Richard W. Weatherhead [eds.], *Politics of Change in Latin America*, pp. 101–25, and in Peter G. Snow [ed.], *Government and Politics in Latin America: A Reader*, pp. 385–403).

the Peruvian scene, this exercise would contribute little to a clearer understanding of the role played by political parties in the nation's politics. In this particular case (no claim is made here for the validity of this approach outside Peru) it may be worthwhile to distinguish between two types of organizations: those whose main objective was or is to serve the immediate electoral needs of an individual or of a clearly identifiable group; and those which are formed around a set of principles, objectives, and proposals which, for lack of a better word, could be called an ideology. Russell H. Fitzgibbon suggested these two types by stating that a valid typology of Latin American parties "might be found, in one direction, in terms of whether a party's ideology is prominent and probably primary in the party's operation or whether, on the other hand, the philosophical basis of the party's organization is only incidental or at least secondary." [2] The latter could be called *ad hoc* parties or "electoral machines," while the former may be identified as "ideological" parties. As usually happens in politics, the line separating the two categories in Peru is neither very clear nor extremely precise, although a strong nationalism may be a distinguishing feature of the "ideological" type.

There are parties that have started as electoral machines:

those which are merely organized around a particular political leader to foster his own political ambitions or to support his regime once he is in power. . . . This kind of group is organized without any particular philosophy or program except that of furthering the interests of a particular political leader. . . . In the nature of the case, such a party is transitory and is likely to disappear along with the man around whom it is organized.[3]

Yet, the inspirer of the party or his immediate lieutenants may, in the process of using the party to achieve their ends, develop a political philosophy (a necessity throughout Latin America, as will be seen), which may become believable to a significant portion of the population, thus assuring the continuation of the party beyond the

[2] "The Party Potpourri in Latin America," in Robert D. Tomasek (ed.), *Latin American Politics: Studies of the Contemporary Scene*, p. 209.

[3] Robert J. Alexander, *Today's Latin America*, pp. 146–47.

political life of the Founding Fathers. On the other hand, it is possible that parties organized for the purpose of promoting a specific ideology either do not survive the test of acceptability and disappear within a short period of time or are taken over by a *caudillo* at a certain point in their existence, to the detriment of their ideological base.

Theoretically, ideological parties could be expected to deal more with the issues at hand, while the electoral machines, by their very nature and objective, should tend to emphasize *personalismo,* as defined by George Blanksten.[4] However, quite often the former become so deeply involved in the complexity and consequences of their espoused philosophical tenets that they seem to lose contact with the nation's immediate needs, as well as with the facts of political life. The latter, on the other hand, are almost forced by the political culture of the Latin American countries to justify their existence on the basis of something that has to pass for the party's ideology. Because of the characteristics of an electoral machine, this pseudopolitical philosophy is often put together as an afterthought and seldom withstands careful analysis or the passage of time. Furthermore, when the electoral machine responds to the will of one man, it is he who dictates the ideology, which usually becomes a necessary but not an important item in his political arsenal. Needless to say, patronage is indispensable to electoral machines, while ideological parties tend to be able to do without it for long periods.

In the 1960's, Peru has had four nearly nationwide political parties, one founded in the early 1920's and the others after World War II. Two of them can be categorized as ideological parties, one is an electoral machine, and the fourth one, in power until 1968, appears to be evolving from the latter to the former. There are also a number of small left-wing parties of only regional significance, mostly of the ideological type. During the nineteenth century, on the other hand, Peru had very few parties of any relevancy; until 1872 the military formed the only successful one. The armed

---

[4] "Politics of Latin America," in Almond and Coleman, *Politics of the Developing Areas,* pp. 482–83.

forces, as they then existed (see Chapter 7), constituted the most important institution of political recruitment, and probably also of political socialization. The Civilista party, which took over in 1872, was, in spite of its broad platform, little more than an electoral machine organized by the traditional upper class to take power away from the increasingly unreliable military *caudillos*; to get the army out of politics, or at least out of the central administration, seems to have been the limit of its ideology.[5]

The relative success of the Civilista party encouraged the formation of a competing political organization, the Democratic party, organized in 1884 by a rival faction within the traditional upper class. The Democratic party, again, was essentially an electoral machine created for the purpose of getting Nicolás de Piérola back to the presidency by any possible method. The party was founded in 1884 (Piérola had already been in control from 1879 to 1882) and achieved its objective in 1895 after an armed insurrection. Although the Democratic party had a charismatic and unquestionably popular leader, at least in the urban centers, there were no basic philosophical differences between it and the Civilistas.[6] The military was unwilling to be left outside the political arena and, under the leadership of General Cáceres while he was still in the presidency, organized the Constitutional party with the support of some civilian elements. In spite of its name, the Constitutional party has also been considered an electoral machine for the purpose of promoting the interests of the military establishment in the political field. It took over the government again in 1894, only to be overthrown the following year by Piérola and the Democratic party. In the opinion of one writer, the Constitutional party "lacked, after its chief's first administration, a definite program, a serene and secure objective, and above all, a more precise vision of reality, which was changing and becoming more complex with the appearance of new and more important problems.[7]

[5] This view is clearly expressed by, among others, José Raúl Cáceres in *El Pasmo de una Insurgencia* (p. 50); see also Chapter 3 of this study.

[6] Jorge Basadre, *Perú—Problema y Posibilidad* . . . , pp. 148–49.

[7] Hernández Urbina, *Nueva Política,* p. 62.

These three parties were not reluctant to make alliances or political coalitions among themselves, according to the circumstances or, more importantly, according to the interests and desires of the leaders. Such were the cases of the alliances between the Civilistas and the Constitutionalists in the election of 1903 (there had been a prior coalition between the same parties), and between the Civilistas and the Democrats in 1895. All three parties disappeared or joined other organizations at the beginning of the twentieth century, after their leaders resigned or had been removed from the political arena.

Liberalism (nineteenth-century style) had existed in Peru since the beginning of the republic; but its political activities had been intermittent, incoherent, unorganized, only partially carried out, extremely theoretical, and concentrated in Lima.[8] Until 1901 liberals had acted within other parties or as loosely organized groups. In that year, because of disappointments with the Democrats, the Liberal party was founded under the leadership of one of Piérola's backers, Augusto Durand. Although the liberals had available a ready-made political philosophy, their party became another electoral machine of brief duration, organized "more to obtain political positions than to defend with conviction the principles of liberalism."[9] Durand died in 1923, and his death signaled the disappearance of the Liberal party.

The only quasi-ideological party which appeared in Peru in the nineteenth century was Unión Nacional, organized by groups of reformist intellectuals in 1890 as an expression of their unhappiness with the political processes. Their political thinking was based on the writings and speeches of Manuel González Prada, one of the most distinguished Peruvian intellectuals and the president of the Literary Circle of Lima. Extremely bright and with an unequaled command of the Spanish language, González Prada attacked everything and everybody that he believed to hinder the development of Peru into a more equitable nation, a nation where rewards and responsibilities were more evenly and fairly distrib-

[8] Basadre, *Perú—Problema y Posibilidad,* pp. 100–105.
[9] Hernández Urbina, *Nueva Política,* p. 64.

uted. He espoused radical if vague changes: a violent revolution in the field of ideas and in the field of action, concurrent with the use of force and the killing of tyrants.[10] He violently criticized the Catholic Church, the armed forces, the police, the university faculty and students, the traditional upper class, the other political parties, the lower class, the newsmen, the country, the Peruvians, and almost everything else. In the words of one of his most fervent admirers:

It is true that he did not provide a systematic program of action, that he did not formulate a philosophical or political doctrine which could serve as the guideline for a new Peru. Prada was neither a politician nor a philosopher; he simply was a literary figure of great sensitivity and patriotism, deeply worried about the destiny of his own people; it was for them that he dedicated his life to point out their errors, so that they could be corrected, to diagnose the wounds, so that they could be cured, to infuse love of truth, of honesty, of freedom, of equality, offering his own life as an example.[11]

An ideological party based on such a negative ideology—which had been rejected by the traditional upper class—could not hold high hopes of survival. The attitude of González Prada, who went to Europe in 1891 and remained there seven years, did not add anything to the electoral strength of Unión Nacional; divided and isolated from the power elites of the time, it disappeared shortly after González Prada's resignation from the party presidency in 1902.

The lack of permanency and of philosophical foundation of the Peruvian parties was evidenced by the facility with which they were prepared to enter into political deals with complete disregard for their prior positions and attitudes. In the 1904 presidential election, the Civil and Democratic parties joined forces against the Constitutional and Liberal parties. In the following election

[10] Manuel González Prada, *Anarquía*, pp. 24–25.

[11] Eugenio Chang-Rodríguez, *La Literatura Política de González Prada, Mariátegui y Haya de la Torre*, p. 96. González Prada was a prolific writer; his political thoughts can be found in *Nuevas Páginas Libres, Horas de Lucha, Páginas Libres, Figuras y Figurones, Propaganda y Ataque, Prosa Menuda*, and the already cited *Anarquía*.

(1908) the arrangement had changed: the Civil and Constitutional parties were on one side and the Democratic and Liberal organizations on the other. These reversals took place on other occasions and were made possible by the narrow leadership recruitment patterns, by the personalistic tone of politics, and by the fact that these parties represented similar groups. More often than not, party endorsement was an addition to the following already enjoyed by a politician, and the public announcement of the decision to support him came from small cliques of active participants in the political struggle.

The Appearance of a Mass Party: The APRA or PAP

Although of very little immediate significance for the country's power elites, the organization of a party that tried to articulate the philosophy of those who wanted drastic social, economic, and political alterations in Peru (Unión Nacional) did spread the seeds from which two ideological parties of a strongly reformist character were to emerge in the 1920's. It can be no accident that both José Carlos Mariátegui and Víctor Raúl Haya de la Torre, founders of the Communist and APRA parties respectively, were faithful disciples of González Prada. Ideologically they took up where he left off in that they proposed specific changes and programs to implement them. The first party chose the road of a select group of intellectuals who appropriated an ideology from Europe. Mariátegui's ideological position was complex and in many ways he was a heretic Marxist. The second party subscribed to the idea that Peru (and Latin America) could not use outside political philosophies and attempted to develop its own; in the process APRA actively canvassed for mass support.

From the time APRA became a relevant force in Peruvian politics it has had a divisive influence not only among Peruvians but among foreigners as well, scholars included. After coming in contact with APRA, the overwhelming majority of individuals are either strongly for or against it, and this is reflected in the studies so far made public. This may be due to APRA's claim to continental, as opposed to national, validity and to the unstable combination of men, styles, and compromises which can be found in the party's history. Whatever the reason, Peruvian politics cannot be understood without a clear knowledge of APRA's role(s).[12]

The Alianza Popular Revolucionaria Americana (literally, "American Popular Revolutionary Alliance") materialized in 1924 in Mexico City, where Haya de la Torre had been exiled by the Peruvian dictator Leguía. However, the organization can be traced to the activities of this Peruvian political leader while a student at the University of San Marcos in Lima. He represented the student body in their contacts with originators of the University Reform Movement at the University of Córdoba, Argentina. When the objectives of that movement were achieved in Peru, in 1919, the students already had developed the basis of a political organization.[13] The pretext to demonstrate their force came four years later, when dictator Leguía went along with the idea of dedicating Peru to the Heart of Jesus Christ, an idea originally suggested by the archbishop of Lima. Elements of varying political beliefs opposed the idea; Haya de la Torre and a group of university students took over leadership of the opposition, organized demonstrations against the project, and forced Leguía to abandon it.

A new force appeared, belligerent before the *Leguiismo,* with popular roots among the youth, separated from the politicians and hostile to them, as was demonstrated in the case of Congressman José Antonio Encinas, whom the students did not allow to speak at the university when he tried to express his support for their attitude.[14]

[12] The best study of APRA is unquestionably Harry Kantor's *The Ideology and Program of the Peruvian Aprista Movement,* and yet the author is considered too pro-Aprista even by members of the party, as some of them told the writer in January, 1965, while viewing a Lima television program in which Professor Kantor participated. On the other hand, Fredrick B. Pike, a well-known specialist in Peruvian history, is hostile to the party; see, for instance, his "The Old and the New APRA in Peru: Myth and Reality." A more profound cleavage appears among Peruvian writers.

[13] On the university reform movement, see Alberto Ciria and Horacio Sanguinetti, *Universidad y Estudiantes: Testimonio Juvenil,* and Carlos Alberto Astiz, "The Changing Face of Latin American Higher Education".

[14] Jorge Basadre, *Historia de la República del Perú,* IX, 4034.

Leguía was not prepared to suffer political defeats of that type; Haya de la Torre was jailed as he ran once again for the presidency of San Marcos' student body (he lost, then was unanimously elected when his imprisonment became known) and later was deported to Panama, from where he went to Mexico and founded APRA. It should be noted that the chosen name indicates an emphasis on Latin America as a whole, and not on Peru. In fact, the Peruvian political arm was and is the Partido Aprista Peruano (in theory only one of the Latin American members of APRA), founded in 1931 in order to participate in that year's presidential election, with Haya as the standard-bearer. The hemispheric influence of APRA was never great, and no important Aprista parties appeared anywhere else in Latin America.[15] Thus, the distinction between APRA and PAP became (probably it always was) academic, although Aprista writers often emphasize this distinction. In reality, the party has played a very important role within Peru; outside the country, however, its influence has been nonexistent. APRA's maximum program has been a declaration, expressed in very general terms, of what ought to happen in all the Latin American countries. Many people could subscribe to it, but the Apristas themselves have done very little to make it a reality. Since APRA is most relevant in Peru (or PAP, since the terms are interchangeable), it is in this context that its minimum program and political actions will be discussed here.[16]

[15] The writer disagrees with those who maintain that Venezuela's Acción Democrática, Costa Rica's Liberación Nacional, and Mexico's PRI are Aprista parties; there may be certain ideological coincidences and similarities of clientele and recruitment patterns (more research is needed to determine whether or not this is the case), but it is absurd to place APRA in a position of superiority or as the source of what have been called the national-popular movements. Any paternity awarded to APRA over other parties needs to be proven by those who claim it. In this line of thought see Pierson and Gil, *Governments*, pp. 319–20; for the opposite view, see Robert J. Alexander, "The Latin American *Aprista* Parties," and Blanksten, "Politics of Latin America," in Almond and Coleman, *Politics of the Developing Areas*, p. 486.

[16] APRA's "minimum program" was its original platform in regard to Peru and included vague pronouncements, such as the abolition of feudalism, and specific ones, such as a national department of statistics and the taking of a census. APRA's "maximum program" outlines the party's international ob-

The Apristas were jailed, exiled, and outlawed in the 1920's by dictator Leguía. When he was overthrown by Sánchez Cerro a period of respect for personal and political rights ensued, and the APRA leadership regained its freedom and drifted back from exile. The party was then officially founded in Peru in March, 1931, with the purpose of participating in the forthcoming presidential election. At approximately the same time the new administration began blocking its political activities, and a number of electoral irregularities followed. When the election was finally held and the results announced, the incumbent was given 155,378 votes and Haya de la Torre, APRA's presidential candidate, 106,551. APRA and some writers have maintained that APRA won the election and that at least 50,000 of their votes were declared void arbitrarily.[17] Shortly after the election, APRA was forced underground once again. The Apristas counterattacked: in 1932 they sponsored a revolt in Trujillo, and the following year a member of the party killed Sánchez Cerro. Since then, APRA has been outlawed almost constantly and excluded from participation in elections. This persecution, carried out by governments headed by the military or the traditional upper class, unquestionably increased the party's popularity, glamour, and believability; with brief periods of legality—the most important was the presidency of Bustamente y Rivero, 1945–48, who was elected with APRA support—the persecution lasted until 1956.

During these long periods of forced abstention from the electoral process, APRA maintained a powerful underground organization and retained and increased its influence over a significant portion of the Peruvian population. Like many other national-popular movements in Latin America, APRA tried at various times to con-

jectives, to be pursued by all Latin American countries; again, it included specific proposals, such as the inter-Americanization of the Panama Canal, and general ones, such as solidarity with all the oppressed classes and peoples of the world, See Harry Kantor, *El Movimiento Aprista Peruano,* chs. 4 and 5. For the original enunciation, see Víctor Raúl Haya de la Torre, *Política Aprista,* pp. 5–75.

[17] Kantor, *El Movimiento,* p. 45; Haya de la Torre, *¿A dónde va Indoamérica?* p. 270.

vert its personal following into electoral strength and to convert this strength into support for a candidate who, regardless of his ideology, was willing to promise better treatment for APRA in his administration; these beneficiaries were Eguiguren in 1936 (the election was cancelled by General Benavides, then in power), Bustamente y Rivero in 1945, and Prado in 1956. These deals made it possible for the party to occupy Senate and House seats under the Bustamante y Rivero and Prado administrations and even some cabinet posts under the former. At the same time, however, these compromises, made by the only party which had developed the image of uncompromising and profound reformism, disappointed some of its followers. The disappointment was especially felt by those who had risked their lives for APRA and had not received or did not expect to receive the patronage jobs that this coparticipation made available. This is particularly true when it is remembered that the administrations elected under APRA's auspices did not carry out any of the fundamental reforms the party had been calling for.

There is one aspect of APRA that should be clearly understood: it is an ideological party, but until the present time the ideology has been—at least on the surface—developed and dictated by its undisputed and seemingly permanent leader, Haya de la Torre. Yet it would be a crucial mistake to assume that APRA is only Haya de la Torre. The ideology that he has publicly given the party faithful, vague and often beyond the comprehension of most of them, has shown numerous signs of lasting for a long time. The development and building of *indigenismo* into a political myth, the condensation of Peruvian politics into an oligarchy-mass antinomy, the theory of "historic space-time," and the repeated use of the exclusivistic slogan "only APRA will save Peru" are small pieces of a complex, confusing, and sometimes contradictory political ideology which Haya de la Torre and his lieutenants have quite convincingly "sold" to a large portion of the Peruvian population. But as the original ideology was slowly modified, often by omission, the proportion of the population that could be considered Aprista decreased; as a writer pointed out:

The APRA of the 1930's pretended at least to have the character of the *dominant party in the nation*. After 1956, and the coexistence agreements, it admitted to being the *dominant party in a majority coalition*. And after the 1962 elections it was only *one of the three major parties,* seeking contacts with its two rivals and declaring to be ready to reach an understanding with them.[18]

Regardless of what the Aprista leadership claims, the ideology has been going through deep changes at two distinct rates: a very mild modification of basic principles, almost imperceptible in the short run, which started in the 1930's and a more abrupt change in behavior which took place in the 1950's. Both changes have been of the same tendency: from left to right. In the first category, the party's position on the Panama Canal and on the need of government involvement in the economy are only two of the many aspects which the Aprista leadership has modified in order to make itself attractive to the power elites.[19] The renunciation of violent attempts to overthrow the government after the 1948 revolt of some noncommissioned officers of the Navy (see Chapter 7) and the willingness to make political "deals" with such a clear-cut representative of the traditional upper class (the "oligarchy" in Haya de la Torre's duality) as Manuel Prado, in order to insure Prado's election as president, illustrate the second kind of change.[20] But these changes, as indicated earlier, have greatly diminished the reformism of APRA and its leader. This widely perceived fact prompted one of the members of the traditional upper class to say, "Haya de la Torre is the conservative leader the country needs." [21]

[18] François Bourricaud, *Ideología y Desarrollo: El Caso del Partido Aprista Peruano,* p. 34 (emphasis added).

[19] For a comprehensive discussion of these changes see Bourricaud, *Poder y Sociedad en el Perú Contemporáneo,* pp. 141–85; Pike, "The Old and the New APRA," *passim;* and Luigi Einaudi, "Changing Contexts of Revolution in Latin America," pp. 14–20.

[20] On the first point see Einaudi, "Changing Contexts," p. 24n., and Víctor Villanueva, *Un Año bajo el Sable,* pp. 32–42; on the second point see Arnold Payne, "Latin America's Silent Revolution."

[21] The statement is attributed to Pedro Roselló Truel, as quoted by M. Guillermo Ramírez y Berrios, *Examen Espectral de las Elecciones del 9 de Junio de 1963,* p. 94.

The most obvious changes of Aprista ideology had been in the area of hemisphere-wide affairs (thus within the domain of APRA's maximum program): attacks on United States imperialism were slowly downgraded, and the differences between *aprismo* and communism—which had existed from the beginning—were emphasized, in part to counter charges of collusion made by some members of the traditional upper class. Thus the emphasis shifted from anti-imperialism to anticommunism. This ideological change had repercussions in the minimum program, since Haya de la Torre and other APRA leaders became better disposed toward foreign investors and less adamant in favoring the nationalization of the La Brea and Pariñas oil fields, under the control of a Standard Oil subsidiary. On the domestic scene:

the new APRA has rejected experimenting with innovations aimed at the immediate redistribution of wealth and instead seeks to strengthen the processes that have been tried and found effective in generating capital. Even if the *Apristas* still cling to their old hope of a redistribution, they are at least not putting the cart before the horse. To the contrary, they are concerning themselves first with the generation of wealth.[22]

Whether these changes are causes or consequences of their newly-gained acceptability among the traditional upper class (as reflected in newspapers such as *La Prensa*) can only be speculated upon. What is clear is that the shift was ordered from the top of the hierarchy, apparently against the will of some of Haya de la Torre's closest associates. In fact, a supposedly secret letter, written to Haya de la Torre by some of them in 1954, comments with regard to Haya de la Torre's ideological changes, "you are perhaps bound by some temporary commitment which limits your public activities." But apparently they did not feel that, whatever the temporary commitment, it could justify such a change, because they also wrote, "let us not postpone with plans for the future the irrevocable demands of a present which requires a frank and com-

[22] Pike, "The Old and the New APRA," p. 37.

bative posture, at the cost of losing the party's position of continental leadership." [23]

The "party's position" could only mean the leadership of the politically-aware elements of the lower and lower middle classes, which was the only leadership realistically at stake. In finally making the 1956 deal with the coastal sector of the traditional upper class in exchange for legalization, a share of patronage, and the possibility of participating fully in the 1962 election, the Aprista high command was apparently prepared to risk that leadership. Thus the Apristas continued with the same general principles, always insisting on the unequivocal continuity of their "doctrine," while de-emphasizing bolder reforms and concentrating their energies on fighting communism and repressing other organizations that threatened to take away their more reformist followers. This fundamental shift in the specific ideological objectives of the Apristas, their willingness to enter into practical political deals with those who benefited from those features of Peruvian politics that they had originally sought to change, and the winds of change coming from the Holy See and the Catholic Church in other Latin American countries (recently reflected in Peru, as discussed in Chapter 8) have initiated a fundamental realignment of the *status quo* elements. There are indications that the traditional upper class is having second thoughts regarding the long-run reliability of the Catholic clergy as the providers and interpreters of the conservative ideology: these second thoughts apply not so much to what has taken place in Peru as to the trends shown elsewhere in Latin America and particularly by international Catholic organizations, such as CELAM.[24] Almost simultaneously, the

[23] Portions of this letter have been translated by Einaudi in "Changing Contexts" (pp. 14–20); the quotations are from p. 16n. and p. 17. The entire letter may be found in Villanueva's *La Tragedia de un Pueblo y un Partido* (pp. 227–57).

[24] Conferencia Episcopal Latinoamericana ("Latin American Episcopal Conference"), created in 1955 by Pope Pius XII. For a report on a crucial gathering of this organization, see *Primera Plana* (Buenos Aires), October 11, 1966, pp. 34–41.

Aprista ideology, when translated into concrete pronouncements, became more and more attractive to the traditional upper class and specifically to its coastal sector; it was based not on their having an enthusiastic preference for APRA's basic political tenets, but on the likelihood that a significant portion of the lower and lower middle classes was prepared to believe them. The willingness of the Aprista leadership—and especially of Haya de la Torre —to make such a deal with the traditional upper class is what made the deal possible at that particular moment.

It would be erroneous to assume that the Apristas "gave in" only in order to be legally accepted and receive a share of the patronage. Even friends of APRA recognize that the party represents approximately one-third of the electorate, and that its electoral strength has been concentrated in the northern part of the country in what the Apristas call the "solid North." It has also been recognized that the significance of APRA's electoral support to non-APRA presidential candidates had been overemphasized in 1945 and, more importantly, in 1956.[25] The rigid discipline and high degree of centralization of APRA has been quite useful in obtaining as many votes as the party faithful can possibly cast, particularly for non-Aprista candidates, but is a drawback in attracting independent or non-Aprista votes for party candidates. Consequently, because of these characteristics of APRA's vote, plus the repeated failures and/or unwillingness to take over power by force, it seems evident that, under competitive conditions, APRA would be unable to win either the presidency or a majority in Congress by itself. APRA's leadership and many of its followers have apparently reached this conclusion after the elections of 1962 and 1963, if not before. Unwilling or unable to reach an understanding with Acción Popular (see below) and the left-wing parties, APRA accepted the offer of the traditional upper class and made a "tactical" agreement with its latest electoral machine, the Unión Nacional Odriísta, immediately after the 1962 elections (see Tables

[25] See Enrique Chirinos Soto, *Cuenta y Balance de las Elecciones de 1962,* pp. 33–39. The author calls himself a "friend of APRA" (p. 12) and was its successful senatorial candidate in 1967.

17 and 18). The agreement was broadened after the 1963 elections and gave this coalition (and the traditional upper class) a majority in both houses of the legislature and the legal power to block

Table 17. Results of the 1962 presidential election, by party

Party	Votes for presidential candidate	Percentage
APRA	557,047	32.94
Acción Popular	544,180	32.19
Unión Nacional Odriista	480,798	28.44
Christian Democrats	48,792	2.89
Others	59,801	3.54
Total of valid vote	1,690,618	100.00

Source: Prepared by the author from published election returns.

Table 18. Distribution of congressional seats, by party, 1962 election

Party	Senate		House	
	Seats	Percentage	Seats	Percentage
APRA	26	47.3	83	44.7
Acción Popular	17	30.9	64	34.6
Unión Nacional Odriista	11	20.0	33	17.9
Others	1	1.8	5	2.8
Total	55	100.0	185	100.0

Source: Prepared by the author from published election returns.

and water down bills which threatened the *status quo* (see Tables 19 and 20).

The observer could engage in almost limitless speculation regarding the reasons behind APRA's abandonment of its reformist tendencies or the motivation of Haya de la Torre in sanctioning the shift. Decisions are often made for a number of different reasons that may carry a given weight in the mind of the decision-maker and a different one in the eyes of the researcher. Furthermore, this distinction implies the assumption that all reasons will become known, which is not always the case. Available evidence,

Table 19. Results of the 1963 presidential election, by party

Party	Votes for presidential candidate	Percentage
Acción Popular–Christian Democrats	708,662	39.05
APRA	623,501	34.36
Unión Nacional Odriista	463,085	25.52
Others	19,320	1.07
Total	1,814,568	100.00

Source: Prepared by the author from data released by the Peruvian National Electoral Tribunal.

Table 20. Distribution of congressional seats, by party, 1963 election

Party	Senate		House	
	Seats	Percentage	Seats	Percentage
Acción Popular–Christian Democrats	20	44.4	50	35.7
APRA	18	40.0	58	41.4
Unión Nacional Odriista	7	15.6	27	19.3
Others	0	0.0	5	3.6
Total	45	100.0	140	100.0

Source: Prepared by the author from data released by the Peruvian National Electoral Tribunal.

however, leads to the speculation that APRA's shift may very well have been caused by a growing recognition on the part of Haya de la Torre and other leaders that the party was not going to gain power by force and did not have enough popular appeal to obtain the support of a majority of the *voting population.* They seem to have believed that their reformist ideology had gotten them as far as it could possibly go under the existing "rules of the game" (literacy as a voting requirement, uneven congressional representation, and the like). Faced with a new military take-over supported by the "coastal plutocracy" in 1948 and the persecution that followed, APRA's leadership seems to have decided that the only alternative really open to them was to move closer to the upper class and the old middle class; apparently APRA's leadership believed —and probably still believes—that they could do it without alienating the bulk of their traditional support. If successful, the shift would increase the possibility of APRA's putting together an electoral majority and would make the party and its leaders acceptable to the upper class, the military establishment, and perhaps even to the Catholic hierarchy.

The mutation of APRA, announced through vague pronouncements and a change of emphasis, was made quite clear by the performance of its congressional delegation on key issues; needless to say, it is here that the traditional upper class expects Apra to carry out its side of the bargain. Thus, since the Belaúnde Terry administration took office, the Apristas have supported a balanced budget through reduction in governmental expenditures—particularly in public works and lower taxes—and currency devaluation, which favors the interest of the coastal plantation owners and mining enterprises. At the same time they oppose the takeover by the government of the oil fields exploited by subsidiaries of foreign companies, and also a protectionist tariff—a position which favors the traditional upper class and blocks the development of an industrial counterpart.[26] But perhaps the more obvious about-face of the Aprista congressional delegation came about in reference to the Agrarian Reform Act, originally proposed by the Belaúnde administration and substantially reduced in effectiveness, scope, and even clarity by the Apristas and the Odriistas. Scholars have demonstrated that the law that came out of the legislature was essentially written by these two parties and that an effective agrarian reform was almost impossible under it.[27] Agrarian reform may have been accepted in principle by the passage of this law

[26] These positions of Aprista senators and representatives have been widely reported in the press; see *Primera Plana* (Buenos Aires), August 1, 1967, p. 32; *Oiga* (Lima), March 31, 1967, pp. 4–5, May 19, 1967, pp. 8–10, June 9, 1967, pp. 4–7, June 30, 1967, pp. 4–7; and *Confirmado* (Buenos Aires), June 1, 1967, p. 29, and July 6, 1967, p. 30.

[27] The most comprehensive study of the Peruvian Agrarian Reform Act and its enforcement is that of Ernest R. DeProspo, Jr., "Administration of the Peruvian Land Reform Program." See also Terry L. McCoy, "The Politics of Agrarian Reform in Peru," and Bourricaud, *Poder y Sociedad,* pp. 331–49.

(the coastal sector of the traditional upper class had "accepted" the principle at the beginning of this decade, provided that its plantations were excluded), but no real redistribution of land has occurred and none is likely to occur under it.

Some of the amendments specifically introduced by the Apristas excluded the large sugar plantations from the application of the Agrarian Reform Act so long as it can be shown that the area covered permits an adequate use of the machinery (Article 38); what is more, the Apristas insisted on placing the Agrarian Reform Institute directly under the legislature's authority (where the landlords are strong and the APRA-UNO coalition can oversee its activities); furthermore, important duties of the program have been awarded to other bodies, such as the national Agrarian Council and the Agrarian Reform Financial Corporation, where private organizations, dominated by the traditional upper class, have an important voice and possibly a majority. In addition to these and other clear obstacles to a true redistribution of land added by the Aprista legislators—and approved with the aid of the UNO congressional delegation—the final version of the law has idiomatic incongruities in most of the important provisions, and most of the text is written in substandard Spanish. It is apparent that these things did not happen by accident, since some of the Aprista legislators are distinguished writers, and since such an important law, discussed in Congress for over ten months, certainly warranted their attention. On the other hand, it is obvious that provisions which are unclear and a few items that apparently are clear can be challenged in the courts, which are not known for their speedy decisions.

Besides fulfilling their side of the political bargain with the traditional upper class, the Apristas were in fact protecting their immediate political interest and that of some of their members. Part of the party's strength in the "solid North" comes from its control of the unions which represent workers on the coastal plantations, either through direct contacts or through the National Federation of Peruvian Peasants (FENCAP), organized in 1960.[28] An

[28] See James L. Payne, *Labor and Politics in Peru: The System of Political Bargaining*, especially pp. 116–24.

effective land redistribution program, particularly if proposed and enacted when a non-Aprista occupied the presidency, would undoubtedly release the plantation workers from APRA's protection and control; it is highly questionable that once they became independent farmers their allegiance to APRA would continue. On the other hand, these uneducated peasants could not have been expected to understand the complexities of the Peruvian lawmaking procedure: if the Agrarian Reform Act fails to solve their plight, the party controlling the executive branch (Acción Popular) will take the political consequences. But in pursuing these immediate or newly acquired goals APRA's leaders have turned their backs on the party's original position.[29] Important elements within the party, and particularly within its youth organization, have reacted against these changes either by abandoning the party—at the polls or in a more militant fashion—or by becoming less active within it.

At the highest echelon of the party, the ideological change which has taken place in APRA caused sharp reactions on the part of the more reform-minded elements. The head of this disappointed reform faction was Manuel Seoane, considered until a few years ago the number two man in the party hierarchy. Seoane had already expressed profound disagreement with Haya de la Torre's ideological shifts in the 1950's.[30] In the early 1960's, after the negotiations with the traditional upper class and with the Odriistas, Seoane indicated his disagreement and displeasure by moving out of the country and accepting a position with an international agency in Washington. After the 1963 election he warned his party that there was only one road open to it: To join forces with the winning parties under a reformist program or to see the erosion of its influence. APRA ignored his advice; Haya de la Torre ignored his death (in September, 1963); and the party newspaper seldom mentioned his name after his public pronouncement.[31]

More important perhaps for the future of APRA is the disappointment felt by its youth and university branches; even those

[29] The best exponent of APRA's agricultural program is Alfredo Saco; see his *Programa Agrario del Aprismo*. It is interesting to note that Haya de la Torre has always been vague in referring to agrarian reform.

[30] Einaudi, "Changing Contexts," pp. 14–20.

[31] *Primera Plana,* January 10, 1967, p. 34.

who have been benefiting from the party's new role and the patronage it produced are sensitive to the ideological shift and its
materialization in the coalition with the Odriistas, and the amendments to the Agrarian Reform Bill. Most of those who remained in
the party seem to be waiting for the top leaders (the generation of
1930, according to Einaudi) to retire or pass away, in order to
gain control of the party and return it to the road of reform.[32]
Whether they will in fact do so is, needless to say, an open question. However, a group of Aprista militants was unwilling to wait
until time would give them a chance to influence the party's policies. Beginning in the mid-1950's many of the most distinguished
elements in the Aprista youth movement developed a growing al-
ienation from the party, which culminated when the party's 1959
National Plenary Meeting refused to adopt their proposed program
of almost complete structural change. At that time, under the leadership of Ezequiel Ramírez Novoa and Luis de la Puente Uceda,
they left APRA and organized what they successively called the
Movimiento Veintiocho de Julio, APRA Rebelde, and Movimiento de Izquierda Revolucionaria (MIR). Finally frustrated by
their inability to achieve their ends within the political system,
they took to the mountains in 1965 and organized guerrilla operations, which were wiped out by the military (see Chapter 7). An
observer has described the mood of one of the young Apristas in
the late 1950's as follows:

At that time Luis de la Puente belonged to APRA, but he already
had—because of his temper and views—serious difficulties with that
organization which, as we remember, was aptly denounced by the representative of the Cuban youth organization "Julio Antonio Mella" as
the "society for repentant revolutionaries;" Luis de la Puente already
knew the individuals with whom he was dealing. . . . And to be a

[32] Einaudi, "Changing Contexts," pp. 11–13. This writer held long discussions with most of the Aprista youth leaders in important party positions, and
their ideological frustration was readily apparent. Some made excuses and
tried to emphasize that the changes were temporary and should be charged to
political expediency; but when prodded further, they unanimously stated that
they did not agree with the shifts and had to accept them because of party
discipline.

leader it was necessary to be first in making sacrifices, something which the old leaders of APRA were not prepared to do, inasmuch as they had double-crossed and given up the principles of that organization, which had tried to be anti-imperialistic and revolutionary.[33]

The degree of centralization and strict discipline within APRA is quite extreme. Most Latin American political parties discourage significant deviations from party policy and strictly control from central headquarters the internal political life, the external activities of members, the role played by the branches, and the selection of candidates at all levels, but APRA is unusually strict in all these aspects. Violations of instructions emanating from the top have often been construed as ideological deviations, and those found responsible have been expelled from the organization. It is likely that this strictness made it possible for the Aprista organization to survive persecution until 1956. It appears, however, that a crucial element in the party's survival was the strength and credibility of its ideology, particularly since the party had not been influential in the Peruvian government until that year (with the exception of the period 1945–47) and thus had been unable to do anything to improve the material well-being of its followers, and even of most of its leaders. The Aprista ideology emanated from a recognized and widely accepted source (Haya de la Torre) and was protected from "diverging interpretations" by the centralization and discipline already alluded to. But since the ideological shift began to develop, centralization and discipline have in fact been increased in order to enforce the "new ideological look."[34] How-

[33] Speech by Juan Nuiry at the University of Havana on January 13, 1966, quoted in Universidad de la Habana, *Homenaje a José Luis de la Puente*, p. 12.

[34] The writer had a number of opportunities to acquire direct personal evidence of this centralization and discipline. On one occasion, when the Aprista youth branch was planning an attack on the University of Iquitos, the operation was authorized, organized, and led by people from the central party headquarters in Lima; the final approval was given by Haya de la Torre, and student leaders were flown to Iquitos, more than 1,000 miles away. Many of these clashes had taken place before, and the decision could have been left to the Aprista authorities in Iquitos, who could be expected to have been better aware of the situation.

ever, what was acceptable to the party faithful in the time of underground activities and physical persecution may not necessarily be acceptable in times of relative party prosperity, particularly when discipline and centralization are employed to coerce support for abandoning the reformist policies which made the party attractive to a large portion of the Peruvian masses and to some of the country's intelligentsia.

The erosion of party strength was clearly in evidence in the defeat suffered by candidates backed jointly by Apristas and Odriistas in the December, 1963, municipal elections (see Table 21). A widely known historian wrote:

Aprista hopes were shattered when Popular Action–Christian Democratic candidates scored a stunning victory over their rivals for municipal office. Even in the one-time "solid *Aprista* North," the APRA-*Odriista* ticket was defeated in many locales, while in the election for the mayor of Lima, María Delgado de Odría, backed by *Apristas* and thought to be extremely popular because of her charitable activities during the *ochenio*, was overwhelmingly defeated by Belaúnde's close friend Luis Bedoya Reyes, an important leader of the Christian Democratic Party.[35]

Table 21. Municipal election results, by party, December, 1963

Party	Total votes	Percentage
Acción Popular–Christian Democrats	616,172	46.8
APRA–Unión Nacional Odriista	580,568	44.0
Others	123,350	9.2
Total	1,320,090	100.0

Source: Prepared by the author from published election returns.

More recent municipal elections (November, 1966—see Table 22) have confirmed this trend, particularly in regard to the continuing loss of electoral strength of the Apristas, whose "solid north" showed new and important cracks, as Table 23 shows.[36] Although

[35] Fredrick B. Pike, *The Modern History of Peru,* p. 317.
[36] See the analysis in *Caretas* (Lima), November 25–December 7, 1966,

Table 22. Municipal election results, by party, November, 1966

Party	Total votes	Percentage
Acción Popular–Christian Democrats	820,662	47.5
APRA–Unión Nacional Odriista	796,446	46.1
Others	109,679	6.4
Total	1,726,787	100.0

Source: Prepared by the author from published election returns.

it may be too early to predict the future of APRA, we can probably say that the party leadership seems to be trading current well-being and respectability for long-run survival.

Table 23. Comparative 1963 and 1966 election returns, selected departments (in per cent)

	June, 1963, presidential election			November, 1966, municipal election		
Department	AP–DC	APRA–UNO	Others	AP–DC	APRA–UNO	Others
Lima	40.6	58.2	1.2	53.2	43.3	3.5
Amazonas *	17.7	79.8	2.5	46.5	51.9	1.6
Cajamarca *	19.4	79.8	.8	41.9	56.8	1.3
La Libertad *	13.4	86.1	.5	29.7	70.3	–
Lambayeque *	19.1	80.3	.6	46.2	48.5	5.3
Arequipa †	58.3	41.0	.7	37.6	41.7	20.7
Cuzco †	45.5	54.3	.2	49.9	37.3	12.8
Puno †	73.9	24.6	1.5	47.3	18.8	33.9

Source: Prepared by the author from published election returns.
* Departments of the "solid North"; the bulk of the votes belongs to APRA.
† Departments of the South.

Acción Popular

The party in control of the executive branch during the period 1963–68 began as another electoral machine under the name of Frente Nacional de Juventudes Democráticas ("National Front of

pp. 17–24. The same conclusions appear in *Primera Plana,* December 13, 1966, p. 34.

Democratic Youth"); it was organized in 1956 to serve as the vehicle for Fernando Belaúnde Terry's election to the presidency. Belaúnde Terry was defeated by Prado, but his hastily organized front received almost 37 per cent of the popular vote. Encouraged by the results, Belaúnde Terry continued his electoral activities with an eye to the 1962 elections and transformed the front into Acción Popular ("Popular Action"). In the late 1950's the party was Belaúnde Terry and he was the party.

Who was Fernando Belaúnde Terry? A member of one of the most distinguished families, originally from the southern city of Arequipa, he belonged to the traditional upper class and had very strong ties to the Catholic Church, mostly through his uncle Víctor Andrés Belaúnde, one of the best-known Catholic intellectuals of Latin America. His father, Rafael Belaúnde, had occupied cabinet posts and had suffered political exile, a fact that enabled Belaúnde Terry to study in France and in the United States, where he received a degree in architecture at the University of Texas. Upon his return to Peru, Belaúnde Terry was sympathetic to the Apristas, without joining the party, and was elected to the House in 1945 on the coalition ticket headed by another Catholic intellectual from Arequipa, Bustamante y Rivero. Shortly thereafter, he split with the Aprista legislators and, after the 1948 *coup d'état*, remained politically inactive until 1956.

It is apparent that although Belaúnde Terry avoided direct references to religion his position was extremely similar to that of the Christian Socialists of Europe or the Christian Democrats of Chile. Protected by his surname and his uncle from charges of Communism and fellow-traveling,[37] he was able to show certain reformist tendencies, mild in the mid-1950's, but becoming stronger as APRA's continuing shift developed a vacuum on the Left of the Peruvian spectrum. He was quite effective in forestalling Church opposition; approximately forty days before the 1963 election the Church published a pastoral letter, dated May 1, 1963,

---

[37] This is recognized by his admirer Ramírez y Berrios, in *Examen Espectral*, p. 109. See also Víctor Andrés Belaúnde, "Mi Posición ante las Elecciones de 1963."

in which it subscribed to the general principles of reform endorsed by Belaúnde Terry in his campaign.[38] The charges of communism, hurled mostly by the Apristas, thus became of doubtful effectiveness, and Belaúnde Terry gained even greater freedom to court the vote of the extreme Left, on the grounds that he was the only alternative to their wasting their electoral strength.

Belaúnde Terry's approach was based on a carefully calculated appeal to the Peruvians' national pride. His best-known book was entitled *La Conquista del Perú por los Peruanos* ("The Conquest of Peru by the Peruvians") and describes in specific terms some of the things he would do if he were given power.[39] Highways, irrigation works, specific economic and fiscal reforms, and other projects are clearly outlined and documented, although the means to carry them out are not so explicitly explained. He took radical stands in matters such as the nationalization of the oil fields; yet, in 1956, he was not only acceptable to but supported by *La Prensa*, and he presented as the essence of his program the necessity "to improve living conditions and consolidate the economy . . . to continue a policy of fulfilling our obligations in order to keep open the doors of international credit, the only way to develop the country at an accelerated pace." [40]

By 1960, however, these orthodox views were being de-emphasized and the AP leader was presenting himself as a new man, changed by his wide travels in the interior of the country. At this time he tried to indicate that he had *national* solutions; he wrote:

We have been able to develop in the citizenry the deep conviction that the source of inspiration of a doctrine exists in our soil, it thus being unnecessary to import political-social ideas into a country which, since the distant past, distinguished itself by producing them. . . . If we are proud of anything, it is precisely of having found a Peruvian solution for our national problems. . . . We are original because we return to the origins, not with the purpose of going back to the past, but with the

[38] *El Comercio* (Lima), May 2, 1963, p. 1.

[39] There is an English translation with the less expressive title *Peru's Own Conquest*.

[40] Ramírez y Berrios, *Grandezas y Miserias de un Proceso Electoral*, pp. 136–37.

purpose of finding in this land solid foundations on which to base the Peru of the future.[41]

Furthermore, Belaúnde Terry indicated his desire to decentralize some of the activities which he felt were extremely concentrated in Lima; in the political field he proposed to revive municipal elections and in the area of finances to provide more bank credit to the rest of the country. Needless to say, this section of his platform appealed to the traditional upper class and the middle class of the Sierra. His emphasis on industrialization and his newly gained confidence in domestic entrepreneurs sounded extremely attractive to the limited group of Peruvian industrialists and small mineowners, as well as to those working in their enterprises. He increased his attractiveness to this group by attacking foreign monopolies and questioning the judgment exercised by the Prado administration in granting further concessions to large foreign investors.

Acción Popular succeeded in 1963 as an electoral machine with the help of the military, which evidently felt that Belaúnde Terry's reforms were acceptable to them; the Church, which probably considered that his victory would prevent the type of cleavages within its ranks evolving elsewhere in Latin America; and the Christian Democratic party, which, convinced of its inability to go it alone, joined forces with AP in exchange for the country's Second Vice-Presidency and certain places in the congressional lists and provided the margin of victory (see Chapter 7). But the mutation of Acción Popular from an electoral machine to a transitional organization, moving in the direction of an ideological party, has been caused by the flow of members of the intelligentsia who, either because of frustration with the other parties or because of attraction to Belaúnde Terry's organization, joined the ranks of AP. Led by Edgardo Seoane, brother of the former Aprista leader, First Vice-President of Peru in the period 1963–68 and secretary-general of Acción Popular, these individuals constituted the left wing

[41] Fernando Belaúnde Terry, *Pueblo por Pueblo,* pp. 164–69 *passim,* cited by Bourricaud, *Poder y Sociedad en el Perú Contemporáneo,* p. 238.

of the party and contributed through their writings and public pronouncements toward giving it a pragmatic ideology of reform which transcends that of President Belaúnde Terry. This trend was reflected among university students, who in 1965 showed a preference for Acción Popular, not only in terms of sympathy, but also in regard to actual party membership.[42]

The pragmatic ideology of these intellectuals was articulated by Seoane:

The characteristics of Peruvian society, that is, of our nation, reflect what we Peruvians actually are: an educated, intelligent, progressive, but extremely selfish minority; and an ignorant, poor, majority whose acceptance of desperate living conditions diminishes daily, a fact which may lead them to seek violent solutions or to become ready materials for the spread of dissociative ideas. . . . There is not the slightest doubt that an authentic Revolution has to take place in Peru so that, in changing our present structures, it will solve the painful situation of millions of Peruvians who lack adequate nourishment, clean housing, education, and healthy leisure activities.[43]

Unlike Haya de la Torre and other Aprista writers, Belaúnde carefully avoids citing foreign thinkers and scholars; he centers his commentaries on the greatness of the nation's past and tries to instill confidence in his fellow countrymen by telling them that the secrets of the vitality of the Inca Empire have not been lost. An outstanding speaker, he employs his oratory to avoid making commitments in regard to specific courses of action. It would appear, as Bourricaud has said, that *"Belaundismo* is an ideology without doctrine."[44] If this is so, if Belaúnde Terry is in fact trying to build a party based on a pragmatic ideology, then the record of his administration will provide the opportunity for Acción Popular to become a long-term feature of Peruvian politics.

[42] See *Caretas,* July 9–22, 1965, pp. 10–13.
[43] Edgardo Seoane, *Surcos de Paz,* pp. 16–17. The book goes on to outline a specific program of reforms, mostly in the rural areas, whose necessity is documented with statistics and charts and backed by references to recent Catholic documents issued in Rome *but not in Peru.*
[44] *Poder y Sociedad,* p. 254.

According to some, Belaúnde Terry has done many of the things he pledged to do. He has started the construction of at least some of the highways he promised in his writings and campaign speeches; he proposed a land-reform bill, prepared by a group headed by Edgardo Seoane, although the version passed by the APRA-UNO congressional majority was significantly amended and toned down. Even with the substantial limitations of the Agrarian Reform Act, the Belaúnde administration has announced the expropiation of some large landholdings, practically all of them in the Sierra; these included the cattle ranches of the American mining concern Cerro de Pasco Corporation, which covered 617,417 acres,[45] although company officials had declared that the company was not interested in its landholdings and indicated willingness to sell them to the government. Belaúnde also revived the autonomy of the local governmental units, allowing them to elect their key officials; most of the municipal elections favored Acción Popular and its allies, the Christian Democrats, but not without some regional defeats, mostly at the hands of independent candidates not necessarily in disagreement with the President's position. He appointed to his cabinet men who were neither landowners nor bankers, mostly in their forties and, in more than a third of the cases, of technocratic backgrounds. The cabinets have included a number of individuals who were born in the Sierra and the Selva, breaking the traditional dominance of the coastal area and more specifically of the capital city. Perhaps more significant was his nationalization of the Registro de Depósitos y Consignaciones ("Registry of Deposits and Consignments"), an agency jointly organized by six of the largest banks for the purpose of collecting certain taxes on a commission basis. Finally, in mid-1967 the Belaúnde administration, with congressional approval, made a general declaration of state ownership of the La Brea and Pariñas oil fields and promised to move toward their take-over. This has long been a national issue with international overtones, since the oil fields have been exploited by a subsidiary of Standard Oil of New

[45] *Oiga,* June 9, 1967, p. 7.

Jersey.[46] Specific steps to implement this promise were not immediately taken.

But, while these measures have been considered important reforms, the feeling of most observers is one of disappointment. It seems clear that the hopes developed by Belaúnde Terry and other members of his party did not materialize. Reporting in August, 1966, Norman Gall wrote in the *Wall Street Journal:*

So far, agrarian reform in Peru has done as badly as similar government programs in almost every place where attempted in Latin America. They have lacked impact either as social welfare programs or as stimuli to desperately needed food production increases. The only significant changes in the land tenure system, and those very few, have come by peasant land seizures.[47]

This tone can be found, week after week, in the magazine *Oiga*, mildly pro-Acción Popular, but expressing the views of the party's developmentalist wing. Perhaps the best evidence of at least partial failure is the speech made by First Vice-President Edgardo Seoane, representing this sector, on the occasion of his election as secretary-general of his party.

My presence in the position of Secretary General will involve, then, the preparation of the party to carry out the reforms. Not only agrarian reform, but also tax reform, credit reform, and corporation reform, because Peru's progress and development exist in these reforms. . . . Fernando Belaúnde spread throughout the country the seeds of many hopes which germinated confidence, and the plants have grown. But as it happens with all plants, they have suffered diseases which have to be cured, and there have grown rotten branches which have to be pruned. . . . We have to recognize the physical works carried out by the present government, the many things done in the area of roads, schools, hospitals, sanitation and irrigation; but this huge physical body,

[46] See *Oiga*, June 30, 1967, p. 7; *Primera Plana*, August 1, 1967, p. 32; New York *Times*, August 13, 1967, p. 31; *La Prensa* (Buenos Aires), December 20, 1967, p. 2; and *International Financial News Survey*, 18:108 (1966).

[47] "Elusive Land Reform," August 18, 1966, p. 7.

grown in these few years, has to be given a soul, and the soul is the reforms, the social justice.[48]

Besides being blamed for the questionable effectiveness of the Agrarian Reform Act, Belaúnde Terry has been criticized for the corruption which has continued to exist under his administration, his tax policy, and the recent devaluation of the sol. The matter of corruption was brought to the fore by an investigation of smuggling conducted by a group of army intelligence officers hired by the textile industry; the investigators concluded that, "everything can be gotten through Peruvian customs, except the ship." [49] Other signs of corruption have appeared, such as the "Datorre-Grimberg affair" which compromised the then Minister of Finance and Commerce.[50] In the area of taxation the situation seems to be worse; published reports indicate that only 17,000 Peruvians pay any sort of income tax—and not necessarily in accord with the law; furthermore, out of 3,124,579 economically active persons, only 25,000 paid taxes on profits in 1965.[51] Practically nothing has been done in this matter, and attempts to alter the tax structure and collection procedures have been rejected by the APRA-UNO congressional majority, thus causing the pressure on the Peruvian sol which finally brought about its devaluation.

The question of currency devaluation is complex, but it does exemplify, perhaps more clearly than anything else, the distribution of economic rewards in Peruvian society. For a long time the value of the sol had remained steady at twenty-seven to the U.S. dollar. As inflationary pressures mounted in Peru—in the last three years

[48] Quoted in *Oiga,* June 2, 1967, p. 9.

[49] *Confirmado* (Buenos Aires), February 2, 1967, p. 31. The evidence of corruption in the Bureau of Customs has been *vox populi* in Lima for some time; airline officials repeatedly pointed out that the Bureau Chief was listed as receiving a salary of a few hundred dollars a month and yet he owned a house in the $100,000 range and travelled to Europe or the United States at least once a year. The stores of the border city of Iquitos (in the Selva) have been full of television sets and heavy clothing, in spite of the fact that it has no television station and a tropical climate.

[50] The affair was reported in *Oiga,* May 19, 1967, p. 11, and June 2, 1967, p. 7.

[51] *Ibid.,* July 16, 1965, pp. 18, 36–37.

at the rate of approximately 9 per cent a year—the purchasing power of the American currency was correspondingly reduced. This reduction in the purchasing power of the sol tended to make the exporting of raw materials less rewarding (thus damaging mining enterprises and producers of cotton, sugar, and fish meal—in other words, foreign investors and the coastal sector of the traditional upper class) and the importation of industrial goods and foodstuffs less expensive. If coupled with favorable and properly enforced tariff protection for finished industrial products, this trend could diminish the domestic cost of food and make the development of an industrial base easily attainable. Peru's balance of payments was favorable throughout the 1960's, thus making it possible for the Central Reserve Bank to avoid downward fluctuations of the exchange rate without applying exchange controls. This policy was being carried out, to a certain extent, at the expense of the exporters, who would benefit from a depreciation since it would increase the amount of sols they would get for the dollars earned abroad. On the other hand, they would not really suffer in terms of the imported products they buy, since their own terms-of-trade ratio in the international market would remain the same. This was the situation of the fish-meal industrialists, who export their product but have been building up their plants and thus importing industrial machinery.

The attack on the sol was mounted at the beginning of 1967. The fish-meal producers delayed their shipments abroad and the other raw material producers retained their dollars, while rumors of a forthcoming devaluation increased the demand for the American currency. The Central Reserve Bank was forced to utilize its dollar reserves to maintain the exchange rate. In March the representatives of the fish-meal industry appealed to the President and to Congress for either the elimination of export taxes or the devaluation of the sol; they did not obtain any immediate satisfaction from Belaúnde Terry, but they were favorably received by the APRA-UNO congressional majority, where their interests were well represented. The reduction of export taxes, particularly in a country where direct taxes were paid by only a few, would have meant a greater budgetary deficit or the curtailment of governmental programs, essentially in the areas of agrarian reform, road-building, education, and so on. At that time, the administration was warned that "if the President does not accept the request of the fishing industry, the pressure of the exporting and financial groups may reach really dangerous levels." The pressure from financial circles originated in the fact that 75 per cent of the money invested in the fishing industry came from the Lima banks; in fact, the banking interests appeared to be the true owners of the fishing industry.[52]

The situation came to a head when the legislature was ready to deal with Belaúnde Terry's budget requests; in May, Congress approved reductions totaling $56,000,000 in the 1967 budget, although more than one-half of these "savings" were earmarked as additional appropriations to the Defense Ministry. The 1968 budget was rejected toward the end of that month, since the APRA-UNO majority was unwilling to vote the new taxes proposed by the executive in order to finance programs such as agrarian reform. It proposed, instead, deep cuts, mostly in those items which were related to the developmental process. This and previous budget deficits had already been anticipated in 1964 as part of the administration's public investment program.[53] However, with pressure on the sol mounting, the traditional upper class seems to have decided that the time was right to end those government programs which were considered a threat to the *status quo*, as well as to control inflation and deficit spending, which it has traditionally opposed. When Belaúnde responded with mild moves to leave the legislature without a quorum and to govern by decree, the military (who apparently had not forgotten the special appropriation of a few months earlier) practically ordered him to negotiate a compromise solution within the constitutional framework.[54]

[52] *Ibid.*, March 31, 1967, pp. 5, 7.

[53] *International Financial News Survey*, 16:415 (1964); see also 19:188 (1967), and 15:399 (1963).

[54] The pressure of the military was reported by *Primera Plana*, August 1, 1967, p. 32, and *Oiga*, June 9, 1967, p. 6. The opposition of the traditional upper class to high taxes and deficit spending can be seen in the editorials

What followed was a series of offers and counteroffers in which Belaúnde Terry was trying to avoid devaluating the sol by going along with some budget cuts in exchange for some sort of tax increase. He finally proposed a tariff increase, which was first accepted by the opposition in committee, than rejected on the floor of the lower house. Simultaneously, the International Monetary Fund and the United States government made loans and credits which could have reinforced the sol subject to fulfillment of either politically unacceptable austerity measures or devaluation.

Belaúnde Terry was politically and economically surrounded on all sides and unwilling to cut the budget as much as the opposition wanted, which would have stopped practically all public works and other politically important programs. At last he gave in to the traditional upper class, and particularly to its coastal sector, and ordered the Central Reserve Bank to cease supporting the sol which went down to approximately forty to the U.S. dollar.[55] Some observers may claim that the devaluation was due to structural balance-of-payment problems, but they should remember that on a number of occasions the general economic situation of Peru, and particularly its foreign exchange reserve and balance of payments, have been considered basically sound.[56] In fact, Belaúnde Terry's economic policy, on the whole, was following the lines drawn by the publisher of *La Prensa*, Pedro Beltrán, when the latter was economic tsar under Prado.[57] The devaluation of the sol was a politically-motivated act, whose main objective was to turn around whatever redistribution of income had been taking place as a consequence of internal rises in prices and salaries and a fixed foreign exchange rate. The coastal sector of the traditional upper

---

of *La Prensa* (Lima) throughout the summer of 1967; see Bourricaud, *Poder y Sociedad*, pp. 186–209.

[55] Bits and pieces of evidence have appeared in the New York *Times*, August 13, 1967, p. 31; *Caretas*, May 12–25, 1967, p. 14; *Primera Plana*, September 26, 1967, pp. 32–33; *Oiga*, June 30, 1967, pp. 4–7, 30; *Confirmado*, June 1, 1967, p. 29; and *International Financial News Survey*, 19:388, (1967).

[56] *International Financial News Survey*, 20:11, (1968).

[57] *El Universal* (Mexico City), September 5, 1965, p. 2.

class could now get almost 50 per cent more sols for their exports; those engaged in the production of foodstuffs for domestic consumption could charge higher prices, because imports would cost more. Industrialists had to pay more sols for their machinery and imported raw materials, and the government could approach a balanced budget with the old indirect taxes. In the meantime the cost of living jumped 10 per cent in the three months following devaluation, and wages did not increase in the same proportion. In a special election to fill two vacant seats in the lower house and some municipal offices, Acción Popular suffered a setback, and the percentage of registered voters who did not vote was unusually high.[58]

It is on the basis of episodes like the 1967 devaluation of the sol that parties which sponsor a pragmatic ideology, like Acción Popular, ought to be judged; indeed, this is the only way they can be judged. The complexities of the constitutional procedure and the ability of all sides to hide their true goals and actions from the average Peruvian voter (who has only an elementary education), plus the contempt and cynicism with which politics and politicians are viewed, make it extremely difficult to maintain popular support while in power, except by unusual charisma or by dramatic improvements. It is still too early to say whether Acción Popular will achieve permanency on the basis of either one, but this seems unlikely unless the party carries out more drastic reforms; since 1967, Belaúnde Terry appeared to have been only trying to survive and complete his term of office.

The Unión Nacional Odriista

Compared with the two parties already discussed, the electoral machine organized to satisfy the political aspirations of former military dictator Manuel A. Odría would seem an anticlimax. And yet, the voting strength the party demonstrated in the elections of

[58] Data on wages and the cost of living are from *International Financial News Survey*, 20:11, (1968). Data on the special election are from *Primera Plana*, November 21, 1967, p. 31; also *Clarín* (Buenos Aires), December 31, 1967, p. 22.

1962 and 1963 (see Tables 17 and 19), under administrations that did not do anything to assist the general, warrants something more than superficial reference to this organization. Traditionally, Peruvian electoral machines succeed in getting their candidate elected when they receive support from those in power, usually through a combination of financial assistance (government jobs and monies) and coercion of competing organizations. This was the case with the Movimiento Democrático Pradista, which carried Prado to his second presidency (although the Odría administration lent its positive support only near the end of the electoral campaign, it did obstruct the activities of the most important competitor, Belaúnde Terry), and with the Convención which elected José Pardo.

The ideology which UNO claims to profess appears to be quite simple: the party relies on the record compiled by General Odría when he occupied the presidency (1948–56). Odría himself has tried to emphasize this approach by repeating during the electoral campaign of 1962, and again in 1963, the slogans "democracy cannot be eaten," "deeds not words," and "bread, a roof, and a job." Remarks made by the party leader and his close lieutenants indicate that they would try to continue the policies already developed in the first Odría administration, which essentially consisted of a few but spectacular public works, concentrated in Lima and other coastal cities; a few irrigation works, which benefited the region's landowners; a balanced budget; plentiful employment opportunities; and low indirect taxes. During the 1963 electoral campaign the present UNO leader in the Senate, Julio de la Piedra, rejected without qualifications all progressive taxes, and indicated that his party intended to reduce income and real property taxes, an apparent appeal to upper and upper middle sectors.[59] And yet it is obvious that the party could not have received 28.44 per cent of the vote in the 1962 election or 25.52 per cent in 1963 from the upper levels of society alone. A careful look at the returns shows that, besides regional preferences in the departments of Piura and Tacna (where Odría concentrated most of his public

[59] Press interview reproduced in César Martín Saunders, *Dichos y Hechos de la Política Peruana*, pp. 95–99.

works outside the capital city), he received the votes of the very rich and the very poor of the urban centers, particularly the Lima-Callao area. His support came and still comes from the people of the shantytowns, a point that was demonstrated when he returned to Peru in 1961 after a five-year residence in Washington, D.C.

The general's return provides the occasion for a well-attended demonstration, with some of his former cabinet members, advisors, clients, and relatives in the first row. But beyond them the people of very humble origin constitute the majority of the public; men and women from the shantytowns have been recruited in large numbers to receive the dictator of the period 1948–56.[60]

In spite of Odría's quarrel with members of the coastal sector of the traditional upper class in 1955–56, UNO was well off financially. Odría was born in the Sierra and seems to enjoy the confidence of the traditional upper class of the interior, as well as of a portion of the dependent middle class. His appeal to the sub-proletariat, mostly of the city of Lima, stems from the good party organization in the shantytowns, some schools and housing developments built under his administration, and the role played by his wife in dispensing charity—although an attempt to cash in on Mrs. Odría's image by having her elected mayor of Lima failed. In general, however, the party seems to be maintaining its organizational structure, although recent divisions can not yet be fully assessed, and financial backing still appears to be generous. Its electoral strength is difficult to ascertain because of the understanding reached with APRA after the 1963 presidential election. In view of

[60] Bourricaud, *Poder y Sociedad*, p. 292. The writer had a few opportunities to observe the composition and operation of the UNO from the inside in 1965 and was impressed with its diverse membership and its strong structure in the shantytowns which surround Lima. It was apparent, however, that party policy was made by Odría and was strongly influenced by traditional upper class contributors, although they seldom appear at party headquarters. In fact, decisions were made at Odría's plush residence, located in the Lima suburb of Monterrico, and to have been there was a status symbol among party leaders.

the diverse composition of its membership, the absence of ideological bonds, and the rigid personal leadership exercised by Odría, it is extremely difficult to predict what would happen were its leader to retire or pass away. So far, General Odría has not discussed retirement (he was born in 1897); rumors in this direction which spread in the second half of 1967 were quickly squelched by the Odriistas.

The Christian Democrats

The Christian Democratic party of Peru became a reality in 1956 when a group of Catholic laymen decided to enter the political struggle directly, with the avowed intention of altering the established role of the Peruvian Catholic Church as supplier of the conservative ideology which supported the privileges of the traditional upper class (see Chapter 8). Encouraged by recent encyclical letters issued by the Holy See and by the new Catholic emphasis on material improvement of the lower class seen in Europe and in other Latin American countries, a group of intellectuals, mostly from Arequipa, founded the party and elected a few legislators in 1956. Although it is difficult to identify an unchallenged leader, Hector Cornejo Chávez was one of its most active original members. The party received the intellectual inspiration of former president Bustamante y Rivero, who had been overthrown by the military with the support of the coastal sector of the traditional upper class. Thus, from the very beginning, what was later to be the Christian Democratic party showed an anti-Odría attitude and, because of its ideological position, was profoundly distrusted by most of the members of the traditional upper class, and particularly by its coastal sector. While probably not the decisive factor, the socioeconomic origin of the Christian Democratic leadership may have had something to do with this encounter, since many of the party's leaders belonged to old families (a regional aristocracy) with limited economic resources, particularly when compared with the bankers, raw material exporters, and fish-meal producers centered in Lima.

In 1949, shortly after being overthrown, Bustamante y Rivero wrote:

There is more and more the impression that too much emphasis on the doctrinaire aspects is often placed from the pulpit, without insisting enough on the usual Christian norms of living. . . . There is sometimes a lack of human emotion and of Christian indignation to harass social injustices and merchants' greed. There is fear of injuring the powerful, and respectful euphemisms are employed to condemn authoritarian abuses. From it grows the widespread belief that the Church goes along with the interest groups and maintains an implicit alliance with the temporal powers. . . . Human contact with urban and rural workers has also been lacking. . . . [The objective should be] to demonstrate *with facts* that, if the priest knows how to comfort a misfortune and pray before a grave, he also knows how painful misery feels deep inside; *to show them that, at the hour of justice, he does not limit himself to preaching submission, but knows how to back with his moral authority the just and human demands.*[61]

The Christian Democratic party of Peru, in reacting against the situation described by Bustamante y Rivero, presents itself as a reformist party which is totally unwilling to employ violence to achieve the changes it favors. Its ideology claims to reject both Marxism and capitalism as it has existed in Peru; it subscribes to the ideological tenets of the Christian Democratic parties of Italy, Austria, Belgium, and other European countries, with the specific changes required by the different environment. While the party has attempted to project a legalistic left-of-center image by backing profound reform programs, its emphasis on the normal constitutional process as the only way to achieve power and carry out reforms and its strictly regional base have diminished its appeal to those who favor urgent and meaningful changes in the *status quo*. It was evident from the beginning that the party was torn between its conservative and liberal wings and pre-empted by Belaúnde Terry's Acción Popular. The latter had been organized almost at the same time, was backed by well-known Catholic intellectuals, and appeared more convincing as the sponsor of structural reforms

[61] José Luis Bustamante y Rivero, *Tres Años de Lucha por la Democracia en el Perú*, pp. 164–65 (emphasis added).

and as a winner in a presidential contest.[62] After the poor showing by the Christian Democrats in the 1962 election, they joined
Belaúnde Terry and provided the margin for his 1963 victory, in
exchange for the ticket's second vice-presidency, some support in
certain congressional races, and the right to select the candidate
for the mayoralty of Lima, won by Luis Bedoya Reyes.

This alliance has continued in Congress to the extent that the
Christian Democrats became almost an appendage of the Belaúnde Terry administration. In 1967, however, the strain between
the conservative and reformist wings of the organization produced
a division, which can be traced back to the party congress held in
November, 1966. In February of 1967, the conservative elements,
led by the mayor of Lima, decided to break away and organize the
Christian Popular party, which announced its opposition to redistribution of privately-owned land and nationalization of the oil
fields and mines. Belaúnde Terry maneuvered to obtain the support of this faction in the special election held in November, 1967,
and the Christian Democrats, still under the guidance of Cornejo
Chávez, interrupted their collaboration with Acción Popular, os-
tensibly on the grounds that the administration had ceased to be
reformist.[63] In view of these difficulties, which cannot yet be accurately assessed, the future of the Christian Democratic party will
probably depend on the future role of Acción Popular and the relation between the two.

The Extreme Left

No description of the Peruvian party structure would be complete without a brief reference to the conglomeration of minute
ideological parties which make up the left wing of the country's
political spectrum. Some of the organizations included in this category have been or will be referred to in discussing APRA (APRA
Rebelde and MIR) and the Catholic Church (The National Liberation Front). Most of these parties have appeared in the last de-

[62] See Hernández Urbina, *Nueva Política*, pp. 123–38; Héctor Cornejo
Chávez, *Nuevos Principios para un Nuevo Perú, passim.*

[63] *Confirmado,* March 2, 1967, pp. 28–29, and *Primera Plana,* November
21, 1967, p. 31.

cade and sometimes collaborate with the now established occupants of this portion of the political spectrum, the Socialists and the Communists. The over-all objective of all these organizations is the elimination of the power elites and radical alteration of the present distribution of political, economic, and social power. Beyond this general goal, however, they agree on very little; there is disagreement about how their revolutionary objectives will come about and, more importantly, about who will lead the masses to their "political redemption." When they have decided to try the electoral road they have been unwilling or unable to join forces; this disunity makes even more evident their limited and highly localized following. When one or two of the organizations selected the road of violent revolution and took to the mountains, the others either refused to collaborate or actually rejected the decision.

The Socialist and Communist parties maintain that they were founded in 1928 by the distinguished Peruvian intellectual, José Carlos Mariátegui, under the Marxist-Socialist label. The split came when Mariátegui died, two years later, and both parties have since claimed that he in fact founded *their* party and that the other organization cannot possibly call Mariátegui its founder.[64] It could probably be stated that neither the Socialists nor the Communists have lived up to their founder's prescription:

Unfortunately, the revolution is not made with fastings. The revolutionaries of all latitudes have to choose between suffering violence or using it. If men do not want spirit and intelligence to be under the command of force, then it is necessary to put force under the command of intelligence and spirit.[65]

In spite of their allegiance to Mariátegui, neither the Socialists nor the Communists have demonstrated a willingness to follow his revolutionary advice. As almost everywhere else in Latin America, they have become "revolutionaries of café society," who, rightly or wrongly, accept as an unchangeable fact the overwhelming power

[64] For conflicting claims along these lines, see Chang Rodríguez, *La Literatura Política*, pp. 161–79, and Hernández Urbina, *Nueva Política*, pp. 82–105.

[65] José Carlos Mariátegui, *La Escena Contemporánea*, pp. 198–99.

of the ruling groups and often dissuade their followers from taking revolutionary steps, instead of leading them in that direction.[66]

It has been this refusal on the part of the established left wing to do something, anything, that can be considered truly revolutionary which has encouraged the formation of other political organizations, whose disagreement with Socialists and Communists is centered not on their appraisal of Peruvian society, but in the strategy that should be employed in changing it and, what is more important, in its concrete application. APRA Rebelde, MIR, Frente de Izquierda Revolucionaria ("Front of the Revolutionary Left") Social Progressive party, Revolutionary Workers party (Trotskyite), National Liberation Front, and others which appear and disappear, merge and split, are organizations that want to apply revolutionary tactics in Peru *now*. But, needless to say, it is easier said than done; besides fighting official repression and the physical and intellectual persecution of the *Apristas,* Christian Democrats, and sometimes Belaundistas, they find it very difficult to get along within their minuscule organizations. In discussing subversive activities mounted by the Frente de Izquierda Revolucionaria in 1962–63, a well-placed observer wrote:

The outcome was tied to the special conditions of the revolutionary structure now being examined. Serious disagreements developed in Lima among the members of the political directorate, and even more serious disagreements between them and the military machine, and, finally, conditions which led to a break between all of them and the international directorate. Two factors were extremely important in these developments. One of them was the question of the destination of the expropriated funds, their use, distribution, accounting, and custody; it was the main point which caused the break with the international directorate. The other, the matter of hierarchy and clear and deep understanding of the tactical line to be followed, was what caused the discrepancies between the political bureau and the military organization.[67]

[66] There are many specific examples of this attitude; see, for instance, Hugo Neira, *Cuzco: Tierra y Muerte,* especially pp. 43, 44–47, 55–56, and 73–74; also Ismael Frías, *La Revolución Peruana,* especially p. 69.

[67] Américo Pumaruna, "Perú: Revolución, Insurrección, Guerrillas," p. 67.

These parties of the Left are politically significant only in that their presence places at the disposal of the politically mobilized portion of the Peruvian population a rallying point, if and when a significant portion of them become frustrated with Acción Popular and are not attracted by the Christian Democrats. This rallying point need not be exclusively for electoral purposes, since the Movement of the Revolutionary Left, the National Liberation Front, and the Front of the Revolutionary Left, among others, are strongly committed to the use of force and generally subscribe to the views expressed by Fidel Castro and, to a certain extent, by the Chinese Communist party. MIR emphasized in its program the importance of waging an armed struggle, and even after the failure of the 1965 attempts, it continued its preference for a violent revolution.[68] Nevertheless, observation indicates that the established ideological parties of the Right and Center and the electoral machines, through charisma and changes of labels, provide the politically active Peruvians with at least the appearance of a channel to articulate their interest, an acceptable myth, and the hope that governmental responsiveness to their wishes will improve for most of them. As long as these parties and machines do so function, the Left will have to continue its dependency on the shelter provided by certain labor unions and outside help, while they wait for those Peruvians to become disenchanted enough with the *status quo* to want to change it at any cost. It may be a long wait, and in the meantime, the parties of the Left may themselves frustrate their few members with their powerlessness.

[68] Movimiento de Izquierda Revolucionaria, *Bases Doctrinarias y Programáticas, passim;* Rogger Mercado, *Las Guerrillas del Perú—El MIR: De la Prédica Ideológica a la Acción Armada, passim;* also Luis F. de la Puente Uceda, "The Peruvian Revolution: Concepts and Perspectives." Finally, see the statement made by the MIR delegation to the 1966 Tricontinental Conference, quoted by Pumaruna in "Perú," p. 86.

7. The Peruvian Military

Almost anyone who has followed Latin American politics for some time or who has studied the topic is familiar with the crucial role played by the military establishment in the political lives of most of the countries. Peru is no exception; indeed, it could be cited as one of the best—or worst—examples. From 1821, when Peru became independent, until 1968, the presidency (or its equivalent) has been held by seventy-six individuals; fifty of them were military men who led the country for eighty-six years. More than half of the civilians achieved the presidency through the use of force and thus depended upon the military to remain in power. The first civilian president was elected to the post in 1872, but his followers had to defeat a coup led by four brothers, illiterate colonels, who could not bear the sight of a Peruvian president who was not a military man.[1]

It should be clear that an institution which has provided most of Peru's presidents cannot be considered simply a pressure group, unless the definition of "pressure group" were to be radically altered. It is also clear that, even if the Peruvian military tried at any one time to act as a traditional pressure group, national history would remind any government that the type of pressure the military can apply far outweighs the ability of the government to resist. Furthermore, the success which the armed forces usually have in associating their interests with those of the nation often

[1] See Víctor Villanueva, *El Militarismo en el Perú*, p. 25. A good historical description of the political activities of the military can be found in Leónidas Castro Bastos, *Geohistoria del Perú: Ensayo Económico, Político, Social*, ch. 10.

makes their "pressure" all the more irresistible. This role of the armed forces as a key power holder (see Chapter 2) is only now being brought up in the literature on Latin American politics; until recently the military were lumped together with institutions such as labor unions or chambers of commerce. In countries, such as Peru, where the rules of the political game are not precisely defined and seem to admit the use of violence, those who are equipped to employ violence and have shown their willingness to use it have placed themselves above the category of pressure groups. This is not simply a question of terminology; true pressure groups are powerless to counterbalance the influence of a power holder such as the armed forces when there is wide agreement within the officer corps regarding the achievement of certain objectives. As will be seen, pluralism cannot, and does not, operate in such a case.

Nineteenth-Century Militarism in Peru

The figures presented at the beginning of this chapter, expressive as they are in reference to the political role of the military in the country, do not have the same significance through time. The domestic struggle for power that ensued after Peru's independence made the line between the national armed forces and the personal troops of various *caudillos* very difficult to draw. Few members of the officer corps were "career officers,"—in the sense that they were willing to remain in the armed forces for a long period of time. As elsewhere, politicians and men with ambitions and power became generals (often self-appointed), and officers who had achieved their personal objectives withdrew, sometimes to administer their newly acquired land or business. The national army happened to be that army whose *caudillo* was in control of the capital city and, therefore, had access to the national treasury. Soldiers and noncommissioned officers joined because there was nothing better to do or because they were forcibly drafted. In brief, throughout the nineteenth century the country had armed groups but not a national army as currently defined. Occasionally, a prominent *caudillo* (such as Ramón Castilla) would achieve a degree of permanence through agreements with other *caudillos* and the traditional upper class and would attempt to unify the armed forces into a national institution; but these attempts produced only temporary positive results because they were based on the *caudillo's* personal power and skill.[2]

The military *caudillos* were not members of the traditional upper class, particularly just after independence. Villanueva has said:

The civilians subordinated themselves peacefully and with pleasure to the generals-made-*caudillos*. The landlord, somewhat impoverished as a consequence of the war, prefers to withdraw to the hacienda to rebuild it and to improve his damaged economy; he does not see the military *caudillo*, who relieves him of acting in politics and gives him guarantees defending his property, in a bad light.[3]

Evidence of this alliance, or at least agreement of interests, can be found in the various measures which in fact reinstated slavery —partially outlawed by the Argentine General San Martín in 1821—until a mestizo dictator, Castilla, abolished it thirty-three years later. There is general agreement that during this time the officer corps was open to all those with courage and a strong desire to move upward in the socioeconomic scale. While the nineteenth-century Peruvian military were willing to risk (and sometimes lose) their lives to improve their individual status, nobody, not even Castilla, took steps to alter the *status quo* or to take power away from the traditional upper class. A tacit accord evidently developed early in Peruvian history between the creoles who replaced the Spaniards and the military officers; its objective and result was the preservation of the structure inherited from the colonial administration in exchange for ample economic rewards and relatively easy admission of distinguished military officers into the group of "good families," plus whatever legitimation the upper class could provide. While it is true that disagreements sometimes developed between some *caudillos* and one upper-class clique or

[2] Villanueva, *El Militarismo*, ch. 1; Liisa North, *Civil-Military Relations in Argentina, Chile, and Peru*, pp. 8–10.

[3] *El Militarismo*, p. 19.

another, it should not be forgotten that the *caudillos* were forced to surround themselves with a clique since only the upper class was adequately trained to administer the country; it would not be an exaggeration to say that education was monopolized by the traditional upper class.[4]

Certain steps taken in the 1850's and 1860's, such as the ending of the guano concessions, upset the relationship between the upper class and the military, and the Partido Civilista took the presidency away from the *caudillos* in 1872. Once its ruling elite occupied the seat of government, the coastal upper class proceeded to counter the influence of the military by creating a National Guard and various military schools, which were to unify and professionalize the armed forces. Now in direct control of the governmental machinery, the traditional upper class was interested in subordinating the armed forces to the civilian authorities (itself) and in converting them into an effective and reliable fighting force. These actions were only partially successful; the defeat in the War of the Pacific and the inability of the upper class to provide effective leadership brought the military back to power, although this time they were less willing to be guided and advised by the traditional upper class. And yet no attempt was made to modify the traditional sources of power, particularly the ownership of land.

Clearly, the military officers wanted to join the upper class and share its privileges, not to destroy it. But the abuses and lawlessness which ensued in building up personal fortunes at the expense of the public treasury caused a reaction against the military *caudillos;* this reaction manifested itself in the coalition between the upper-class Partido Civilista and the Partido Demócrata, a conglomeration of lower- and middle-class elements led by a charismatic leader, Nicolás de Piérola. In 1895 the army was defeated by bands of civilians that put Piérola in the presidential palace. And, as they had done with the military before, the coastal upper class influenced the civilian *caudillo,* who continued the attempts of the

[4] On this point see François Bourricaud, "Remarques sur l'Oligarchie Peruvienne," pp. 694–95, and North, *Civil-Military Relations,* p. 9.

Partido Civilista to control and improve the armed forces. President Piérola hired a French military mission in 1896, created the Military School at Chorrillos and training centers for noncommissioned officers, supported a Law of Obligatory Military Service, and rationalized somewhat the system of promotions. The net result was a higher degree of professionalism in the armed forces and a loss of popular support, which led to partially effective civilian control.

These developments altered the political thinking of the military officers, who apparently realized that they were unable to oppose successfully a popular leader who was backed by the upper class —specifically, by the coastal plutocracy. But the presidential election of 1912 marked the beginning of a split between the upper class and the Partido Demócrata. That party's winning candidate, Guillermo Billinghurst, managed to widen the split—particularly by his willingness to go along with the eight-hour working day and his reduction of the military share of the national budget from 24.75 per cent to 21.60 per cent [5]—and developed an obvious community of interest between the upper class and the armed forces. The Lima garrison revolted in February of 1914 and Colonel Oscar R. Benavides, escorted by the Prado brothers, his "civilian advisors," took over the presidency. This event marks the beginning of an effective collaboration between the armed forces and the coastal sector of the traditional upper class, with the acquiescence of the Sierra landowners.

Many have claimed that the 1914 coup which overthrew President Billinghurst marks the moment when the military became the defender and protector of the upper class. This may in fact be the case, as later revolts against the dictator Leguía, who enjoyed strong popular support, particularly in the urban areas, and President Bustamante y Rivero, who obtained a significant electoral majority after a deal with the then outlawed APRA, tend to show; but it cannot be considered the whole case. The military had come

[5] For accurate accounts of these events see César Lévano, *La Verdadera Historia de las 8 Horas . . .* , *passim;* Villanueva, *El Militarismo,* pp. 40–50; and Leonidas Castro Bastos, *¡Golpismo!,* pp. 40–46.

to realize that the traditional upper class could, when allied with a popular movement, subject them to civilian control or at least deprive them of the legitimacy provided by the approval of the "good families" and the "distinguished citizens." They also knew that there was no reason to believe that a government which challenged the interests of the upper class would be more responsive to the budgetary needs of the armed forces than a government which had attained office as a consequence of a coup, particularly if it was led by a military man or if the military establishment participated in it. Former dictator Leguía had been encouraging the development of a competing industrial base at the expense of the traditional upper class, but he also gave military commissions and rapid promotions to his followers, created a Civil Guard, and bought expensive military equipment for the Navy and the Air Force to counter the political power of the Army. This redistribution of military funds becomes particularly important in the light of the great fluctuation in this statistic. President José Pardo, of the Partido Civilista, who was re-elected in 1915 with military backing, had reduced the military share of the national budget from 25.2 per cent to 17.9 per cent when he was overthrown in 1919. Leguía increased this to 22.1 per cent during his first year in office, but the figure had dropped to 17.6 per cent when he was overthrown in 1930.

The different factors which pushed the upper class and the armed forces toward each other were made clear by their spokesmen in 1914. The proclamation issued by the military leadership of the coup that overthrew Billinghurst emphasized the poverty that existed in the military establishment, the ragged appearance of the troops, and their need for shoes: "they still lack summer uniforms in the month of February." [6] On the other hand, at a banquet organized by the peers of the Prado brothers in their honor (the brothers had been the "political commisars" of the revolt) the keynote speaker concluded that the military revolt had been fundamentally directed "against the irreverent, insolent, and devastating

[6] José Urdanivia Ginés, *Una Revolución Modelo [del] Ejército Peruano*, p. 17. Urdanivia Ginés was one of the leaders of the 1914 revolt.

audacity of the lower classes, which had almost eclipsed the ruling class." [7]

Other *coups d'etat* in this century further demonstrate the existence of this community of interests. Dictator Leguía was overthrown by Colonel Sánchez Cerro, a cholo from the Sierra and a classic product of the dependent middle class. But the Colonel was rapidly co-opted by the traditional upper class, which "makes Sánchez Cerro dizzy with the glamour of its gatherings, swells him with pride with its flattery, seduces him with the 'love' of some of its ladies, and places the commander totally at its service." [8]

Sánchez Cerro also raised the military share of the budget to 24.1 per cent, at the expense of other sectors, had himself elected President in 1931, and was killed in 1933. But his place was taken by General Oscar Benavides, who had shown his responsiveness to the wishes of the traditional upper class. A number of abortive revolts were attempted in the thirties and early forties, many of them sponsored by APRA. In the process, APRA made the mistake of appealing to the noncommissioned officers and the soldiers against the officer corps; in the Trujillo revolt of 1932, organized by Aprista elements, most of the officers were executed, and two years later a "conspiracy of the sergeants," again under APRA sponsorship, was discovered in Lima. Particularly after the Trujillo revolt, APRA became unacceptable to the armed forces, and because of its reformist purposes (see Chapter 6), it was also unacceptable to the traditional upper class. Thus, at least until the 1950's, the desire to keep APRA out of power reinforced the community of interests between the military establishment and the upper class. [9]

The successful *coup d'état* of 1948 shows a similar pattern. President Bustamante y Rivero, a provincial intellectual with strong Catholic leanings, was elected in 1945 with APRA votes in ex-

[7] Urdanivia Ginés, *Una Revolucion Modelo*, p. 65; the phrase "political commisars" is from Villanueva, *El Militarismo*, p. 45.

[8] Villanueva, *El Militarismo*, p. 66.

[9] The revolts of this period are described by Castro Bastos, *¡Golpismo!*, part I; Villanueva, *El Militarismo*, chs. 2–5; and Jorge Basadre, *Historia de la República del Perú*, vols. VIII and IX.

change for APRA's participation in the legislature and in patronage appointments. But the alliance was extremely shaky: Bustamante y Rivero got along neither with APRA nor with the traditional upper class, and his own popular support vanished when Peru suffered postwar economic dislocations. APRA attempted numerous conspiracies and made contacts with young officers and noncommissioned officers. It did not appear to have been successful with the officers, but elements of the Peruvian Navy revolted on October 3, 1948, with mostly noncommissioned officers leading the movement; the revolt ended in failure and triggered a reaction on the part of the traditional upper class, which, fearful of APRA's victory, had already joined forces with senior Army officers. The result of these efforts was the overthrow of Bustamante y Rivero on October 27, 1948.[10]

Here, again, "the community of interests" seemed to be in operation. The military establishment feared the inability and/or unwillingness of the President to handle APRA, which had broken relations with Bustamante y Rivero and was plotting to overthrow him. Whether or not these fears were justified is debatable, since in the last month of his administration the President outlawed APRA, jailed many of its leaders, and moved tanks into San Marcos University to control Aprista students. On the other hand, it may be that these moves were made under pressure from the army and the traditional upper class, in order to gain their support. The proclamation of the revolutionary government also mentions, somewhat vaguely, attempts to "weaken the power, diminish the prestige, and destroy the unity of the armed forces," and accuses the Bustamante y Rivero administration of "not having built even

---

[10] For further details on the 1945–48 political maneuvering see Oscar Bueno Tovar, *Las Fuerzas Armadas y el APRA* . . . , *passim;* Víctor Villanueva, *El Militarismo,* chs. 5–6 and *La Tragedia de un Pueblo y un Partido, passim;* José Luis Bustamante y Rivero, *Tres Años de Lucha por la Democracia en el Perú, passim;* Harry Kantor, *El Movimiento Aprista Peruano,* ch. 2; and Enrique Chirinos Soto, *El Perú Frente a Junio de 1962,* ch. 1. For details of the *coup d'état* which overthrew Bustamante y Rivero see the New York *Times,* October 28, 1948, pp. 1 and 4; October 29, 1948, p. 18; October 30, 1948, pp. 1 and 5; and October 31, 1948, p. 38.

one military base," of refusing to purchase "weapons, materials, equipment, and even elements which are needed for military training," and of having adopted "the inconceivable project of reducing the military forces by one-third, for economic reasons." [11] In reality, the military share of the national budget had descended from 25.6 per cent to 19.9 per cent during the three years of the Bustamante y Rivero administration.

The grievances of the traditional upper class, and particularly of its coastal sector, were equally important. APRA was still a reformist party with large popular support; it wanted to alter the nation's structure radically, and land reform was its chosen method of doing so. The party had been willing to use violence before and was plotting again, particularly among the noncommissioned officers. But there were other reasons for being unhappy with Bustamante y Rivero: he had enforced exchange controls, which in fact were a tax on exports—a tax that could not be passed on to the buyers because of competition from other countries. And the money, particularly the hard currencies, thus obtained by the government was being used to subsidize industrial development.

Evidence of the connection between these grievances and the *coup d'état* is provided by the key measures taken by General Odría shortly after assuming the leadership of the new government: he persecuted the Apristas ruthlessly; he increased the military share of the budget to 23 per cent, gave the officers opportunity to engage in business operations (legal or otherwise) and to buy automobiles at special prices, and awarded them sizable bonuses upon retirement; and he eliminated the exchange control system, thus more than doubling the net profits of Peru's exporters.[12]

Suspension of the Community of Interests

Perhaps because history repeats itself the foundations of joint action by the armed forces and the upper class to eliminate gov-

[11] *El Comercio* (Lima), October 29, 1948, p. 1.
[12] Enrique Chirinos Soto, *El Perú Frente,* pp. 75–86; Villanueva, *El Militarismo,* pp. 121–29.

ernments that were insensitive to their respective interests came to an end sometime in the 1950's. This may have been owing to the abuses and the growing unpopularity of the Odría regime, his attempts to develop a more permanent political base, or his application of repressive legislation (intended for the Apristas) against individual members of the coastal upper class with whom he did not get along. Although the military were on occasion badly needed, "they become difficult to handle. First, they refuse to leave, when their services are needed only for a limited period. Furthermore, their actions cannot be predicted and anything can come out of their erratic initiatives." [13]

On the other hand, the alliance became less and less necessary when the reformist party lost its reformist zeal and turned to fight communism. After all, it is always more impressive, both at home and abroad, to control the government through an "honest" electoral victory than through military action. And it may very well be that this *rapprochement* between APRA and the coastal sector of the traditional upper class caused an unfavorable reaction within the military establishment, particularly after the military had been encouraged by the upper class to persecute APRA. By 1955 the break between the Odría government and the coastal sector of the traditional upper class, which "guided" him to power, was complete. *La Prensa* attacked the regime constantly, and most of those close to the newspaper were leading the opposition. Their candidate, Manuel Prado, received the APRA vote and defeated Hernando de Lavalle, who was preferred by Odría. The armed forces supervised the elections and saw to it that the incumbent administration did nothing to perpetuate itself in power. In exchange for their electoral support, the Apristas received political patronage and the right to exist legally and to participate in the 1962 presidential elections.[14] It may be more accurate to speak of a break in relations between Odría's military clique and members of the tra-

---

[13] François Bourricaud, *Poder y Sociedad en el Perú Contemporáneo*, p. 193.

[14] This is recognized by pro-APRA writers, such as Kantor (see *El Movimiento Aprista*, p. 14).

ditional upper class, led by *La Prensa*'s publisher Pedro Beltrán. In any case, the armed forces were left in the middle, and their role did not please anyone—least of all the officer corps itself.

Clearly, the events prior to the 1956 election implied the repetition of the late 1890's coalition between the traditional upper class and Piérola's Partido Demócrata, with a "domesticated" APRA providing popular backing. It was also clear to the officer corps that one of the objectives of this coalition had to be the settlement of scores with the military establishment: the coastal sector of the upper class might not have been prepared to forget the closing of *La Prensa*, the police action against the Club Nacional, and other affronts; and APRA certainly would not forget the killing, torture, imprisonment, and exile of most of its leaders and many of its followers (beginning with the five years that Haya de la Torre spent in embassy asylum).[15] While both APRA and the upper class reassured the armed forces, the armed forces started a profound re-examination of their role in Peruvian society and politics.

The Center of High Military Studies

One of the key elements in the re-examination that took place after 1956 within the military establishment was the Centro de Altos Estudios Militares (CAEM). Created in 1958 to prepare the high military command for national defense, the Center became a military school of public affairs. The faculty, mostly civilians, represented almost all political views and, at least at one time, included one individual who was considered to be a Communist.[16]

[15] Haya de la Torre entered the Colombian embassy in Lima on January 3, 1949, and asked for political asylum; the Colombian government granted the request and petitioned the Odría regime for a safe-conduct so that the Aprista leader could leave the country. The safe-conduct was denied for more than five years and caused international frictions and a case in the International Court of Justice. It was finally granted, and Haya left the country on April 6, 1954. Among the numerous accounts of this controversy is Haya's article, "My Five-Year Exile in My Own Country." For an analysis of the legal aspects see Amalia Zavala Álvarez, "La Corte Internacional de Justicia y el Asilo Diplomático."

[16] In a conversation with the author, one of the members of the CAEM faculty (a civilian), pointed out that it was "the only school of political

In any case, it is clear that the Center concentrated on the study of social, political, and economic problems in Peru. At the same time, the attendance of younger officers at the universities increased, and it is possible to assume that contacts developed between them and the civilian students. The military attending CAEM concentrated on studying the problems faced by the country and prospects for the future. Their findings were quite distressing and displeased a good number of officers; these intellectual pursuits were reflected in the articles published by the *Revista Militar del Perú*, the journal of the officer corps of the Peruvian Army. A comparison of articles published in the years 1949–51 with those included in the early 1960's shows that approximately one-sixth of those published in the later period deal with national development or with the country's sociopolitical problems. No reference to these topics can be found in the earlier issues. The general thesis of the articles indicated that

the new military ideology proposes the improvement of social and economic conditions so that the grievances on the basis of which revolutionary groups can obtain support will be eliminated. If the new perspective toward development is a nationalistic one which includes purely military aims, it also includes a modern economy and social structure as the necessary supports of a modern military organization.[17]

The interest of CAEM faculty and students in socioeconomic problems was not received favorably by the traditional upper class. In the late 1950's the curriculum of the Center called for a

science in Peru." The curriculum, while not too sophisticated by American standards, was quite advanced for Latin America, where political science is only beginning to exist as an independent discipline. The faculty member considered a Communist was Gregorio Garayar, and the point was made by an Aprista leader, Andrés Townsend Ezcurra in his article, "Frente a la Ley, los Tanques," p. 59.

[17] North, *Civil-Military Relations,* p. 53. See also Villanueva, *El Militarismo,* pp. 174–89. For specific examples of military writing in this field, see José P. Calderón M., "El Comandante y la Comunidad," and Lisandro Mejía Zagastizábal, "Acción Cívica en el Campo Laboral."

ten-month course, with seven months dedicated to social, political, and economic matters, and only three to military subjects. In 1960, when Pedro Beltrán became Prime Minister in the Prado administration, the curricumum was changed to nine months of military and one month of nonmilitary topics.[18] This sensitivity of the traditional upper class to the activities of the Center may have been prompted by the antiaristocratic sentiment which apparently was developing among the officer corps under the realization that they had been "used" by the traditional upper class without being given an adequate share of the benefits.[19]

This feeling was undoubtedly encouraged by the social origin of the majority of the officer corps. The Peruvian armed forces have been completely opposed to allowing any kind of survey or data-collecting activity within any portion of the military establishment, but all available information indicates that the majority of the officers come from the middle class, with an apparent overrepresentation of the interior over the capital city. In fact, all observers agree with this view, which is also partially reinforced by informal observations in Peru and by data collected in other Latin American countries where the armed forces have been willing to release this type of information.[20]

[18] Reported by William F. Whyte, *La Mano de Obra de Alto Nivel en el Perú,* pp. 51–52.

[19] Richard Patch, "The Peruvian Elections of 1962 and Their Annulment," p. 16.

[20] In a number of visits to Peru the author was able to come in contact with military officers, mostly of the intermediate ranks. Depending on the situation, discreet inquiries into the personal background of the officers were made. While the results cannot be considered reliable scientific evidence, a pattern of dependent middle-class background clearly develops, weighted in favor of the cities and towns of the Sierra. This pattern was corroborated by the fact that most of the officers contacted appear to belong to the mestizo group, from the ethnic point of view. For testimony on this point see Aníbal Ismodes, "La Conducta Política de los Militares"; Jacques Lambert, *América Latina: Estructuras Sociales e Instituciones Políticas,* pp. 358–62; John J. Johnson, *The Military and Society in Latin America,* p. 105; José Nun, "A Latin American Phenomenon: The Middle Class Military Coup," in *Trends in Social Science Research in Latin American Studies: A Conference Report,* pp. 55–99; Castro Bastos, *Geo-Historia del Perú,* pp. 148–54; North, *Civil-*

But there is a common-sense explanation of the social background of the Peruvian military officers. Military life is simply too regimented and disciplined for the youngsters of the upper class, who already have at their fingertips almost all of the rewards which a successful military career could bring them; and obviously, only a minority reach the highest ranks. The same reasoning may be applied to a large portion of the upper middle class, which is found for the most part in the large urban areas. On the other hand, practically all those who belong to the lower class are excluded because they are unable to meet the formal educational requirements of the Peruvian military academies or to pass their admission examinations. These factors virtually reserve the military academies for the middle class. However, Lima and the other large cities offer alternative educational and business opportunities, which often are more pleasant and comfortable, at least in the short run. Those opportunities are scarce in the small towns, and the abundance of scholarships at the service academies (this is not the case at the universities) further attracts those who have financial difficulties.

This argument is corroborated by the results of a survey of the occupational preferences of high school students throughout Peru. After interviewing students in exclusive private schools (upper-class) and in public institutions (almost solidly middle-class), the study reported:

It is interesting to note the substantial popularity of military careers among the students of *public schools.* The military career has, for some time, made available the means of social mobility to those who do not find favorable opportunities in other fields.[21]

Nevertheless, the significance of the social background of the military has probably been exaggerated. There appears to be something mysteriously powerful about the forbidden data. Most writers in the field accept the idea that given a certain social ori-

---

Military Relations, p. 51; and Basadre, *Historia,* X, 4735–43. For comparative data on the Argentine and Brazilian armed forces see José Luis de Imaz, *Los que Mandan,* pp. 45–84; and Mario Afonso Carneiro, "Opinião Militar."

[21] William F. Whyte, *La Mano de Obra,* p. 56 (emphasis added).

gin, only one kind of political behavior will take place, at least among the officer corps of the Latin American armed forces.[22] This deterministic cause-effect relationship simply does not exist in Peruvian politics. If the middle-class origin of the overwhelming majority of the military officers is accepted—and it has to be until the military itself is willing to release data that proves otherwise —this origin does not explain the changes in political behavior and the cleavages which have existed and continue to exist in the Peruvian armed forces. The issue is not in what class the officers were born, but whom they represent, whose values they share, and what view of the ideal Peruvian society they hold. If the problem is seen in these terms, then it can be said that the country's armed forces may tend to reflect some of the contradictions of its middle class, but heavily mediated by the institutional interest of the military establishment itself.[23]

The military establishment, then, is the most solid and cohesive of all organizations of middle-class origin, much more so than the few white-collar workers' unions and the small businessmen's organizations. And the officers are not brought together by a common economic interest, although the protection of the institution's economic well-being is an important factor in their political actions. But rather, the future officers enter the military schools between the ages of sixteen and eighteen, and from that point on, their contacts with the civilian world are kept to a minimum. While this is probably good from the professional point of view, since it increases the specific socialization process, it greatly reduces the officers' ability to deal with civilian matters, particularly in the field of politics. The ultimate goal of the process of military socialization is the development of a strictly military outlook,

[22] This oversimplified interpretation of Marx can be found, among other places, in S. E. Finer's *The Man on Horseback,* p. 40. For a documented criticism of this abusive employment of social background data see Lewis J. Edinger and Donald D. Searing, "Social Background in Elite Analysis: A Methodological Inquiry."

[23] This point is also made, in reference to other Latin American countries, by Nun in "A Latin American Phenomenon" (*Trends in Social Science Research,* p. 86).

which sets the military establishment apart from and above the rest of the national society, equating it with "the sacred interests of the fatherland." All available evidence tends to corroborate, in reference to Peru, Lambert's dictum that in the last forty years the military officer corps has been socially "as distant from the aristocracy as from the masses." [24]

A further element of potential discord between the military establishment and Peru's traditional upper class is the image the military officers have of their institution as a fighting force. Placed between the extremes of Argentina or Brazil on the one hand, whose armed forces consider themselves—rightly or wrongly—capable of carrying out the traditional mission of protecting their country's security from almost any type of aggression, and El Salvador or Honduras on the other, whose armies cannot possibly believe that they can withstand any serious attack, the Peruvian military appears torn between its needs for domestically manufactured supplies and the traditional upper class's reluctance to encourage industrialization. Thus, if the Peruvian military officers consider themselves closer to their Argentine or Brazilian counterparts— and personal observation tends to indicate that they do—they are forced to move in the direction of becoming industrial promoters, regardless of the usual social, economic, and political consequences of rapid industrialization. On the other hand, there are signs that the traditional upper class is quite aware of the consequences of rapid industrialization (in Argentina, for example) and is unwilling to allow the military or anybody else to promote it. This discord has been reflected in the studies conducted at CAEM and in the program changes introduced by Prime Minister Beltrán. The discord acquired overt political manifestations in the 1962 *coup d'état.*

The 1962 Military Revolt and Its Aftermath

In exchange for the electoral support given to Manuel Prado in 1956, APRA was permitted to participate without limitations in the elections of 1962. APRA's traditional *caudillo* and founder of the

[24] *América Latina,* p. 359.

party, Haya de la Torre, became once again its presidential candidate. Former dictator Odría was, of course, the Odriísta party's hopeful, and Belaúnde Terry led the Acción Popular ticket. There were four other candidates from minor parties, of whom only Cornejo Chávez of the Christian Democrats was running in earnest. The military were frankly unhappy about the organization of the election. There was almost unanimous agreement in not accepting Haya de la Torre, and numerous remarks were made before the election to the effect that he was not going to be allowed to consummate his expected victory. Beyond this virtual veto, the military appeared to have been divided in their pre-election preferences. The officers active in CAEM favored Belaúnde Terry; those who had benefited under the previous Odría administration were naturally inclined toward him, and a large number seemed to have doubted the whole process and remained undecided.

It would be too complicated to detail here the armed forces' involvement in the electoral process. It began with their investigation of irregularities in voter registration, including electoral surveys, and ended with the rejection of the results and the overthrow of the Prado government, which had accepted them. The military takeover took place on July 18, 1962, ten days before Prado was to have turned the presidency over to the victorious candidate; obviously the coup was not directed against Prado, but against his successor—Odría, according to an agreement reached the day before. Since none of the candidates had been able to obtain one-third of all valid votes cast, as required by the Peruvian constitution (Article 138), the election was to be thrown into Congress, which has the constitutional authority to choose the president from among the three candidates with the largest number of votes. As Tables 17 and 18 indicate, no party could have its candidate elected by Congress without assistance, a fact which was compounded by the armed forces' veto of Haya de la Torre, who had obtained the largest number of votes and controlled the largest bloc in both chambers. The veto was made explicit at the beginning of July (Haya himself announced it on July 4), and after conversations between the three leading candidates, the leader of

APRA instructed the party senators and representatives to vote for former dictator Odría, a decision which insured the latter's election.[25]

Clearly, General Odría was the candidate most acceptable to the traditional upper class (see Chapter 6), in spite of his difficulties with it in the mid-1950's. After an unsuccessful attempt by some of them to organize their own electoral machine (the National Independent Movement), the large landlords distributed their support between Odría and Haya de la Torre. They were evidently aware, however, of the military's position regarding a possible victory by the latter, and when the veto materialized, the influential representatives of the upper class were essential in getting APRA to support Odría, who had persecuted the party ruthlessly until the mid-1950's. As one writer put it:

The *coup d'état* finally took place. It took place regardless of the understanding between Haya and Odría. There are those who believe that it would have taken place in any case, even if the understanding had been reached sooner. It took place, above all, against Odría, who at noon of July 17 virtually was President-elect.[26]

It was also evident that the only candidate acceptable to the officers who led the coup was Belaúnde Terry, whose electoral tactics parallel those of the military. Even before the election Belaúnde Terry had openly recognized the military's role as election arbitrator by stating that he would accept defeat at the polls only if

[25] There are numerous accounts of these events; the best one is Arnold Payne, *The Peruvian Coup d'Etat of 1962: The Overthrow of Manuel Prado.* Other accounts include Humberto Ugulotti Dansay, *Las Elecciones de 1963 y la Lección del 62;* Enrique Chirinos Soto, *Cuenta y Balance de las Elecciones de 1962;* M. Guillermo Ramírez y Berrios, *Examen Espectral de las Elecciones del 9 de Junio de 1963;* Castro Bastos, *¡Golpismo!;* Edwin Lieuwen, *Generals vs. Presidents* . . . , pp. 25–36; Bueno Tovar, *Las Fuerzas Armadas y el APRA;* Luis Humberto Delgado, *Drama del Perú;* Luis Antonio Eguiguren, *La Fuerza Armada y el Proceso Electoral de 1962;* William Obelson, *Funerales del Apra: El Fraude Electoral y Fiscal;* Aníbal Ismodes, "La Conducta Política de los Militares"; and Townsend Ezcurra, "Frente a la Ley, los Tanques."

[26] Chirinos Soto, *Cuenta y Balance,* p. 77.

the armed forces accepted the result.[27] Since it was apparent that his main competitor was Haya de la Torre and that APRA's victory was not going to be accepted by the military establishment, Belaúnde Terry was in fact counting on the military to extricate him from an electoral defeat, as well as to guarantee his victory, which is what actually happened.[28] The day after the election, Belaúnde Terry, on the basis of early returns, thanked the Peruvian population by radio and television for their votes and the National Electoral Jury and other authorities for having conducted a clean election. As later returns changed the picture, he denounced the electoral process and openly encouraged the military to intervene. His invitations became louder after the understanding between APRA and Odría became likely.[29] It is extremely difficult to establish whether Belaúnde Terry led the military or simply announced publicly bits of political gossip. But the *coup d'état* took place, Odría did not become president, and Belaúnde Terry was given a new opportunity in 1963, which he did not waste.

The New Military in Power

From the moment the 200 Peruvian rangers (counterguerrilla troops) took over the presidential palace, it was evident that this differed in important ways from traditional military revolts. While the Army was still the most important of the three services, true collective leadership existed in the junta: four co-presidents—the chairman of the Joint Chiefs of Staff and the commanders of the three branches—acted jointly on all policy decisions, with the chairman, General Pérez Godoy, acting as Chief of State. No individual *caudillo* appeared, and when Pérez Godoy showed an inclination to become one, he was abruptly dismissed from the junta,

[27] *Ibid.*, pp. 63–64.

[28] See Ramírez y Berrios, *Examen Espectral*, pp. 51–53.

[29] Belaúnde's erratic behavior has been widely reported in the daily press; he went so far as to barricade himself with a few youngsters in the center of his home town, Arequipa, while announcing that he was beginning the movement to overthrow the Prado government and annul the elections. The government ignored him, and without any reaction from the armed forces, he gave up and went home. See Payne, *The Peruvian Coup d'Etat*, ch. 3.

and his ceremonial responsibilities were transferred to General Lindley, the Army commander.[30]

Another break with tradition was the unusual effort made by the three services to consult the officer corps, and their desire to show total unity, or at least a pretense of unity, in the military establishment. In the three or four months prior to the coup, numerous steps were taken by the military leadership to familiarize itself with the views of officers at all levels in regard to the political situation which was then shaping up: gatherings of officers with direct command of troops, tours of the commanders-in-chief to all bases and units, and even a written questionnaire, which all officers had an opportunity to answer anonymously. Evidently, the military leadership used this information to select a course of action satisfactory to the great majority of the officers *in active service*. In this sense, it can be affirmed that the 1962 *coup d'état* was institutional in its inception and in the policies it produced, at least in the first few months. The military had no popular backing, and they did not pretend that they had it; but popular support against the coup could not be mustered either. An attempt by APRA to call a general strike elicited almost no response, although the party controlled a large number of labor unions, or at least their leadership.[31]

It seems apparent that the members of the military junta and their backers, particularly at the level of the colonels and majors, had either been involved in CAEM or had been influenced by its activities. During the first few months of the junta's administra-

[30] The overthrow of Pérez Godoy and his replacement by Lindley appeared to have been a consequence of the cleavages within the armed forces—cleavages which materialized *after* the military took over. The institutional agreement which existed at the time of the overthrow of the Prado regime was certainly not present in Pérez Godoy's replacement. It would appear that the coastal sector of the traditional upper class benefited from a reduction in certain taxes imposed by the junta on income, corporations, and fish production. The tax reductions were decreed within three weeks after Pérez Godoy was ousted. For a detailed discussion of these events see Villanueva, *Un Año bajo el Sable*, ch. 8.

[31] On this question, see Chapter 9 and also James L. Payne, *Labor and Politics in Peru: The System of Political Bargaining*, chs. 6 and 8.

tion, there was no repression of individuals or ideologies and, perhaps owing to outside pressure, fair elections were promised within a year. Although the declared objective was to invalidate the 1962 election, the military announced their desire to try to solve some of the problems identified as most pressing according to the files developed at CAEM. Some of the objectives were: an agrarian reform, a better distribution of wealth, an improvement of the educational system, and a reduction in the price of foodstuffs and basic items.[32]

From July until December, 1962, the military government avoided practically any measure that would violate individual rights. The opposition attempted by APRA and a few minor parties during the first few days was handled quite effectively; delegations representing most unions were invited to visit the presidential palace and meet with key officers, and on August 21 a decree-law ordered pay increases and other benefits for white- and blue-collar workers in industry, commerce, and service. This action pacified discontented union members. Other workers were promised a minimum salary statute as soon as studies were completed. A new plan to teach reading and writing was devised, and 1963 was decreed "Literacy Year." Taxes on corporations, income, and the fishing industry were enacted, and there was talk on the part of the Minister of Government, General Bossio, regarding the annulment of the La Brea and Pariñas oil concessions.

However, as time went on, the measures announced or enacted by the junta were either forgotten or altered. In the last weeks of 1962 and the beginning of 1963 the compromising attitude was abandoned and a large number of left-of-center elements, some of them involved in the articulation of miners' and peasants' interests, were summarily imprisoned; it is no accident that these groups had not yet received the salary and other improvements promised earlier by the military rulers. The educational reforms which were

[32] The writer has seen some of the files, which are also mentioned by Justo Piernes in his article "Democracia Directa," *Leoplán,* August 15, 1962, pp. 12–15. Mr. Piernes even warned his readers that "Nasserites" had taken over a Latin American country.

to be carried out during the "Literacy Year" were somehow shelved after the expression was printed in all official correspondence; only the equivalent of $400,000 was appropriated to get the program under way. The new taxes were unanimously opposed by commercial, industrial, and landowners' organizations and by newspapers that articulated their views; the revenue measures were either reversed or substantially altered for the benefit of the prospective contributors. Finally, General Bossio, who had publicly announced his intention of proposing the annulment of the foreign oil concessions, resigned in mid-October "for reasons of health" but the text of his resignation was never made public.

The imprisonment of left-of-center politicians and labor leaders was particularly indicative of the changing mood of those running the military government and of the success of the upper class in bringing about this change. The latter, after disagreeing with the *coup d'état,* challenged the legitimacy of the government and demanded that it prove itself by taking measures which would diminish or eliminate the effectiveness of the reforms which CAEM considered necessary. In the area of labor policy, *La Prensa* emphasized the danger of a Communist takeover of the labor movement; it also emphasized that, things being what they were in Peru and since the labor organizations were going to be involved in partisan politics anyway, these groups might as well be led by men of "democratic tendencies." Inasmuch as the power struggles within the labor movement were between APRA and the Communists, it was clear that *La Prensa* was asking the military to assist APRA in ousting the Communists. General Bossio, who represented CAEM thinking within the military government, left his cabinet post after having been opposed by *La Prensa* particularly on the significance of a peasants' movement in the Cuzco area; following his departure the newspaper continued its denunciations of Communist involvement in both labor and peasants' organizations and of proposed deficit spending by the junta.[33] The exhortations

[33] It would be fruitless to identify any one editorial, or any one speech made by junta members. Almost every day, from July 19, 1962, on, *La Prensa* (Lima) had something to say on these subjects. On the "Communist menace"

were finally heeded by the military leaders, who moved forcefully, first against the peasants and later against the miners and other workers who had gone on strike. After constitutional guarantees were suspended, a widespread dragnet in the first week of 1963 brought in close to 2,000 political prisoners accused of planning sabotage, subversive activities, and the violent overthrow of the government. The prisoners were slowly released, and as far as can be ascertained, not one of them was ever found guilty of these charges by either a civilian or a military court; in fact, only sixty-two were brought to trial before a military court in highly irregular proceedings, with the junta unable to provide the evidence it had claimed.[34]

The military leaders thereby achieved a number of objectives: First, they satisfied what probably enjoyed highest priority among the demands being made by the traditional upper class. The repressive measures greatly diminished the effectiveness of organizations which articulated lower-class interest, particularly in the rural areas. It was there that the peaceful occupation of haciendas was threatening the landowners' economic base. Secondly, powers derived from the suspension of guarantees were directed against the National Liberation Front and other left-of-center minor parties and nonpartisan organizations; their voting strength was small and diffused (approximately 50,000 votes), but in the absence of participation by these parties and organizations most of those votes would have to go to Belaúnde Terry, the candidate acceptable to the majority of the officers in control and the least repugnant to the left-of-center voters. In view of the results of the 1962 election, these votes could have made the difference. Finally, the junta quieted the fears of powerful foreign investors (particularly oil companies and mining enterprises) over the nationalistic tone prevalent in some CAEM studies, which were publicly articulated

---

see particularly the editorials and the first-page news in the period December 21–29, 1962, just before the dragnet.

[34] The best description of events in this period can be found in Villanueva, *Un Año bajo el Sable,* chs. 6 and 7; for an account of the repression by one of those jailed, see Genaro Ledesma Izquieta, *Complot, passim.*

during the first three months by General Bossio. At a time when the United States government was quite cold toward military coups, this demonstration of "anti-Communist zeal" could and did help in improving relations.

While managing these and other changes and counterchanges, the military did not forget their own economic interest. The Prado administration had decreed salary increases for the military approximately a month before it was overthrown, with the provision that they go into effect in 1963. The military junta, however, ordered the increases into effect immediately, but only for those on active duty, thus excluding retired officers and violating what had been legally mandated heretofore; furthermore, it deprived retired officers of a number of privileges, including free medical treatment at the military hospitals and the opportunity to purchase low-price, duty-free goods at military stores. This change of policy regarding retired officers provides one more evidence of the wide difference between those who carried out the 1962 *coup d'état* and the previous military leadership.

One promise that the military did fulfill was the holding of free elections within a year of its take-over. The voting registration procedure was improved, and the number of registered voters dropped—indicating that at least some of the irregularities denounced before, during, and after the 1962 election may in fact have existed. A new electoral law was passed, and the total number of Senate and House seats was reduced, with some redistribution among departments. But unquestionably the most important electoral event was the agreement reached between the Acción Popular and the Christian Democratic parties: in exchange for some congressional slots in safe districts, the latter agreed to vote for the Acción Popular presidential candidate, Fernando Belaúnde Terry. This coalition, together with the decision by minority, left-of-center parties to back Belaúnde Terry, gave him the presidency as indicated in Table 19.

The military turned power over to Belaúnde Terry; but it is important to recognize that the individuals who performed the ceremony of July 28, 1963, had moved substantially away from the mandate which produced the 1962 *coup d'état*, even if some of the top political offices were occupied by the same individuals. The reformist zeal pushed by the CAEM alumni and particularly by the so-called Nasserites had not been linked to those civilian political groups which could have popularized it among those who were always suspicious and resentful of men in uniform. This inability of the reformist military officers to carry out any of the proposed reform programs was not an accident; it was the consequence of an outstanding campaign of division, and psychological warfare which brought enough key officers around to the traditional upper class's point of view and drove a wedge between the military establishment and the civilian reformists.

The Military Under the Belaúnde Terry Administration

Since Belaúnde Terry was the most popular—or least repulsive —of all presidential candidates, his victory in 1963 in an election which none of the leading participants challenged appeared to have satisfied the political desires of the military. Apparently, they returned to their bases and surrendered the government to what many Peruvians considered the country's new modernizing elite. In reality, however, the military, since July, 1963, have been sharing in the decision-making process, not only in those matters related to national defense but on every major political move made by the Belaúnde Terry administration. And although it is apparent that the President expected, probably on the basis of the 1962 events, that the military were going to assist him in having his proposed reforms approved by a legislative branch dominated by a conservative APRA-UNO alliance, in fact the opposite happened. The traditional upper class, which had effectively divided the military establishment and backed the group that shared its view of Peruvian society, continued its *rapprochement* with the military leadership by signaling a new community of interests: they were allied against the danger of a Castro-Communist takeover, which was said to be starting in the Sierra as an outgrowth of the occupation of landholdings being carried out by the peasants' organizations. There was enough truth in the claim to make it believable, particularly to a Peruvian military which could not forget the way Castro handled the Cuban officer corps.[35]

A combination of police repression, poor organization, and a weak and confusing land reform act pushed some of those involved in the peasants' organizations into guerrilla warfare. Early guerrilla attempts in Jauja, Puerto Maldonado, and La Convención Valley in 1962–63 had been handled easily by the various police organizations and did not require the intervention of the military establishment. Apparently the guerrillas learned their lesson, and after widespread advertisement, they went into operation in June, 1965, in La Convención Valley, Junín, and Piura. This time, however, the rural constabulary was no match for them; fairly well equipped and organized, the guerrillas acted ruthlessly in their operations, wiped out entire patrols of the Guardia Civil, and forced the armed forces to take upon themselves the responsibility for handling the situation.[36] The Belaúnde administration, for reasons of prestige, refused to recognize the existence of guerrillas (the President seems to have felt it would damage his image as a reformer), while the opposition parties and most newspapers exaggerated the threat, either to damage the President's image or, in the case of those who articulated the point of view of the traditional upper class, to use the military in a final clean-up operation which would eliminate not only the guerrillas but the peasants' or-

[35] A solid report on the land invasions can be found in Hugo Neira's *Cuzco: Tierra y Muerte*. On the peasants' organization, see Aníbal Quijano O., "El Movimiento Campesino del Perú y sus Líderes." The increasing community of views between the traditional upper class and the military leadership was confirmed by the forced retirement of General Bossio in 1964; see *Caretas* (Lima), January 8–21, 1965, pp. 24–26.

[36] There are few and broken accounts of the guerrilla operations of 1965; as reported in the New York *Times*, September 12, 1965, p. 1, the military authorities closed the "war zones" to outsiders and arrested and expelled foreign and Peruvian newsmen who violated their orders. The best account can be found in Américo Pumaruna, "Perú: Revolución, Insurrección, Guerrillas." Interesting bits and pieces of information appeared in the magazine *Oiga* from June to December, 1965. Part of the information possessed by the author has not been published anywhere and was transmitted by individuals connected with the events being discussed.

ganizations as well. Senator Martinelli Tizón, who represents one of the departments of the Sierra, stated:

Let the "rangers," the Army, and the Air Force go after the guerrillas! We shall back them, because we cannot allow the constitutional regime to suffer sabotage, subversion; we cannot allow it to fall into the hands of reds. Half-measures are out of place! [37]

Even pro-Belaúnde Terry publications felt the pressure of events and advanced the idea that the guerrillas were "a challenge to the efficiency of the armed forces," and that "if they were not bloodily repressed by the Peruvian Army, the revolt might provoke in the long run an ominous intervention by the United States armed forces." The military soon came around to see it that way too and, as Bourricaud put it, "made the liquidation of the guerrillas a point of honor." [38] In July of 1965, the Joint General Staff presented an ultimatum to the Belaúnde Terry government, demanding that all constitutional guarantees be suspended and that the military be put in charge of the repression, with authorization to do whatever they considered necessary. At the same time, General Oscar Benavides, Jr., son of the officer who led the 1914 *coup d'état* and presided over the country during the period 1933–39, was put in charge of the Intelligence Service and mentioned in military circles as Belaúnde Terry's replacement, if a change was considered necessary.

The emergency measures were happily approved by the APRA-UNO congressional majority and reluctantly signed by the President. Antiguerrilla units, reportedly advised by members of the U.S. Special Forces, went into action and badly mauled the guerrillas and killed or captured practically all their leaders after a few months of fighting. The effectiveness of the military was underwritten by the traditional upper class, which rapidly bought 200 million sols (approximately $8,000,000) of government bonds especially authorized by Congress at the end of August to finance

[37] Quoted in Pumaruna, "Perú," p. 73.

[38] *Oiga,* July 9, 1965, pp. 1, 8; and Bourricaud, "Les Regles du Jeu en Situation d'Anomie: Le Cas Péruvien," p. 348.

counterguerrilla operations; *La Prensa's* Pedro Beltrán is reported to have contributed one million sols ($40,000). By early 1966 the guerrillas had been almost completely wiped out, although a few groups had not been accounted for in the military communiqués; probably for this reason, an armed forces report closed with a warning: "The struggle is not over. The danger remains." [39]

The appearance of guerrillas, who constituted a threat to the established order and whose objective was to bring about the Peruvian version of the Cuban revolution, provided a new link between the traditional upper class and the military establishment. The equation that developed in 1965–66, was, at best, highly unstable, because the traditional upper class felt that it needed (or at least it wanted to keep) both its alliance with APRA and its community of interest with the military. However, while it is true that all members shared in their opposition to communism and to Castroism, and that the Apristas had been the strongest backers of the military's antiguerrilla operations and provided them with a certain measure of popular support, it is evident that the military did not make gestures indicating acceptance of Aprista support or even implied that they were ready to forget the "Trujillo massacre." The instability of the situation has been reflected in recent reports, which indicate that the Peruvian military leadership "envelop[s] with the same sharp repugnance the largest party, Acción Popular; its weak ally, the Christian Democrats (now divided); and certainly the right-wing forces: Haya de la Torre's APRA and former President Odría's UNO." [40]

[39] *Confirmado* (Buenos Aires), November 17, 1966, p. 40. It appears that the military rapidly identified and captured all peasants who were acting as contacts between the guerrillas and the rest of the population, thus isolating the former. After getting substantial information out of the contacts, they moved against the guerrilla bands with artillery and air strikes, including napalm (Pumaruna, "Perú," pp. 74–80; New York *Times*, September 12, 1965, p. 1, and October 11, 1965, p. 14; *Política* (Mexico City), November 15, 1965, p. 32). Simultaneously, the secret police and the intelligence service jailed actual and potential urban contacts, including the wives of guerrilla leaders (*Oiga*, July 23, 1965, p. 6). Beltrán's contribution was reported in *Confirmado,* September 8, 1966, p. 30.

[40] *Primera Plana* (Buenos Aires), August 1, 1967, p. 32.

Although the military was happy to show its ability and fighting spirit in defeating the guerrillas, as well as in saving the nation from communism and in protecting their institution in the process, they are not looking forward to further demonstrations of this kind. The self-image developed by the Peruvian officer corps is that of a traditional military establishment responsible for the safety of national boundaries; it is clear that the armed forces have accepted responsibility for internal security (to what extent this acceptance has been the product of outside influences is an open and extremely attractive question), but observers are left with the impression that they are not interested in intervening every time a group of individuals decides to go outside "normal channels" in their search for political power. Politically, the military would like to be recognized as the arbiter of political disputes, and to a certain extent this is justified by Article 213 of the Peruvian constitution, which entrusts the armed forces with "the protection of the rights of the Republic, the enforcement of the constitution and the laws and the maintenance of public order." What is perhaps more important: if this role of the military is not recognized as something that ought to be, it is certainly recognized as something that is—and necessarily so, in the attitude of many Peruvians. Consequently, only a handful of those who participate actively in politics question the principle of the military as referees of political disputes; what different people question at different times is the choice the military makes. But, by the same token, there are always political figures who benefit from the involvement of the armed forces and therefore praise them. Belaúnde Terry followed this course in 1962, while APRA, UNO, and the traditional upper class cheered the military in 1965–66.

On the other hand, although the armed forces would like to arbitrate disputes only when there is total agreement within themselves, it is difficult to see how they would go about keeping national controversies from taking hold inside the military. While unquestionably a card-carrying member of the Communist party would not be able to remain in the officer corps (control is extremely strict, with at least one representative of the intelligence service in every unit), the fact is that even at the height of the military hatred of the Apristas between 1930 and 1950 there were seven attempted revolts by military units tied to Aprista elements. And the elimination of General Pérez Godoy from the military junta in early 1963 shows that not even the 1962 *coup d'état* (often cited as the example of an "institutional move") constituted a perfect compromise of the different political philosophies within the military. At any rate, the temporary agreement within the military which made the overthrow of the Prado regime possible broke down shortly thereafter, and the different positions reflected the cleavages existing in the country at large, and particularly between the different groups of Peru's middle class.[41]

It would seem, then, that the current political role of the Peruvian armed forces does not fit any of the traditional patterns outlined by most scholars.[42] In a country with the deepest political cleavages, both country-wide and along class lines, the military seems to have set itself apart from, and from its point of view, on top of, the domestic political struggle. With an overwhelming superiority in the management of violence, which it does not hesitate to employ in the political arena, it is presently in a position to lend its support to the ever-changing groups that are trying to influence national policy. As has been indicated throughout this chapter, successful political involvements by the military have had the solicited or unsolicited backing of different sectors at different times, such as the coastal sector of the traditional upper class in 1948 and most Belaúnde Terry partisans in 1962. This "adaptability" of the military establishment has not been overlooked by any political group, and in many cases even those victimized by military involvement in politics are reluctant to criticize it publicly, at least not strongly, in the hope of benefiting the next time around. Even Apristas and Communists, who would be expected to have lost all hope along these lines, cannot be said to be consistently critical of

[41] Along the lines suggested by José Nun in "A Latin American Phenomenon" (*Trends in Social Science Research*, pp. 55–99).

[42] See, for example, Lyle N. McAlister's "Civil-Military Relations in Latin America" (also reprinted in Peter G. Snow [ed.], *Government and Politics in Latin America: A Reader*, pp. 277–85).

the military.[43] And the truth is that at one time or another and with varying success, almost all politically active groups have "knocked at the door of the military bases" to ask them to replace the government of the day. Consequently, on most occasions one finds an unusual unanimity in praising the military. This unanimity, together with the natural admiration of the Latin American masses for the true *macho* (a strong and fearless man), has made possible the existence of a "civilian militarism" which leads people to distinguish between the sometimes blameworthy action of certain military officers in the political realm, and the military institution, which is always blameless.

Under these conditions, it appears that the political role of the military as the domestic "balancer" has been tacitly legitimated, at least by default. In reality, however, this role is heavily influenced by the interests of the military establishment itself, as defined and identified by the leadership. The extent to which the identification of those interests is the product of inputs from the lower level or the consequence of forceful consensus backed by strict military discipline is quite difficult to ascertain accurately because of security regulations, and in any case it probably changes with time. Regardless of the type of decision-making process in existence within the armed forces, they continue to be the most influential political party, the most effective labor union, and probably the key power holder in Peruvian politics; nothing currently within the political system offers a realistic possibility of altering that fact.

[43] The Apristas provide the best example of this military idolatry, which molds the outlook of the population. See, for instance, Luis Alberto Sánchez, *El Perú: Retrato de un País Adolescente,* pp. 141–47, and the statement made by the Aprista leader Silva Solís in *Caretas,* January 8–21, 1965, p. 16.

8. The Church

The Spanish conquistadors arrived in Peru (as in the rest of Latin America) under the protection of the Cross and the Sword; the take-over of the country was essentially a joint enterprise between the military and the clergy. A large portion of their relative influence has remained, although the methods may have been modified. Many Peruvians have fatalistically accepted this dominance, calling it their "historical destiny":

No Western Hemisphere country can show an older, brighter, and more glorious Catholic tradition than Peru. The Cross, together with the Sword, was one of the symbols of the Conquest which opened the spiritual horizons of Latin culture and Catholic faith to our Fatherland.[1]

At the time of the discovery and conquest of what is today Latin America, the Roman Catholic Church was playing a crucial role in the expulsion of the Arab invaders from the Iberian peninsula. The Church was in fact one of the arms of the Crown and of the state and was rewarded for its loyalty and effectiveness with land grants and other economic benefits that made it an extremely wealthy institution. At the same time, the clergy set a pattern which was to be followed on the new continent.

It would be a grave mistake to assume that the Catholic Church of Spain was in any way in control of the state or that it was the power elite that it later became in countries such as Peru. Since the right of the Spanish kings to rule had very little relationship to the will of the majority, the influence of religion on the common

[1] Roberto MacLean y Estenós, *Sociología del Perú,* p. 49.

man was not at that time the element of political power into which it was transformed in Latin America in the last two centuries. If anything, the Catholic Church of Spain was completely subject to the Crown, and this control was recognized by the papal bull issued by Julius II in 1508, which gave the Spanish Crown the right to select and appoint clerics to church offices in the territories under its juristiction. Previous bulls of Alexander VI, issued in 1493 and 1501, had given the kings of Spain and Portugal the exclusive role of Christianizing the native inhabitants of the Western Hemisphere and to the Spanish monarchs the right to collect tithes in exchange for establishing and maintaining the Church in the new territories.

Consequently, the conquest of the Western Hemisphere was not only military, but also political, economic, and cultural; conquistadors and priests came together and worked toward the same end: to place the new lands and their inhabitants under the control of their emperor and leader. Peru, as one of the two most important centers of Spanish power, was an outstanding example of this joint enterprise. It was perhaps symptomatic of things to come for the Catholic priest accompanying Pizarro, Father Valverde, to have been deeply involved in the capture and execution of the Inca, Atahualpa, and to have provided the rationale for this action.[2]

As indicated earlier, the Indians had a pantheistic religion with the Inca as the head of the faith on earth, in his role as son of the sun. The Catholic Church at first made a decisive attempt to destroy all aspects of the cult of the Incas and to replace it with the "right" faith. The Indians, were ambivalent and quite flexible; unable for the most part to understand the philosophical foundations of the new religion but convinced of the new God's powers to benefit those who believed in Him, they were willing to grant Him a place in the old religious structure and, if pressed by the Spaniards, even to place the new God at the top of the list.

The religious zeal of the first priests was subject to the trials of

[2] José Carlos Mariátegui, *Siete Ensayos de Interpretación de la Realidad Peruana,* pp. 146–47; see also Luis E. Valcárcel, *Ruta Cultural del Perú,* pp. 142–43.

coping with thousands of missionaries, many of whom had their eyes on the Church as one of the few channels of socioeconomic mobility in Spanish society. Many of the newly arrived missionaries went through the motions of converting the Indians, but they were more interested in increasing the number of fee-paying individuals than in saving souls. In a legal system where the elder son inherited the titles and properties of the family (the *mayorazgo*), other sons were often destined to the priesthood, with or without vocation. In the Spanish colonies, they had a better opportunity to serve their faith and themselves. An observer has written of the period of Spanish domination:

Privileged was, then, the priestly class; its property and income, huge; its rank, very high; its authority, almost equal and sometimes superior to that of the civil power, with which it had frequent friction; and its spiritual power, unlimited as representative of God.[3]

Although most accounts of the role of the Church are strongly colored by the religious (or antireligious) convictions of the observers, it is apparent that while some priests protected the Indians from extreme abuses, many assisted the Spanish power structure in the exploitation of the native population. Once the Indians became at least nominal Catholics they were often forcibly required to receive as many sacraments as possible. Every community had to reserve a certain portion of land to pay for collective religious services, and although that plot was supposed to remain fixed, there is evidence that it increased in acreage when ambitious priests were in charge.[4] Masses were celebrated not only every Sunday, but on numerous festive occasions, which sometimes varied from town to town. Naturally, there was a charge for the celebration of each Mass, and although the income of the plot was intended for the ceremony, this sum was often insufficient, and the

[3] MacLean y Estenós, *Sociología,* p. 53.

[4] To cite one example, in the Andean community of Muquiyauyo, the land allocated to the Church increased from 27¼ acres, or 1.5 per cent of the total area, in 1742, to 90 acres or 5.2 per cent of the total area, in 1819 (Richard N. Adams, *A Community in the Andes: Problems and Progress in Muquiyauyo,* pp. 20–21).

community was responsible for making up the difference out of personal income. Special officials, known as *mayordomos,* were appointed for important celebrations, and one of their key duties was to make sure that the priest's pay was available; they were responsible for making up shortages out of their personal patrimony. Although in some communities the appointment was considered an honor, there have been reports of those who refused to serve and suffered physical punishment.

Personal services by the priest required extra compensation, paid by those receiving them according to predetermined price scales. Although the Crown had decided that certain sacraments were to be administered free of charge, the clergy continued to collect fees from the Indians and mestizos for services such as baptism, matrimony, and burial. Forced marriages, sometimes at age 13 or 14 and without the right to choose the spouse, night inspections to identify and marry those who were living together, and the appointment of local assistants to keep track of births and deaths—all for the purpose of fee collection—were some of the activities which permitted the colonial clergy to benefit, as individuals and as an institution, from the *status quo.* The abuses were so flagrant and the power of the clergy so great that one of the most distinguished viceroys of Peru wrote to the Spanish king:

Your Catholic Majesty: when I arrived in this kingdom I found that bishops and priests were masters of everything, both spiritually and materially; they neither knew nor had superior authority. And your Majesty spends his royal money sending in each fleet a large number of priests to preach and convert the Indians. In reality what they do is enrich themselves at the Indians' expense, cleaning them out of what they have in order to gain wealth. They collect all tithes themselves, although the *encomenderos* should do it; in order to be paid in silver or food, they pressure Indians and *caciques* with abuse and violence. They have jails, instruments of torture, and guards, and they imprison and punish at will those who refuse to pay.[5]

[5] Viceroy Francisco de Toledo in *Memorias de los Virreyes que han Gobernado el Perú durante el Tiempo del Coloniaje Español,* IV, 46. For a comprehensive study of the reaction of the Andean Indians to the newly

Assignments to wealthy areas, such as Peru, were bought and sold like many other public offices in the colonies and in Spain. Like other officeholders, priests neither expected nor desired to remain in Peru for a long time unless they were assigned to Lima with an adequately compensated position. The nature of their offices made it almost mandatory for them to exact as much as possible from the lower classes, as many public servants, including some viceroys, did. What made the priest a special type of corrupt representative of the new power elite was the flagrant contradiction between his preaching and his actions; it is unquestionable that this duality, rapidly perceived by Indians and mestizos, has molded the cynical view of the clergy found throughout Peru.

During colonial times the Catholic Church had a branch of its repressive arm located in Lima (further indication of the significance assigned to Peru). The Tribunal of the Inquisition opened in Lima in 1570 and operated continuously until the institution was dissolved in 1813. While the announced objective of the Inquisition was to root out heresy, in fact it fulfilled the functions of a secret police and became involved in everything in which the inquisitors had an interest. It acquired responsibility for press censorship, clerical misbehavior, violations of Catholic dogma, and threats to Catholicism from other faiths. All these items were subject to the interpretation of Inquisition officials who, as often happens, tended to enlarge their jurisdiction and power. Furthermore, the new overseers of corruption sent from Spain soon learned what seemed to be the mores of the viceroyalty of Peru: the second inquisitor rapidly became famous for his greed and huge profits in silver operations, his numerous love affairs with single and married women, and his conflicts with the governmental bureaucracy and the regular church hierarchy. Needless to say, his powers as head of the Inquisition in Peru were extremely useful and freely taken advantage of in all these enterprises. A modern account states:

the land was at the mercy of the Inquisitorial officials who murdered, robbed, and took women at their pleasure, and those who complained

arrived Catholic faith see Luis Millones, "Introducción al Estudio de las Idolatrías: Análisis del Proceso de Aculturación Religiosa en el Área Andina."

were fined or were chained in prison. . . . The government officials, however highly placed, who sought to curb Inquisitorial arrogance, could have slender hope of support from their royal master.[6]

Realistically speaking, the Inquisition did not have many heretics to persecute and prosecute in Peru. Those heresies that were present were swiftly eradicated in the first few years of its existence; the arrival of potential heretics in the Spanish colonies was controlled by the metropolitan branch of the Inquisition, leaving the agents in the Western Hemisphere free to dedicate their energies to the persecution of civilians and members of the clergy who deviated from the "official line," always as interpreted by those on the scene. As can be expected, the Peruvian Inquisition was particularly ruthless toward those who threatened its power; in this sense, the main role of this institution was strictly political and consisted of stamping out actual, suspected, and potential opposition and/or dissension. The Inquisition was a close equivalent of today's secret police organization in totalitarian states, but its role was further strengthened by its spiritual responsibility toward the official faith. This peculiar institution was made possible by the powers granted by the pope to the Spanish Crown, and it clearly exposes the political involvement of the Catholic Church in colonial Peru, as well as in the rest of Latin America.

The Church during the First Century of Independence

The independence movement which expelled the Spaniards from Peru, their last stronghold in South America, in the early 1820's deeply divided the country's clergy. The overwhelming majority of the high officers was clearly opposed to the independence forces and tried to defeat them not only with the Church's spiritual influence, but with its financial support and organizational skills as well. This faction of the clergy, practically all of them born in Spain, owed their positions to the Spanish Crown and immediately perceived the threat which the change in government was bringing about. The lower clergy, which at the beginning of

[6] Henry Charles Lea, "Inquisition in Colonial Peru," in Fredrick B. Pike (ed.), *The Conflict between Church and State in Latin America*, p. 42.

the nineteenth century included a sizable percentage of Creoles and even some mestizos, appeared divided; some favored the Spaniards, others backed the (mostly non-Peruvian) revolutionaries, and a third group remained more or less neutral. The archbishop of Lima at the time of independence, Monsignor Bartolomé María de las Heras, exemplified the attitude of the high clergy; as an expression of contempt for the new regime, he boarded a ship bound for Spain and never returned.[7]

The new political leadership immediately compensated those members of the lower clergy who had shown sympathy toward the pro-independence forces. The republican authorities maintained that they had inherited the right to appoint the clergy formerly granted to the Spanish Crown and proceeded to state that all appointments, promotions, and transfers were to be filled with "patriotic priests," excluding those considered "enemies of the system of independence, because of the *unquestionable influence which they exercise over the consciences of their parishioners, owing to their sacred role.*"[8]

The political activities of the Catholic Church and its ever-present involvement in all aspects of life during the colonial period, plus the new liberal ideas developing in Europe, caused a reaction on the part of certain elements within the new ruling groups that had replaced the Spaniards. These elements had unquestionably been a source of anxiety for many members of the clergy, at least at the lower level, who would otherwise have found a reduction of centralization and of the king's powers to their advantage. After the danger of a Spanish counterattack disappeared, these "liberal" elements moved to achieve some of their internal objectives, which were quite limited; they included the abolition of the ecclesiastical *fueros* (immunity) and the limitation of the church's monopoly over such activities as marriages and burials. In the words of Víctor Andrés Belaúnde, a leading Catholic thinker, this early Peruvian liberalism should be considered "timid," since it favored the maintenance of Catholicism as the state religion, the preservation

---

[7] MacLean y Estenós, *Sociología*, p. 68.
[8] Simón Bolívar, quoted in *ibid.*, p. 69 (emphasis added).

of Church property, and most privileges. In any case, when these "liberal" elements threatened to become influential, the Church hierarchy, or what was left of it after the post independence purges, reverted to the more conservative elements of Peruvian society, in an attempt, as Belaúnde has said, "to limit itself to keeping the positions it already had." [9]

The Catholic hierarchy had assessed the "liberals" correctly; they were not anti-Catholic, and their only desire was to free the state from its legal responsibilities toward the Church, to eliminate unwarranted privileges. In any case, they were relatively unsuccessful in altering the economic and political influence of the Church. Only sporadically were some of the economic obligations of the parishioners reduced or lifted, and when the change was economically significant, the state took upon itself to make up the revenue lost to the Church. This is what happened to the 10 per cent of the harvest that was given to the clergy under Spanish rule; after numerous attempts—effectively fought by the Catholic hierarchy—to reduce or eliminate this forced contribution, a compromise was reached whereby the state paid salaries to bishops, other Church officials, and parish priests in lieu of the contribution. This compromise benefited the landowners, who carried the largest share of the burden for this contribution, and to a certain extent the clergy, who did not have to worry about collecting it. However, representatives of the Church strongly criticized the measure.[10] Other actions intended to reduce by law (or decree) of civil authority some of the charges imposed by the clergy for their religious services either failed to materialize (usually because of congressional inaction) or were not enforced after being enacted; such was the destiny of a bill diminishing marriage fees and eliminating burial charges and a law passed December 15, 1864, which was intended to reduce the rent being paid by those who worked Church land.[11]

[9] Víctor Andrés Belaúnde, *La Realidad Nacional,* pp. 98, 96.

[10] Among them was Father Rubén Vargas Ugarte; see his *Historia de la Iglesia en el Perú,* V, 159.

[11] See the details in *ibid.,* V, 268–69 and 293–96.

Because of the extremely low level of education of the population of Peru during the nineteenth century, and particularly in the period immediately after independence (a condition which existed throughout Latin America), the clergy constituted one of the few sources of educated men. Accordingly, they were well represented in many of the congresses, constitutional assemblies, and other political gatherings. In the first Peruvian Constitutional Convention, which lasted from 1822 to 1825, twenty-six of the ninety-one delegates or 28.6 per cent, were priests; the interests of the Church were adequately articulated, and the delegates declared that Catholicism was the religion of the state.[12] The Constitutional Convention of 1855–56 confirmed this precept, but the "radical" attempts to limit forced religious contributions and to eliminate the *fueros* doomed its final product to political failure, which came at the hands of a *coup d'état* the following year; subsequent constitutional documents repeated the precept, although the present constitution only mentions that the state "protects" Catholicism (Article 232). The political influence of the Church was further demonstrated by the approval of a constitutional prohibition to practice publicly any other religion, passed by the "liberal" conventions of 1855–56 and 1867, in the first instance without a dissenting vote.[13]

It would be incorrect to assume that the Church remained exactly as it had been under the Spanish Crown. Certain powers were in fact lost, not out of "revolutionary" measures, but as a consequence of new ideas and philosophies, which provided new frameworks to contemplate and analyze reality. Perhaps the most important change was the loss of the power of censorship within the country for Peruvian and foreign publications. Father Vargas Ugarte, one of the most articulate scholars of the Peruvian Catholic Church, pointed out that "there are two sources which for a long time have been dropping poison in our midst: one is the freedom with which books contrary to our Religion are being brought in and circulated, thus demoralizing the youth; and the other, the almost infinite freedom of the press." And he explains a few pages

[12] Raúl Ferrero, *El Liberalismo Peruano* . . . , p. 21.   [13] *Ibid.*, p. 25.

later that "the liberal and antireligious press, more or less Red, did not cease its attacks against the Church and its ministers, condemning many of the praiseworthy customs approved and sanctioned by the Supreme Authority." [14]

After more than 300 years of total monopoly or at least absence of disagreement, the Catholic Church of Peru has failed to develop the staff and the attitude needed to fight dissent in the realm of ideas. During the nineteenth century it chose to try to combat dissenting ideas by using its influence over the governments of the day, hoping that they would provide the force which the Church had lacked since the Inquisition ceased to operate in the country. The Church's ability to achieve its objective varied with the times and the individuals in power; but whatever objections were raised against it were directed at some of its benefits and privileges and seldom, if ever, at the basic concepts of Catholic philosophy. Most of the attacks were directed at the Peruvian clergy, not necessarily at the religious beliefs they espoused.

That was the case with the few intellectuals who dared to write denunciations of some of the abuses committed by individual priests. Two of the best examples of this group were Manuel Lorenzo de Vidaurre y Encalada and Francisco de Paula González Vigil, but they had no following, either among the lower class, who did not understand them, or among the bulk of the traditional upper class, who benefited from the role of the clergy.[15] An important element in this general lack of success was the fact that the intellectuals limited themselves to criticizing the misbehavior of priests without challenging the conditions which made this misbehavior possible or—what is perhaps worse—without offering a workable alternative that could be attractive either to the traditional upper class or to the oppressed peasants. They were nothing more than "angry young men" of their time, whose only mark on

[14] *Historia de la Iglesia,* V, 155, 158.
[15] Their ideas can be found in Vidaurre's *Discurso a los Habitantes del Perú* and González Vigil's *Opúsculo de la Libertad de Cultos, con Religión del Estado.* Vidaurre could not stand the clergy's reaction and retracted many of his views in *Vidaurre contra Vidaurre;* his change of heart was not acceptable to the Church.

Peruvian society was their attempt to challenge Catholicism as a
political philosophy on the grounds that it had the main effect of
providing continuity to itself and, therefore, to the *status quo*.
Their ineffectiveness was demonstrated by the continuation of the
Church's privileged position in Peru throughout the nineteenth
century, and even to this day. On the other hand, their influence
on most of the few true political thinkers Peru has produced in
this century is indisputable. In any case, the ability of the Church
to maintain its influence over the lower class, particularly in the
rural areas, and its understanding with the traditional upper class
(discussed in the following section) made its continuing role possible.

The Peruvian Catholic Church in the Twentieth Century

The present century brought relatively few concrete changes to
the political power of the Catholic Church. It is true that some of
its economic benefits were diminished by law or eroded by inflation and that some of the most extreme aspects of its religious monopoly have been challenged by the presence of Protestant missionaries, mostly from the United States. But its landholdings have
not been challenged (although the Church has relinquished some
of them, as will be seen), and its role in the field of education, particularly at the elementary and secondary levels, remains extremely strong. It can be said that the growth of a deficient public
school system has, in fact, increased the significance of the private
sector, in which the Catholic schools figure prominently. The social prestige that some of these institutions convey and the desire
of a large sector of the middle class to seek this prestige within the
existing structure make it possible for the Church to have influence over social groups which have been shown, in practice, to be
less responsive to Catholic dogma and liturgy. The long existence
of a Catholic university with authority to award valid degrees (a
situation which, until recently, did not exist in most of the other
Latin American countries) increased the influence exercised by
the Catholic Church over the upper and middle classes and made
the formation of a group of lay Catholic scholars possible.

While the historical and traditional factors already discussed help to explain the origin, sources, and development of the political role of the Catholic Church, those who have dealt with the subject have failed to indicate concretely how the Church actually kept the social and political power it had had in colonial times and how it increased that power to a certain extent by reducing its *de jure* and *de facto* subjection to the Spanish Crown and its successors. In other words, most discussions describe the contributions made by the various groups to the Church, but ignore the reasons for which these contributions were made.

In brief, it would seem that the Catholic Church gave the lower class a pageantry and a comprehensive philosophy not only of this life, but also of a better one to come: a future life in which all injustices of this world are going to be compensated. It is not surprising, then, that in the minds of the Indians and mestizos of the Sierra, "Heaven is conceived as a fertile region of productive land and abundant harvests." [16] Thus, in the words of a contemporary observer, "Catholicism created within the religious world a state of spiritual slavery, which is able to attract man's attention toward the dream of happy heavens and all that can be inspired by the words that are preached in the name of the doctrine." [17] To the middle class Catholicism gave a set of moral criteria which tended to ratify its status and mores, especially in regard to the family, without being too stringent in its enforcement of these criteria, particularly in reference to male violators. To the upper class the Catholic Church gave a political philosophy which provided moral and religious support for their pre-eminent position, and ratified with the force which only faith can give the inordinate share of socioeconomic rewards that the upper class reserved to itself.

Although all three aspects are deeply interrelated, the last one

[16] Oscar Núñez del Prado, "Aspects of Andean Native Life," in Dwight B. Heath and Richard N. Adams (eds.), *Contemporary Cultures and Societies of Latin America*, p. 120.

[17] F. M. Arriola Grande, *Discurso a la Nación Peruana*, p. 47. The only reference to Catholicism as the political ideology of Latin American conservatives is made by Ivan Vallier, who wrote, "in one sense, Catholicism was pushed down one level of social control, taking on the color of an ideology for the conservative groups" ("Religious Elites: Differentiation and Development in Roman Catholicism," in Seymour Martin Lipset and Aldo Solari [eds.], *Elites in Latin America*, p. 195).

has been and is paramount in assessing the role of the Church in Peruvian politics. Writers of different political status and varying degrees of commitment have repeatedly held that the traditional upper class lacked an ideology. In view of the now recognized role of ideology in politics, this is indeed surprising, especially if one remembers the power of the country's traditional upper class. The contribution of the Church to the political power of the traditional upper class has consisted in making available to the latter a ready-made structure of thought, which lends itself to different interpretations according to circumstances and which, in essence, tends to confirm the social, economic, and political *status quo* by emphasizing the sanctity of private property and by leaving the elimination of inequalities to charity. The emphasis on the destiny of the soul after death tends to reduce the significance of earthly suffering in the minds of those who sincerely believe. At the same time, those who do not believe need not follow the recommendations of the clergy regarding charity, as they did not follow other recommendations mildly conveyed to them by priests who were not prepared to alienate men who could pass judgment regarding their prospective promotions, at least within the country. And those members of the traditional upper class who are believers— that is, who more than go through the motions of the Catholic rites —seem to apply to certain aspects of Catholic dogma what their predecessors applied to some royal decrees: they are accepted but not obeyed.

It is within this framework that one should insist on refuting one of the most important mistakes made by those who have analyzed Peruvian politics and the role of the Catholic Church to date: that the traditional upper class has been unable to develop its own ideology.[18] The statement is a paradox. It is true in that the traditional upper class never actually developed an ideology *of its own;* it is false in that it conveys the impression that the traditional upper class did not have an ideological foundation. Peru's ruling elite did not have to develop an ideology of its own because, from

---

[18] For instance, François Bourricaud, *Poder y Sociedad en el Perú Contemporáneo,* pp. 186–87.

the very beginning, it had available a set of beliefs which, as interpreted to the laymen by intermediaries sympathetic to the *status quo* and benefitting from it, almost always tended to provide religious sanction to the interests and actions of the ruling elite.

This is not to imply that the Catholic faith, in its universal aspects, favors the traditional upper class everywhere. Like most religions, Catholicism seems to have something for nearly everybody, although even at the supranational level there are certain aspects which appear to de-emphasize change, at least by downgrading life in this world to a simple stage toward an infinite salvation or condemnation.[19] What is maintained here is that these general principles of Catholicism, when applied to specific instances of Peruvian political reality by the only ones who can properly do so according to the dogma, almost always tend to come out in favor of the *status quo* and to confirm the position of the traditional upper class. It is not necessary to go far back in time to find examples: In the early 1960's during the campaigns organized by peasants to obtain redress of their grievances by occupying portions of certain landholdings claimed as belonging to them, Catholic priests refused to hear confession, administer the sacraments, and say Mass for those involved in these activities.[20] This attitude of the local priests cannot be considered an isolated incident if it is remembered that thirty years ago the archbishop of Peru emphasized poverty as the road to eternal happiness and based the solution of social problems on the ability of the state to make the poor recognize the value of their economic situation.[21]

Although recent pastoral letters have made reference to the convenience of improving the economic conditions of the Peruvian lower class, they have not gone beyond vague, general exhorta-

[19] On this point see Glaucio Soares and Robert L. Hamilton, "Socioeconomic Variables and Voting for the Radical Left: Chile, 1952," p. 1054. In reference to Brazil see Emanuel de Kadt, "Religion, the Church, and Social Change in Brazil," in Claudio Véliz (ed.), *The Politics of Conformity in Latin America*, pp. 192–220, especially p. 203.

[20] See Hugo Neira, *Cuzco: Tierra y Muerte*, p. 89, and Víctor Villanueva, *Hugo Blanco y la Rebelión Campesina*, p. 149.

[21] *Carta Pastoral de Pedro Pascual Farfán con Motivo de la Próxima Festividad de Santa Rosa de Lima, passim.*

tions, not directed to anyone in particular. One such letter read: "Because we love, we are required to interest ourselves in the temporal well-being of our brothers; to dress the naked, to feed the hungry, to visit the ill, to help the poor, to teach the ignorant." [22] A superficial view of the distribution of wealth in Peru shows that either the admonition was not directed to the upper class or this group did not think very much of it. Furthermore, these generalities contrast with the political advice given in the same document to assist the faithful in their choice of political parties. The pastoral letter in question makes quite clear that it is a political error to favor laicism in public life or in state activities, to maintain the absolute sovereignty of the state, to grant the state unlimited power over human beings or intermediate organizations or property, and to affirm that public authority does not derive from God but from the masses, or that it is the mere addition of numbers or comes from the will of the population. And there is no ambivalence in the prohibition to all Catholics against joining a party which espouses any of the "errors" or which in any way contradicts the Catholic doctrine, as defined by the hierarchy. The political instructions also specify:

Neither is it licit to reach political compromises which include substantial aspects of the organization of the state, changes in the Constitution, or new alliances with other countries, etc., since these things belong to the Nation and cannot be the subject of what amounts to party deals.[23]

These pronouncements, which the Peruvian prelates have made on a number of occasions, should not be confused in terms of effectiveness with those of political parties, interest groups, or other holders of power. It must be emphasized that they carry the impri-

[22] Los Católicos y la Política: Carta Pastoral del Episcopado del Perú a los Sacerdotes y Fieles, pp. 1–2.

[23] Ibid., p. 17. The reading of this document will provide a clear idea of the order of priorities of the Peruvian hierarchy. The implication seems to be: social, economic, and political betterment of the masses, yes; but not at the expense of the existing structure. Needless to say, no alternative procedure is offered.

matur of a religious faith, and they are issued in that manner; they are not to be analyzed, discussed, interpreted, or contested. They are to be obeyed, and those who do not do so place themselves outside the Catholic faith. In theory, this power should apply only to the spiritual realm, but in practice the Peruvian clergy (like that of other Latin American countries) has found it very difficult to draw any sort of line, arbitrary as it would have been. Realistically speaking, there has been no line, and the representatives of the Church have involved themselves in every important political controversy and have seen fit to instruct the faithful in regard to the "right" and "wrong" choices.

In theory, these pronouncements, whether they are political, social, economic, or strictly religious, are addressed to all inhabitants of Peru, white and Indian, upper, middle, and lower class. It has already been indicated that the specific instructions of the clergy tend to reinforce the *status quo* and consequently are more convenient to those who receive a greater share of the rewards offered by Peruvian society. But there is an added factor that intensifies the consequences of Church pronouncements, particularly in the political realm: the degree of obedience and acceptance by the various classes. Unfortunately, specific data is extremely difficult to obtain; but certain things are obvious: the Peruvian upper class has not divested itself of its wealth in order to redress economic wrongs, as advised by Catholic dogma and by the clergy, if only in vague terms.[24] Some rudimentary data in the area of birth control, an issue on which both the pope and the Peruvian clergy have taken a strong stand, tends to prove what has been suspected: the upper class ignores Church pronouncements more than the middle and the lower classes. A recent survey found that 62.2 per cent of upper-class women were employing contraceptives, while only 46.5 per cent of middle-class women and 31.9 per cent of lower-class women were doing so. In terms of education, the study showed that university-trained women had almost three

[24] See, for instance, *Carta Pastoral del Episcopado Peruano sobre algunos Aspectos de la Cuestión Social en el Perú, passim;* also *Carta Pastoral de Pedro Pascual Farfán, passim.*

and one-half times more abortions than women with three years of elementary education or less.[25] Surely, it can be said that lower-class and uneducated women may not be materially capable of violating Catholic dogma as much as upper-class women, but the figures are so overwhelming and the techniques required to violate the dogma so simple that the hypothesis of an inverse relationship between socioeconomic status and religious obedience appears to be at least partially confirmed.

Because the key contribution of the Catholic Church to the Peruvian political arena has been in the area of ideology, the main threats to its influence have come not from anti-Catholic liberals but from competing political ideologies. Inasmuch as those competing ideologies also challenged the right of the traditional upper class to continue enjoying its advantageous position, the challengers originally reinforced the alliance already described between the Church and the traditional ruling groups. This is what happened when the APRA organization came into being and developed a believable and acceptable ideology which proposed, if in vague and verbose terms, a course of action completely different from that outlined by the Catholic Church and which promised to provide much more attractive immediate rewards for the majority of the Peruvian population (see Chapter 6). The Apristas were soon joined by the Socialist and Communist parties, and more recently by other left-of-center groups. An observer writes:

But the competition at the level of values turned out to be the only one of those threats posed by those new value movements. Besides offering a whole new framework of "salvation," new meanings, and new categories of evaluation, they also provided the adherents with a "program" and a "strategy of action" in society.[26]

The Catholic hierarchy did not take very long to perceive the threat that these new ideologies constituted. There is a marked difference between the nineteenth-century liberals who merely

[25] This study was published in *Caretas* (Lima), Dcember 20, 1965–January 13, 1966, and is also cited by Fredrick B. Pike in "The Catholic Church and Modernization in Peru and Chile," p. 286.

[26] Vallier, "Religious Elites," in Lipset and Solari, *Elites*, p. 195.

wanted to eliminate a few of the privileges enjoyed by the clergy, and the twentieth-century reformist ideologues, one of whose objectives was and is to separate politics from religion and to neutralize the latter.[27] Both sides understood that this objective could be achieved only if the Catholic faith ceased to provide ideological justification for the *status quo;* this step could only be taken by giving new interpretations to important portions of the dogma.

It should be apparent that the Peruvian clergy was not about to react against any and every anti-Catholic thinker who appeared on the horizon. Inasmuch as the Church had provided a political ideology that appeared to be widely believed among the lower class —although their understanding of the dogma and the rites may have been less than perfect—it was interested in reactions against those ideologies that showed a chance of taking hold in this constituency. It was among the lower and middle classes that APRA developed its following and where APRA's ideology, backed by the charisma of Haya de la Torre, made its most impressive gains. Whether or not this was APRA's main objective is debatable; the fact is that APRA rapidly acquired a large following among the mestizo peasantry and controlled most of the labor unions which, to this day, have given the party a large proportion of its electoral strength. On the other hand, APRA has not been too successful with the middle class and, as can be expected, was opposed by the upper class.[28]

Since APRA provided its followers with a complete political philosophy, both in domestic and international affairs, and since this philosophy runs counter to many of the ideas presented by the Peruvian clergy as part of Catholicism, it was natural for the representative of the Church to attack violently its ideological competi-

[27] APRA's position during its first two decades of existence is best outlined in Luis Alberto Sánchez, *Aprismo y Religión.* See also Manuel Seoane, *Nuestros Fines, passim.*

[28] On the following of APRA in the lower class see Bourricaud, "Syndicalisme et Politique: Le Cas Péruvien"; in regard to the middle class see Pike, "The Old and the New APRA in Peru: Myth and Reality"; on the topic in general see Bourricaud, *Ideología y Desarrollo: El Caso del Partido Aprista Peruano,* particularly pp. 23–25.

tors and at least tacitly approve of their persecution by the traditional upper class and the military establishment. The APRA
leadership, on the other hand, realized from the beginning that
their ideology had to displace Catholic political thinking if it were
to succeed; consequently, they challenged the Peruvian Catholic
hierarchy from the very start and tried to drive a wedge between
the upper and lower clergy. An Aprista intellectual, Luis Alberto
Sánchez, wrote 35 years ago, "this lower clergy shows a clear and
logical preference for the Aprista movement, while the high and
the foreign-born clergy, a sort of imperialism and landownership
wearing cassocks, reject *aprismo*." [29]

The attempt to split the Peruvian clergy along Aprista lines has
been unsuccessful. With a few exceptions, the lower clergy remained under the Church's traditional hierarchy and was instrumental in counterattacking vigorously. They accused APRA of
planning to assassinate priests and the faithful, to burn places of
worship, and to rape nuns; at election time the priests used the
Sunday Mass to threaten with retribution those who violated the
Church's instruction and backed APRA. Pastoral letters issued
from time to time, but often shortly before an election, reminded
the faithful of the errors contained in APRA's ideology and platform and of the consequences, both in this world and in the next
one, of subscribing to those errors.[30] Even after it became clear
that the military establishment stood ready to block APRA's every
attempt to gain power (through the ballot or through force), the
struggle for the minds of the Peruvian lower class continued between the Catholic Church and the party leadership: It was
clearly an ideological struggle.

In the period between the two World Wars the only real threat
to the ideology of the Peruvian Catholic Church came from APRA.
To a certain extent, the growth of APRA during that period paral-
leled a relative decline of Catholic influence, although the hier-

[29] *Aprismo y Religión*, p. 39; see also Pike, "The Old and the New APRA,"
p. 11n.

[30] The events referred to here are described by Sánchez in *Aprismo y
Religión* and mentioned by Harry Kantor in *El Movimiento Aprista Peruano*,
pp. 168–73.

archy did not seem too worried by it. The Socialist and the Communist parties were extremely weak, poorly understood by the lower classes and, consequently, had little popular following. They were no menace to the established order and its ideology. However, in the fifties and sixties, as APRA abandoned its revolutionary ideals and reached an understanding with the traditional upper class, the banner of reform was transferred to an array of left-wing organizations, which included the Communist party, APRA Rebelde, MIR, and a few peasant organizations. The ideological conflict continued, but now these new rivals replaced APRA.

At the same time, however, it is necessary to remember that the Catholic Church is an international institution, and no national church can isolate itself completely from the others or from Rome. It is well known that important ideological changes (if formally of an interpretative nature) have taken place in the last two decades, mostly in the socioeconomic field. The trend, sponsored in the Holy See and in some Latin American countries by younger priests and laymen, calls for a more direct relationship between Catholic doctrine and "the revolution of rising expectations." The more progressive members of the clergy appear to feel that if the interpretation of Catholic doctrine conveyed in most Latin American countries continues to serve as the ideology of the *status quo,* the influence of the Church among the lower and lower middle classes is going to decrease substantially. The loss of ground is likely to be intensified when the Church is faced with reformist political philosophies which take into account the more immediate social, economic, and political needs of the majority of the population. In essence, what these individuals proposed was that the Catholic Church incorporate into its doctrine and activities the most popular measures espoused by these reformist philosophies: they wanted to become, according to one expression, "more reformist than the reformers." Members of the clergy and laymen moved boldly in this direction, particularly after recent papal pronouncements which gave a qualified green light; these pronouncements culminated in the encyclical *Populorum Progressio,* issued by Paul

VI in March, 1967. To a certain extent, this and other pronouncements have reproduced some of the points made by the younger
bishops in the recent Ecumencial Council and also by revisionist
Catholics in countries such as Chile and Brazil.[31]

Although the pressure for reform from within the Peruvian
clergy appears to be limited and ineffective, the example coming
from the Vatican and from some of Peru's Latin American neighbors, plus the apparent success first of APRA and more recently of
other organizations in attracting the younger generation—even to
the point where they may risk their lives for their political convictions—has generated a reformist pressure from within certain mo-
nastic orders of the Peruvian Catholic Church. At the same time,
the profound change in the position of APRA, from the leader of
reform to a party which subscribes to the *status quo* (see Chapter
6), has produced a vacuum on the Left, which may substantially
increase the size of the Peruvian Communist party or of the pro-
Castro MIR. Catholic elements, influenced by world-wide changes
in the Catholic Church and by the danger they see within the
country, have taken a reformist position which conflicts with that
of the Peruvian Catholic hierarchy. If there is, as has been maintained, a bloc of voters that opposes the *status quo* and favors renewal and change, estimated as a little more than one-third of the
population,[32] these reformist Catholics fear that disenchantment
with Belaúnde Terry will send the pro-change bloc into the arms
of the anti-Catholic extreme Left. Their objective is to provide a
Catholic alternative. According to one of their spokesmen:

The objective is to shape a new type of revolutionary man, capable of
engaging in structural transformation, but with the will to freely give,
with a service spirit, with a loving look which will never destroy the

[31] The complete text of *Populorum Progressio*, plus some comments by
Catholic revisionists, can be found in *CIAS*, No. 163–64 (June–July, 1967).
See also, in regard to Chile, the pastoral letter by the Bishop of Talca, Manuel
Larraín Errázuriz, *Desarrollo: Éxito o Fracaso en América Latina*. In reference
to Brazil, the topic is best treated by de Kadt, "Religion," in Véliz, *Politics of
Conformity*, pp. 192–220.

[32] The point is made by Enrique Chirinos Soto in *Cuenta y Balance de las
Elecciones de 1962*, pp. 22–39.

existence of man for his own purposes or convert persons into means for an abstract end; a type of man capable of carrying out a revolution in concrete countries, like this one, with a rational understanding of the execution of plans to be fulfilled.[33]

Another representative of this group calls in more specific terms for direct taxation of a progressive nature, special land taxes for landlords, workers' participation in the operation of enterprises and

a true agrarian reform which, without demagogic bragging or false prudence, resolutely tends to the subdivision of the large landholdings, without losing sight at any time of a double objective: to increase the number of owners and to raise productivity.[34]

These reform Catholics have gained relatively little ground in Peru (the opposite is true in Chile and northeastern Brazil). The frustration caused by their inability to win acceptance of their views either among the clergy or the faithful has led some of them into becoming active leaders and/or ideologists of revolutionary or quasi-revolutionary organizations. The best-known case is that of Father Salomón Bolo Hidalgo, president of Peru's National Liberation Front, a pro-Castro organization that has developed some following among the miners and controls a few peasants' organizations. The NLF was also led by a retired military officer, the late General César Pando Egúzquiza, who was its presidential candidate in the 1962 election. This group was considered important enough by the military junta to be the main target of the January, 1963, dragnet of left-of-center elements (see Chapter 7). Bolo Hidalgo himself escaped capture by living underground for a number of months, while another priest, Father Masías, was jailed in this police action.

The frustration of those Peruvian Catholics who belong to the revisionist groups is expressed in their views of the established clergy. Father Bolo Hidalgo writes in his open letters, many of

[33] Conrado Eggers Lan, *Cristianismo, Marxismo y Revolución Social,* p. 95. This is one of the most interesting essays touching on the ideological competition between communism and the Catholic doctrine.
[34] César H. Belaúnde, *Reforma de Estructuras,* p. 17.

which are addressed to Cardinal Landázuri, head of the Peruvian clergy:

I see with great surprise that the Catholic hierarchy, instead of complaining against inhuman abuses, remains silent. What is the matter with the pulpits which shouted against Cuba? with the pastoral letters? . . . Is the Church an accomplice of dictators? Dictatorships are not eternal, *Monseñor.* I expect to listen to your voice of Christian integrity. Only he who fulfills his duty deserves respect. Fulfill it. . . .

God is infinite, is the purest spirit, and omniscient. The Church is a society formed by men who are sinful and subject to error. It is very often said that the Church believes and defines, when he who defines and believes is a simple individual of narrow views.

I consider that it is absolutely necessary for the clergy to place themselves decisively on the side of the peasants, on the side of the unprotected and the forgotten, instead of prostituting themselves before grants spotted with blood. It is very sad for me to see that, when there appears a priest who, conscious of his duty, follows Christ in his condemnation of imperialism and the oligarchy, those at the top of the Church hierarchy are the ones who condemn an attitude which they should back. . . . I feel that, if Christ were to come to this earth today, he would take the side of the Peasant Leagues, he would take the side of those who earn their food with their sweat, of those who earn salaries of hunger and misery.[35]

Father Bolo Hidalgo disclaims repeatedly the accusation, made by the more conservative newspapers such as *La Prensa,* that he is a Communist. He uses the argument that constitutes one of the potentially most powerful weapons of the Catholic Left: that they cannot be Communists because they are devout Catholics.[36] He points out that communism has little to do with the political insecurity that exists in Peru:

The agitation at La Convención, La Oroya, and Pátapo has a common denominator: misery and injustice; the miserable salaries received by

[35] Salomón Bolo Hidalgo, *Cartas de Mi Refugio,* pp. 29, 85, 114.
[36] *Ibid.,* pp. 136–37.

peasants and workers; and the conviction that they are not being treated like human beings, but like beasts. The number of those who understand that the wealth of our soil should not be for a few privileged ones or for the large monopolies grows daily.

He goes further and relates these revolutionary elements to the position of the Church hierarchy, criticizing at the same time the political role of the clergy:

Those bishops who issue pastoral letters to take votes away but do not issue them to require the wealthy to give something to the poor, to pay just salaries, to stop the exploitation of miners, peasants, and workers: those bishops who photograph themselves with the "jet set" but who forget the undernourished children and do not issue pastoral letters against those responsible for the massive illiteracy and tuberculosis; those bishops who gain plenty of weight but only remember in their pastoral letters to favor the powerful of this country; those bishops, I repeat, are only merchants of religion.[37]

Father Bolo Hidalgo is not the only priest taking a revolutionary attitude, although he probably is the best known "doer" in Peru. The Jesuit Father Romeo Luna Victoria, professor of political science at the Superior Normal School "Enrique Guzmán y Valle" has recently published a manual of revolution, addressed to Peruvian political leaders, which is both an intellectual justification and a description of the techniques to carry out a revolution. Father Luna Victoria rejects the idea that Catholic doctrine forbids participation in strikes or bloody revolution: he maintains that the contrary is true and that the advice "to offer the other cheek" does not apply to social matters. He says:

there may arise the unfortunate and sad situation in which, to carry out that which is experimentally correct, unquestionably just, and extremely urgent, which we are sponsoring throughout this study, there may not be, in some areas of the world, another alternative but to resort to armed revolution.[38]

[37] *Ibid.*, pp. 25, 139–40.
[38] *Ciencia y Práctica de la Revolución,* p. 280.

Luna Victoria maintains that the conditions for violent revolution appear in a country where (1) natural resources are controlled by a small minority and (2) elements who oppose change use their economic and political power to block it and to impede progressive elements from gaining control of the government, thus causing damage over a long period of time. He also proposes a redistribution of certain types of property (what he calls "elastic" property) through the confiscation of the rent produced by natural resources.[39] Finally, he shows the same frustration expressed by other Catholic reformists toward his own Church; he feels that when the faith receives money or other economic advantages from the state, the result is "A 'satisfied' and 'silent' Church."

I do not wish to cite contemporary names because I prefer to avoid damaging discords and arguments. The spectacle of a religious hierarchy that does not speak up when it should, that remains silent when it must denounce the obvious violation of sacred human rights, is extremely depressive.[40]

Some of these Catholic reformers tried to channel their political grievances through the Christian Democratic party, a solution which gained strength after the 1964 presidential victory of its Chilean counterpart. However, the Christian Democrats of Peru have not been able to develop the popular following the Catholic reformers hoped for and in recent times have been partially co-opted by the Acción Popular party of President Belaúnde. For this reason, the party has not lived up to expectations, and political action remains the responsibility of the few reformist members of the clergy who are unable to concentrate on strictly religious activities.[41]

[39] *Ibid.*, pp. 282–83 and 190–203. Although the author attempts to give universal applicability to his manual, it is apparent that he believes that the conditions described exist in Peru; this is particularly true when his previous writings are consulted (for example, *El Problema Indígena y la Tenencia de Tierras en el Perú*).

[40] *Ciencia y Practica,* p. 26.

[41] Vallier, "Religious Elites," in Lipset and Solari, *Elites,* p. 209, suggests that the reformist clergy could concentrate on religious values and action if

Thus, the Peruvian Catholic reformers now appear to feel the necessity of making Catholicism directly and personally congruent with the interests of those groups that consider it convenient or urgent to modify the *status quo*: in the words of Ivan Vallier, "to fuse religion with the idea of social revolution" and to "provide the basis of a Catholic ideology of social change." [42] Specific attempts to adapt the Catholic doctrine to these new ideological needs have been repressed by either the hierarchy or the Peruvian government; the cases of Fathers Lebret and Portain, and of Abbé Pierre, who attempted to move closer to the lower class, in the late 1950's and early 1960's, constitute clear examples of the obstacles put in the way of the reformers.

Nevertheless, whether they are motivated by foreign examples, by greater social consciousness, and/or by the realization that the old methods of resistance to the non-Catholic reform ideologies are doomed to failure, the fact is that Catholic reformers continue to exist and to play a political role, minute as it may be, in the Peruvian arena. In some cases it is not yet clear whether the renewal these Catholic reformers favor is limited to the strategy employed in reaching the masses (such as the use of modern opinion survey techniques and of mass media) and whether it really reaches the substance of the doctrine being transmitted; it appears, however, that the substantive differences are moving up within the hierarchy with the assistance of encyclicals such as *Populorum Progressio*, as well as the results of some surveys.[43]

Finally, the willingness of the traditional upper class to make political deals with ideological movements such as APRA, which the Church fought at least partially at the instigation of the upper

a Christian Democratic party exists. See also his "Religious Elites in Latin America: Catholicism, Leadership, and Social Change".

[42] "Religious Elites," in Lipset and Solari, *Elites*, pp. 210 and 213. However, Mr. Vallier does not seem to see clearly the implications of some of his statements and the contradictions of some of the positions he describes: it will not be possible for those he calls "papists" to provide the ideological base for change and, at the same time, to "pull the Church out of politics" (p. 213); the "papists" will be as much in politics as before.

[43] See the article by Juan Carlos Martelli, "La Iglesia ya no Quiere que Soben a los Santos."

class, tends to reinforce the position of those Catholic reformers who feel that the only secure political position for the Catholic Church is one which has popular support among the Peruvian urban and rural lower class. Furthermore, these reformers have not failed to notice that the upper class—and to a certain extent the middle class, too—are the most constant violators of Church dogma, possibly because they have the means to do it. The absence of clerical opposition to the Belaúnde regime, regardless of the influence of the President's uncle, appears to be an attempt by the Catholic hierarchy to show political flexibility and independence from the traditional upper class.[44] So are some of the steps taken by some Catholic orders to divest themselves of the land they own in order to move in the direction of agrarian reforms.[45]

It is evident that these steps, important as they might be, cannot be considered Church policy, nor even a general trend. In the opinion of a Catholic scholar:

It is in the realm of suggesting flexible solutions to the problems that responsibility and obligations are more commonly ignored. It can be argued that a fundamental reason for this is that Church spokesmen in their social and economic intervention of the post–World War II period are repeating the mistakes made by their predecessors a hundred years ago.[46]

Whether or not the Peruvian Catholic Church will, should, or can avoid the repetition of these mistakes is a matter that will have to be answered in the near future, and whatever the reply, it will leave its mark on Peruvian politics.

[44] The reference is to Víctor Andrés Belaúnde, one of the most distinguished Catholic intellectuals and uncle of President Fernando Belaúnde Terry; on this point see M. Guillermo Ramírez y Berrios, *Examen Espectral de las Elecciones del 9 de Junio de 1963*, p. 109. A reported personal friendship between the President and Cardinal Landázuri, primate of the Catholic Church of Peru, also helped; see Rosendo A. Gómez, "Peru: The Politics of Military Guardianship," in Martin C. Needler (ed.), *Political Systems of Latin America*, p. 307.

[45] Specific examples are given by Leopoldo Zea, "El Perú, Lima y Belaúnde," p. 447.

[46] Pike, "The Catholic Church and Modernization," p. 278.

9. Interest Groups and the Problems of Interest Articulation

All political systems receive and respond to demands from their subjects; the process of making demands on the political system is known as interest articulation, and it is done by groups and individuals, the latter often claiming to assume the representation of important groups or of the whole society.[1] Obviously, the articulation of demands does not guarantee a positive response from the political system, but it is clear that the inability to make certain interests or desires known eliminates even the possibility of a response. Consequently, the problem of being in a position to articulate certain interests becomes crucial in any political system, and Peru is no exception.

Ultimately the concept of state interests must have as its reference point the concrete interest of people, either as individuals, as groups, or as aggregates of groups in some ordered structure of a concentrically radiating consensus. The policies of the state, external and internal, register unevenly upon the interests of various individuals and groups in society, and represent in effect a societal distribution of power reflecting either an informal or a formal consensus pattern or a non-consensual structure of active and passive coercion.[2]

It is apparent that all political systems have "groups of individuals who are linked by particular bonds of concern or advantage

[1] This chapter follows the terminology (but not necessarily the views) of Gabriel A. Almond and G. Bingham Powell, Jr., in *Comparative Politics: A Developmental Approach*.

[2] Vernon V. Aspaturian, "Internal Politics and Foreign Policy in the Soviet System," in R. Barry Farrell (ed.), *Approaches to Comparative and International Politics*, p. 215.

and who have some awareness of these bonds." [3] But these groups' representativeness of the total population differs widely and sets the tone of their respective political systems. In Peru, the interest groups appear to coincide with the identifiable segments of the social structure; that is to say, interest groups are dominated by a given class and, more often than not, articulate interests that contradict those of the classes not represented in them. Thus, the compromising of conflicting interests is made more difficult (whether it is desirable or not is questionable), and very often the responses of the system are made as much against certain groups as they are in favor of others. Furthermore, to the extent that a certain stratum overwhelmingly dominates the political system it is likely that the interest-articulation structure will itself constitute an obstacle to the articulation of interests that conflict with those of the ruling stratum. On the other hand, the upper class will have at its disposal both formal and informal channels of access to the decision-makers. The situation fits the general description made by David Easton:

not all members are equally likely to give voice to a demand. Because of their general social status, some individuals or groups are more inclined to feel efficacious enough to articulate a political position. If this is so, persons occupying these roles in the social and political structure will have an important measure of control over the number of demands put into the system. . . . They are gatekeepers who stand athwart the admission channels to a system. . . . It is clear that the volume or variety of demands that initially get into a system and begin to move along toward the point of output (the authorities) will depend upon the characteristics of these gatekeepers.[4]

In many cases the "gatekeepers" do not limit themselves to controlling the inflow of demands; they also censor the information and support that come from the national society—and from outside the country as well—in order to guarantee the continuity of the system of priorities to which they subscribe. Thus, the "normal" political processes tend to convey essentially the same pic-

[3] Almond and Powell, *Comparative Politics*, p. 75.
[4] *A Framework for Political Analysis*, p. 122.

ture: a picture that confirms and reinforces the views of those who have access to the interest-articulation structure, regardless of the changes which may take place in the environment. Thus, it is not surprising that when Peruvian middle- and lower-class groups attempt to make their interests known through other than "normal" means (strikes, mass demonstrations, land occupation, violence), the charge of communism (it used to be aprismo) rapidly appears and is actually accepted by many of those in positions of authority. Usually, the cry is started by the "gatekeepers," who are trying to insure or reinforce the support of the military, of the Catholic Church, and of those who see communism behind every alteration of "law and order."

Unquestionably, Peru's interest groups can be classified as institutional, associational, and nonassociational, but this classification, while academically interesting, makes a limited contribution toward the understanding of the nation's politics.[5] A much clearer view emerges when the various interest groups are arranged according to the class that controls them and whose interest the groups transmit.

Upper-Class Interest Groups

The Peruvian upper class has formed some of the same organizations that exist today in many other countries under the same or similar labels. The National Agrarian Society, for instance, groups the coastal landowners whose main interest is the exportation of the raw materials produced on their plantations; the Sheep Growers' Association of Peru tends to represent the highland landowners who produce mostly for the domestic market; the Chamber of Commerce, the National Industrial Society, and the Association of Peruvian Businessmen unite the small industrial upper class, owners of large business establishments, executives of large corpora-

[5] This classification appears in Gabriel A. Almond's essay "Introduction: A Functional Approach to Comparative Politics," and is applied specifically to Latin America in George I. Blanksten's "The Politics of Latin America," both in Almond and James S. Coleman (eds.), *The Politics of the Developing Areas,* pp. 33–38 and 501–11. The classification has been reproduced in, among other places, Almond and Powell, *Comparative Politics,* pp. 74–79.

tions (mostly foreign-owned), and financiers; Action for Development brings together young managers of large enterprises, located mostly in the Lima area; and the National Fishing Society expresses the interests of the important fishing industry, dominated by the fish-meal producers. The latter and the National Agrarian Society have healthy and powerful treasuries since they collect from their members what amount to compulsory contributions, based on production.

These organizations fulfill some of the functions which have become characteristic of interest groups throughout the world: they lobby; they handle public relations on behalf of their members; they try to convince the rest of the population of the righteousness of their positions; they emphasize the coincidence of their interests and those of the nation and its citizenry, or at least most of it; and they otherwise "sell" their point of view to those inside and outside the government. What makes these pressure groups—or some of the more effective ones—rather different from their counterparts in the Anglo-American systems and in other advanced European countries is the degree to which they resort to personal and private connections to gain access to the policy-makers and their success in obtaining positive responses from them. Tied to this aspect of interest articulation in Peru is the overwhelming influence exercised by some of these groups over certain political parties, or at least over clearly identifiable factions and leaders within the parties—not to mention their relationship to the military establishment and the Catholic Church, already discussed in previous chapters.

The dominance exercised by the upper-class interest groups over some political parties, from the Civilistas to the Odriistas, and the unanimity of the various groups' views on all important political subjects also serve to explain their success. The close ties of important newspapers and television and radio stations increase the ability of these groups to mount "popular" campaigns and to obtain the backing of some middle- and lower-class organizations, as well as of a portion of the general population. The influence over political parties and the mass media all but cancels the ability of these political elements to aggregate and compromise conflicting interests; the mass media and the political parties only articulate the interests of the upper class, or those of which the upper class approves, pretending they are aggregates or compromises of all views. Thus, in most instances, the upper class appears to be compromising and understanding, while in fact it is translating its interests into national policy. The role of the National Fishing Society in the recent devaluation of the sol (discussed in Chapter 6) is a remarkable example; the Society mobilized a delegation of one hundred members who were received by the senators and representatives led by the presiding officers of both houses in a ceremony which took place in the main reception hall of the Peruvian Congress. The delegation's views were immediately made public by the newspaper *Correo* and echoed by all the important Lima dailies. What is perhaps more remarkable is that the fish-meal producers obtained exactly what they had asked for regardless of the opposition and the alternatives proposed by the executive branch of the government.[6]

The explanation of this outstanding success may sometimes be traced to what amounts to a political interlocking directorate. A recent case is that of Pedro Beltrán, a member of one of the most important landowning families, publisher of *La Prensa*, full member of the National Agrarian Society, and Prime Minister under President Prado after 1959. But, obviously, this type of situation is not likely to occur too often, and the traditional upper class has known it for some time; consequently, it has institutionalized unofficial channels, although their political significance does not seem to have been perceived by many observers. These unofficial channels are the upper-class clubs which exist in Lima, where upper-class interest articulators and representatives of the mass media and the policy-making circle meet, informally and continuously, shielded from public view and free to communicate without being encum-

---

[6] The episode is described in *Oiga*, March 31, 1967, pp. 4–5. See also the coverage given to this issue in the newspaper *Correo* (Lima), particularly in the edition of March 22, 1967, pp. 1 ff. The campaign was kept up in the following days and echoed by *La Prensa* (Lima) and other newspapers.

bered by the need to explain their conversations. Three such clubs stand out in Lima: Club Nacional, Club de la Unión, and Jockey Club del Perú. They have long enjoyed upper-class recognition, but reliable evidence of that status has been almost impossible to obtain because none of the clubs makes available its membership roster to outsiders, and this policy is enforced by the members.

Nevertheless, it was possible for this study to have access to a copy of the Jockey Club's annual report for 1963, which included the complete roster of all members in good standing, their membership numbers, addresses, and, in some cases, business affiliations. It was also possible to obtain the membership lists of the key organs (the ruling board and the qualifying board) of both the Club Nacional and Club de la Unión. When compared with one another and with lists of coastal and highland landowners, politicians, intellectuals, bureaucrats, and representatives of domestic and foreign corporations, they provided extremely valuable insight into the political role of the clubs.[7]

To begin with, a comparison of the list of full members of the National Agrarian Society with that of the Jockey Club reveals that 80 per cent of the families represented in the Society are members of the club in question. When the ruling board of the Society is compared with the club list it is discovered that all the members belong to or represent families who are on the Jockey Club's roster. Even when a comparison is made with the regular membership of the National Agrarian Society, it can be established that almost 65 per cent of them represent families or corporations which are also represented in the Jockey Club. Comparing the list of the 165 largest landowning families or corporations with the

[7] The author had access to Jockey Club del Perú, *Memoria Correspondiente al Año 1963*, which contains a list of its members in pp. iii–cxxxv. He also utilized one-page announcements from the Club Nacional and Club de la Unión, listing their authorities for the years 1965–66. The lists of landowners, members, leaders of the key pressure groups, and other influential individuals were compiled from Banco de Crédito del Perú, *Vademecum del Inversionista;* Perú, Ministerio de Agricultura, Dirección de Aguas de Regadío, *Padrones de Regantes de todos los Valles del Perú;* Andrés Vernal, *Guía Vernal del Perú; Indice Perú;* and especially Carlos Malpica, *Guerra a Muerte al Latifundio.*

Jockey Club roster shows that eighty-one of them (or 48.2 per cent) are directly represented in the latter, although this proportion is likely to be substantially higher, since it was not possible to identify all family connections through marriage because of the secrecy which cloaks membership in this club. It is possible to conclude, then, that the large coastal landowners and the National Agrarian Society are very well represented on the Jockey Club roster.

The findings are not too different when the composition of the Sheep Growers' Association of Peru is analyzed: nine of the ten members of the ruling board represented families or corporations also represented in the Jockey Club; and eighteen of the forty largest Sierra landowners (45 per cent) were so represented. As was true of the coastal sector of the traditional upper class, this percentage would undoubtedly be higher if comprehensive biographical data were made public. When the owners of large tracts of undeveloped land near Lima are similarly analyzed, the results are even more definite: of the sixty-nine families or corporations indentified as owning 250 acres or more, forty-eight (69.6 per cent) were found on the membership roll of the Jockey Club. This figure, too, is probably higher in reality. There are also members who are intellectuals, such as Carlos Miró Quesada Laos and Percy MacLean y Estenós, and representatives of the new industrial upper class, such as the Banchero family, one of whose members presides over the National Fishing Society, and Eduardo Dibos, acting president of the National Industrial Society.

Further examination of the membership list of the Jockey Club reveals that the institution's political and economic significance has been perceived by the most important elements in Lima and the rest of Peru. Banks, foreign investors, newspapers, and even some political parties are represented in it; clearly, however, the landowners constitute the most important single group. Of a total membership of 2,479 individuals, 354 (14.3 per cent) belonged to landowning families; here again, complete biographical data will most likely increase this ratio. Although it is rather unusual in organizations of this type, some members identified their business base (or at least one of them): twenty-two members associated themselves with private banks, twenty-four with various commercial enterprises (including nine with the Wiese Corporation, six with Grace Enterprises, and three with the International Petroleum Company), fifteen with the mass media (including twelve with the newspaper *El Comercio* and its printing establishment), and five with the executive branch of the national government, mostly in regulatory agencies. However, those who identified themselves commercially were few. It should be emphasized that some families have more than one representative on the club's roster (the Aspillaga family, one of the wealthiest in Peru, has at least fourteen members, including those carrying club numbers 1, 2, and 3); there are, then, probably no more than 500 or 600 families in the club, and membership turnover appears to be extremely slow. In that type of environment, and with such an exclusive membership, everybody knows the business activities of everybody else or can get the information without a formal registry. In fact, reference to the members' business activities seems to have been in some cases a by-product of their desire to utilize their office addresses.

The club roster also includes some high military officers, all of whom have recently occupied key positions. Among them are General Pérez Godoy, president of the military junta in 1962; General Oscar Benavides; General Julio Doig Sánchez, Army Chief of Staff; General Carlos Linares Molfino, chief of the tank division; and Admiral Jorge Barreto Alván, commander of the Pacific force. Other important military officers, such as General Julio Luna Ferreccio, Minister of War, or Admiral Jorge Luna Ferreccio and Air Force General Vargas Prada, a member of the 1962 junta, have immediate relatives in the Jockey Club.

The politicos are also well represented in the club. There are cases here of landowners who are also politicians, mostly belonging to the Odriista party, such as the senator from Lima, Julio de la Piedra, or his counterpart for Callao, Carlos Carrillo Smith. But the Odriistas do not have a monopoly: of the nine senators from Lima, four are listed as members and three others belong to families who are members; besides the UNO, they represent the Christian Democrats and AP. The two senators who cannot be traced to the Jockey Club belong to APRA. A similar situation exists with the Lima members of the lower house. The list also includes Pedro Beltrán; Manuel Odría, dictator from 1948 to 1956 and leader of UNO; Luis Bedoya Reyes, mayor of Lima and leader of the conservative faction which broke away from the Christian Democratic party and formed the Christian Popular party; and the family of the Aprista leader León de Vívero.

It appears likely that if the information were made available, the situation in the Club de la Unión and Club Nacional would not be very different. A comparison of the 1965–66 ruling board and qualifying board lists for these two institutions with the Jockey Club roster shows that twelve of the thirteen members of Club Nacional's qualifying board are members or belong to families who are members of the Jockey Club, and four of the ten members of the ruling board, including the president, are in the same situation.[8] The figures for the Club de la Unión are five out of nine on the qualifying board and two out of seven on the ruling board, but in this last case the two are the president and first vice-president. In less exclusive but still selective organizations, such as Lima's Rotary Club, which draws membership from the upper- and the upper-middle sectors, the presence of the Jockey Club is felt. In the Rotary, twenty-one of the twenty-eight individuals who served as presidents from 1920 to 1956 (including four who served more than one term) were members or belonged to families which were members of the Jockey Club; approximately the same ratios exist in other ruling positions.[9]

The picture thus painted, imperfect and limited as it may be, conveys clearly the idea of the Jockey Club as the institutionalization of personal contact channels for the articulation of inter-

[8] It should be added that one of the few families of the coastal sector of the traditional upper class not listed in the Jockey Club roster, the Benavides de la Quintana brothers (with investments in banking and mining) is represented in the Club Nacional's ruling board.

[9] The data for Lima's Rotary Club is from Ricardo Mariátegui Oliva, *Historia del Rotary Club de Lima* (1920–1955), pp. 59–65.

ests in the Peruvian political system, and the available evidence indicates that the Jockey Club is monopolized by the traditional upper class, and particularly by its coastal sector. The same situation seems to exist at the Club de la Unión and Club Nacional, although a recent article claims that the latter's political significance has been in decline for some time. The same study also says, however:

The paradoxic vision of unity appears when we observe how, in spite of all the differences due to opposition and isolation, the majority of regional businesses and all public and private services (public administration, banks, etc.) is organized and controlled from Lima, economic, political, and social center of Peru. It is here that, in mixed lobbies, interact the captains and the servants of the various private groups, international, national, and regional, as well as the most important bureaucrats.[10]

These lobbying activities seem to be carried out in the tranquility of these clubs, away from public control and from the counterbalancing action which may be exercised by middle- and lower-class interest groups. Episodes like the one which forced the fishing industry to engage in a formal lobbying effort, leading finally to the devaluation of the sol (see Chapter 6), are exceptional, and while they show the ability of the coastal sector of the traditional upper class to have its way against an unresponsive administration, they also constitute a qualified failure of the channels of personal connection. The fact that episodes of this type are so unusual and scarce, and the distribution of socioeconomic rewards being what it is in Peru (see Chapters 4 and 5), bears testimony to the general effectiveness of these channels of interest articulation. Furthermore, in those few instances when the administration does not respond favorably to the interests thus articulated, the relationship which exists between these clubs, the interest groups, the mass media, and service organizations makes it possible to produce liter-

[10] Jorge Bravo Bresani, "Mito y Realidad de la Oligarquía Peruana," pp. 60n. and 60–61. The author, who would seem to be related to members of Club Nacional and Jockey Club, provides no evidence that the political significance of Club Nacional is declining.

ally hundreds of communiqués, editorials, and reports that essentially reproduce the position of the traditional upper class, and particularly of its coastal sector. One study has made the following observation:

In Peru the established *Fuerzas Económicas Vivas* have become so structured that the presidents of some ten functional associations hold regular meetings where they discuss differences among member organizations, attempting to resolve disputes privately whenever possible. At these meetings reactions of the several participating groups toward proposed governmental action also are considered and collective action is decided. . . . These private governments acting in concert can generate a tremendous amount of covert pressure, for their members pay a very large share of all taxes collected in Peru and have many other ways of breaking a particular regime.[11]

These expressions of support and agreement from the *fuerzas vivas* are likely to be extremely convincing, particularly to those with limited education (formal and political), or to individuals who depend psychologically and economically on the traditional upper class. If the source of disagreement is a complex one, or if it is presented in a complex fashion, it may even be possible for the upper-class interest groups to rally substantial public support to their side.

The process which led to the enactment of the first Agrarian Reform Act is a good example of the smooth operation of these interest groups, led by the National Agrarian Society. The desire for a program of agrarian reform had first been articulated by the Apristas in the 1920's. It was also made an important part of the Socialist and Communist parties' platforms at that time. After World War II the political system apparently could not ignore the pressures any longer and, with the evident acquiescence of the traditional upper class, proceeded to issue decrees and organize commissions and study groups in order to give the appearance of acting on the demands, without really altering the *status quo*. That

[11] Robert E. Scott, "Political Elites and Political Modernization: The Crisis of Transition," in Seymour Martin Lipset and Aldo Solari (eds.), *Elites in Latin America*, p. 138.

was the case, at least at the beginning, of the Commission for Agrarian Reform and Housing, which was organized by President Prado in 1956 and placed under the control of the National Agrarian Society.[12] By the early 1960's it became apparent that these delaying tactics had run their course, and the peasants were presenting their demands more powerfully, under the combined leadership of some of their own mestizos and representatives of the urban middle class; this will be discussed later in this chapter. They were, to a certain extent, encouraged by the then candidate Belaúnde, who strongly subscribed to their demands. Land invasions and repression followed, but neither solved the problem. The military junta, again with the apparent consent of the large landowners, attempted to implement a regional agrarian reform program in the La Convención area. The junta's Minister of Agriculture announced that twenty-three landholdings were going to be distributed among 14,000 peasants; in fact, however, only one piece of property was expropriated and distributed among 262 peasants, and the owner was at that time conducting negotiations to sell his hacienda to them anyway.[13]

After Belaúnde won the 1963 election and assumed the presidency, the organized peasantry, either because it felt that he was going to redistribute the land forthwith or because it wanted to force his hand, increased the tempo of land occupations. The first step taken by the traditional upper class was to create the impression of a nationwide uproar for "law and order." This was not difficult, in view of their control of the mass media and their membership in numerous organizations of *gente decente;* widespread labeling as Communist helped convince the doubtful, and Be-

[12] The members of the Commission included landowner Pedro Beltrán, and representatives of the Cerro de Pasco Corporation, the Grace Corporation, and others who belonged to the National Agrarian Society; see Víctor Graciano Marta, *Política Agraria;* and Alvin Cohen, "Societal Structure, Agrarian Reform, and Economic Development in Peru." An earlier example of these attempts to postpone action was the decree issued by Odría authorizing the government to expropriate idle landholdings, a decree which was never utilized.

[13] The announcement was made at a press conference reported in *El Comercio* (Lima), March 30, 1963, p. 4. The details of the episode are described by Víctor Villanueva, *Un Año bajo el Sable,* pp. 144–46.

laúnde authorized the jailing of the peasant leadership and the use of force in repressing land invasions. At the same time, he pushed his land reform bill, which had been sent to Congress, in August, 1963, where it competed with five others.[14] Furthermore, the program was unacceptable to the traditional upper class, and particularly to its coastal sector which, of course, controls the National Agrarian Society.

The Society had already accepted the "principle" of agrarian reform when it contributed some of its most distinguished members to the aforementioned Commission for Agrarian Reform and Housing; Belaúnde's electoral victory, the position taken by First Vice-President Eduardo Seoane on the subject, and the increasing intensity and scope of the land invasions apparently convinced many coastal landowners that the practical applications of that principle could not be postponed any further.[15] Since the unrest was localized in the Sierra and had not spread to the key sources of income of the members of the National Agrarian Society, the decision seemingly was to have some sort of agrarian reform at the expense of the Sierra landowners.

The National Agrarian Society collected numerous pledges of support and agreement from regional agricultural organizations and other interest groups. It soon claimed to be the only voice of all farmers who were not invading landholdings. In fact, however, there was substantial disagreement among small farmers as to whether or not the National Agrarian Society really articulated their interest.[16] The Society's position of accepting agrarian reform if productive units were exempted and technical improvement included was outlined in ten editorials published by Beltrán's *La Prensa* and repeated elsewhere, either voluntarily or through paid ads.[17] The National Agrarian Society thus opposed some of

[14] See *Hispanic American Report,* 16:798 (1963), and Ricardo Letts Colmenares, *Reforma Agraria Peruana: Justificación Económica y Política,* pp. 9–11.

[15] Seoane's views are clearly expressed in his book *Surcos de Paz.*

[16] Some of these pledges of solidarity were announced in full-page ads in *El Comercio,* September 19, 1963, p. 6, and December 20, 1963, p. 8.

[17] The editorials were published almost daily from August 13 to August 23; ads appeared in *La Prensa* and *El Comercio* (for instance, on August 13, 1963, p. 7).

the most important features of Belaúnde Terry's proposed program and subscribed to the one presented by the Unión Nacional Odriísta, a party which, as has been indicated, was highly influenced by the traditional upper class. Even the Aprista proposal was more acceptable than the executive branch's bill.[18]

In order to reconcile the six land reform proposals, the House of Representatives appointed a special committee of thirteen members: six from the AP-DC alliance (Belaúnde Terry's supporters), six from the APRA-UNO coalition, and one from Father Bolo Hidalgo's National Liberation Front. The committee held hearings and accepted testimony from a large number of interest groups; finally, it unanimously reported a compromise bill in December, 1963. In view of the committee's composition, the concept of party discipline in Peru, and the relative positions of the parties involved, the representatives of the governmental alliance might have been expected to adjust their bill to duplicate that of the NLF, whose provisions would have brought about profound structural reforms; this procedure would have made sense not only in terms of the programs themselves, but also in political terms—Belaúnde Terry had won the election thanks to his reformist image— and one of the key items in the development of that image was agrarian reform. Compromises with proreform elements to get the margin of victory in committee would have been understood by his followers regardless of developments on the floor of the House and the Senate. Nevertheless, the unanimously reported bill, which was passed by Congress and signed into law by the President, was very close to the Odriísta proposal, which one observer labeled the most reactionary of all bills, rejected by everyone, and making no contribution whatsoever.[19]

18 The choice was reported in a full-page ad, published in *El Comercio*, November 2, 1963, p. 19.

19 Letts Colmenares, *Reforma Agraria Peruana*, p. 10. It is not necessary here to demonstrate the similarities between the UNO bill and the Agrarian Reform Act; it has already been done in the excellent study by Ernest DeProspo, Jr., "Administration of the Peruvian Land Reform Program." I am unable to explain the vote of the NLF representative; a party official would only say that "they were tricked."

The National Agrarian Society showed its skill as an articulator of the interests of the coastal sector of the traditional upper class by objecting only to certain key provisions of Belaúnde Terry's bill, and thus seeking a compromise of a compromise, since the executive branch's bill was already a middle ground between the stands of reformist and conservative wings of the AP-DC alliance. Thus, the only possible "intermediary" was the APRA-UNO coalition, which was dominated either by those who articulated the interests of the National Agrarian Society (UNO) or by those whose political interest lay with the maintenance of the large coastal plantations (APRA), because of the party's control of their peasants' organizations and the electoral support derived from it. In view of the situation, it is not surprising that issues such as the exemption from the law of productive units—essentially the sugar and cotton plantations—reproduced in the Agrarian Reform Act the view of the National Agrarian Society. Furthermore, the responsibility of enforcing the law is divided among a number of agencies, with the groups which articulate the interest of the traditional upper class given direct representation in practically all of them and in some even possible control. This, again, was the position of the National Agrarian Society, which objected to the "abusive powers" granted by the executive branch's bill to the "bureaucratic organs in charge of agrarian reform." [20] On the question of compensation, the means of payment for expropriated property (bonds and cash) was controlled by the Agrarian Reform Financial Corporation and, indirectly, by the Industrial Bank, thus limiting further the tempo of the program, as the National Agrarian Society had requested.

These examples should suffice to show the power wielded by upper-class interest groups, of which the National Agrarian Society is one, if not the most powerful, example. The tone of upper-class interest articulation in Peru is set by the tightly knit personal relationships at the level of social entities, such as the Jockey Club, and by the sharing of social life by the traditional upper class

[20] From a half-page ad published by the National Agrarian Society in *El Comercio,* September 1, 1963, p. 5.

(and particularly its coastal sector) in these settings with intellectuals, public servants, politicians, businessmen, and military officers who are admitted as a consequence of their political weight. The effectiveness of uniting the interest articulators, their supporters, the "gatekeepers," and some of the decision-makers in prestigious organizations where the values of the traditional upper class are dominant seems to have been demonstrated in Peru. The result of this process is the constant positive reaction of the political system to the individual and collective demands of these interest groups, in most cases without the use of overt coercion; it bears witness to the success of this approach.

Middle-Class Interest Groups

Isolated from the more significant interest groups and from the channels of interest articulation, and at the same time dependent to a certain extent on those who control them—not only for material well-being, but in terms of values as well—the middle class seems to have built interest groups with much more humble objectives. Although members of the middle class do join clubs and other organizations, these associations are almost never used to articulate class or any other political interests. A rapid look at the interest-articulation process in Peru shows that the middle class relies mostly on unions, apparently similar to those which represent the interests of the urban and part of the rural lower class, and sometimes loosely associated with them through organizations such as the General Confederation of Workers or the Peruvian Confederation of Workers. However, these consolidations of unions have seldom been effective in merging the interests of the white- and blue-collar workers.

One reason why they have not been successful is the preferential treatment of the white-collar workers (*empleados*), an advantage which the latter are not prepared to give away even if it means a stronger voice in public policy-making (a by no means certain proposition). A significant aspect of this preference is the fact that class membership is determined by type of employment, a fact which has not escaped even students in Peruvian secondary schools. A study of students in academic and commercial high schools revealed an "overwhelming preference" for the status of white-collar worker, which is not too surprising since the students were training themselves for just those positions. But even in vocational high schools, where blue-collar workers supposedly were being trained, only 13 per cent of the sample indicated willingness to work in that capacity for pay equal to that of white-collar workers, and 67 per cent of them either explicitly or implicitly rejected the possibility of willingly becoming *obreros*.[21] On the other hand, it would be erroneous to assume that the difference between *empleados* and *obreros* is strictly one of prestige; *empleados* generally receive higher salaries, enjoy longer paid vacations, receive larger annual bonuses, have greater job stability, better fringe benefits, more convenient retirement conditions, more paid holidays, and make lower social security contributions for the same services. It has been estimated that fringe benefits add 41 per cent to the white-collar worker's salary and only 25 per cent to the earnings of his blue-collar counterpart.[22] These differences are established by law; they tend to be more pronounced in reality, though, because minimum wage and fringe benefit laws go unenforced for *obreros*, but it is unlikely that they can be ignored in regard to *empleados*. This difference in compensation was reflected in another survey, in which 25 per cent of white-collar workers expressed satisfaction with their wages, while only 10 per cent of the blue-collar workers did so.[23]

Two extremely clear facts stand out as one looks at the middle-class interest groups in Peru: their large number and the narrowness of their goals. Since most of the middle-class interest groups are unions, many of them have imitated their blue-collar counterparts; that is, they have become organized by firm and/or activity, but separated and often independent from the *obreros* in the same activity. In addition, there are the traditionally middle-class

[21] William F. Whyte and Graciela Flores, *Los Valores y el Crecimiento Económico en el Perú*, p. 11.

[22] Ronald J. Owens, *Peru*, p. 75.

[23] William F. Whyte and Lawrence K. Williams, "Supervisory Leadership: An International Comparison."

groups, such as public servants, teachers, retail store workers, private office employees, and the like. The teachers provide a good example of this fractionalism: they are divided into four unions: National Union of Elementary School Teachers, National Union of High School Teachers, National Union of Physical Education Teachers, and National Union of Manual Arts Instructors, all of whose activities are supposed to be coordinated by the National Federation of Public School Teachers. Private school teachers and students who are preparing themselves to become teachers have their own organizations, usually by institution (such as the Student Association of La Cantuta Normal School). The employees of the central government are even more divided; a feeble attempt in 1959 to coordinate the activities of their unions grouped twenty-one member organizations (such as the Association of Customs Agents, the Association of the Ministry of Education, and the Association of Judicial Branch Employees) under the National Association of State Civil Servants, whose ineffectiveness as a unifying force became apparent when it called its first general strike.[24]

The goals of middle-class interest groups do not go beyond the respective group's immediate interests, such as salary increases, more fringe benefits, and extra paid holidays. In trying to achieve them, the middle-class interest groups employ practically the same union tactics resorted to by the unionized *obreros:* mainly, strikes and demonstrations. What is often different is the reaction of the political system to these demands and the methods employed to have them accepted. It has been clear for some time that the authorities are extremely reluctant to use force against middle-class interest groups when there is a confrontation; this reluctance does not seem to exist when the lower class—peasants, shantytown dwellers, or unionized workers—resorts to similar methods. Since the government of the day is unwilling or unable to coerce the middle class and to enable its most representative interest groups to employ methods usually reserved elsewhere for the urban workers, the middle class, as a result, often succeeds in obtaining fa-

[24] James L. Payne, *Labor and Politics in Peru: The System of Political Bargaining,* p. 236.

vorable responses to its demands. In view of its record during the last three or four decades, it is legitimate to wonder why the demands articulated by the middle-class interest groups have in fact been so unambitious. The only answer that can be offered is that the Peruvian middle class, as emphasized in an earlier chapter, is basically conservative and satisfied with the *status quo*. The great majority of the demands constitute adjustments and accommodations rather than threats to the political system.

It is possible to think that middle-class interest groups restrain their demands because of their weak power position and the realization that greater aggressiveness in their demands will bring about a strong reaction; while the possibility of this occurring should not be discounted, it has not deterred the middle sector of other Latin American countries such as Argentina, Uruguay, Cuba, and Mexico from seeking changes in the distribution of power. It may be more likely that

the exchange of favors, family connections, "protective" relationships, the distribution of sinecures through the political party, and other forms of primary relations, formed a complex network through which "patronage" continued to operate in favor of the middle class status.[25]

One clear characteristic of the Peruvian middle class is its dependency on the government for employment. The figures given in Table 13 (p. 63) may be clarified by indicating that some of those listed as employed in commerce and finance are in reality working for what is known as the Independent Public Sub-Sector; it is likely, then, that more than 50 per cent of the Peruvian middle class—approximately 200,000—are employed by the Peruvian government. As a comparison, a survey of the industrial establishment in the Lima-Callao area (where most of these establishments are located) discovered that only approximately 12,000 individuals could be considered as belonging to this stratum.[26] There appears

[25] Luis Ratinoff, "The New Urban Groups: The Middle Classes," in Lipset and Solari, *Elites,* p. 71.

[26] The figure has been extrapolated from U.S. Department of Labor, Bureau of Labor Statistics, *Labor in Peru,* p. 27. It is almost impossible to obtain precise data on the Independent Public Sub-Sector; in the 1964

to be no appreciable difference with the middle class which existed at the turn of the century, although it has been affirmed that the Leguía dictatorship enhanced it and altered its composition.[27] In any case, it is clear that its reliance on public employment continues; and since the traditional upper class exercises overwhelming influence over the political system, and public service positions are awarded without regard to merit and achievement,[28] it seems that individual anti–*status quo* attitudes on the part of members of the middle class would require a spirit of self-sacrifice which is seldom found among human beings. Taking into account the fear of the unknown found in most individuals who believe they have something to lose, it is natural that the demands made by the middle-class interest groups are limited to "more of the same" and do not enter the realm of a radical alteration of the distribution of social rewards and of the methodology employed in carrying it out. Faced with such a "responsible" middle class, which confines its demands to obtaining a little bit more under the existing structure, the political system acquiesces, usually after a *pro forma* struggle (so as to remind the petitioners that it is not too easy), without resorting to coercion.

Careful analysis of the process of articulating middle-class interests makes four things abundantly clear. First, a review of demands submitted by bank employees, public school teachers, organizations of public servants, and representatives of commercial and industrial white-collar workers shows a conscious attempt to stay away from areas not clearly involved with their immediate needs; their position on crucial issues such as land reform, taxation, *coups d'état*, and the like is often one of complete silence. Their support for forceful action by unions of blue-collar workers

---

national budget the Minister of the Treasury indicated that only approximately one-fifth of the 246 entities had sent in their budgets; see Perú, Dirección del Presupuesto, *Presupuesto Funcional de la República para 1964*, II, 11.

[27] See Víctor Andrés Belaúnde, *La Realidad Nacional*, pp. 194–96. This position is taken by, among others, Luis Alberto Sánchez in *El Perú: Retrato de un País Adolescente*, p. 135, and rejected by Fredrick B. Pike in *The Modern History of Peru*, p. 218.

[28] This point has been adequately documented by Jack Walker Hopkins in "The Government Executive of Modern Peru," *passim*.

and peasants amounts only to broad oral backing and often not even that. It is not unusual to avoid direct involvement even in conflicts affecting other middle-class interest groups, unless the questions are clearly ones which are likely to have direct applicability to the narrow interests of the groups providing support. Apparently, there is more identification between the upper-class elements in control of a given economic activity and their middle-class employees than between the latter and other members of this stratum employed in different activities. As Luis Mercier Vega has indicated, there seems to be

more solidarity between the bank clerk and the banker than between the same clerk and the depositor or the man in the street who needs the services of a financial establishment. The majority of the compensatory movements begun by bank employees' associations are directed toward a distribution of the profits earned by the employers and not toward the reform of the banking system, even though it may be exploitative.[29]

Second, a review of this type also shows the reluctance of the decision-makers to use force to prevent organized or spontaneous steps, such as strikes, lockouts (in the case of small businessmen), and demonstrations. The 1961 teachers' strike included the closing of all schools, a march on the congressional building and the placement of permanent pickets in front of it, hunger strikes, demonstrations by high school and university students, and other acts of disobedience; but, as usual, the objectives were quite limited, a few percentage points between what the government offered and what the teachers wanted to get.[30] While it would seem unwarranted to identify a direct relationship between limited goals and the absence of coercion, it should be emphasized that attempts at general strikes by public employees have been met by sterner action, although it fell far short of the repression unleashed against similar actions by the lower class.[31]

Third, an analysis of the middle-class interest-articulation pro-

[29] Luis Mercier Vega, *Mecanismos del Poder en América Latina,* p. 37.
[30] Payne, *Labor and Politics,* pp. 241–53.
[31] An example of such action was the total strike called by the National Association of Civil Servants in October, 1959; see *ibid.,* p. 236.

cess also makes clear that the groups belonging to this stratum can generally expect a certain degree of objectivity from the mass media; usually a position is taken only on editorial pages of newspapers and magazines and in commentaries on radio and television. Even here a certain balance is found, and substantial restraint is exercised by the commentators, whether for or against the particular demand being argued. This is probably a recognition of the fact that, while newspapermen and television commentators may share the values of the owners of newspapers and television stations, they tend to understand (although not necessarily agree with) the position of that sector of the middle class they are commenting upon.[32] This understanding is noticeable in the different treatment given by the mass media to demands formulated by such middle-class interest groups as the retail clerks and the teachers on the one hand, and those formulated by sugar plantation or mine workers, not to mention the Sierra peasants, on the other.

Finally, in what could be called the day-to-day articulation of interest, the individual demands personally espoused by the prospective beneficiaries have a substantially greater chance of receiving favorable consideration when they come from members of the middle class. After all, it is only natural for a middle-class bureaucrat to be inclined to act favorably and expeditiously on a request by an individual who dresses, speaks, and behaves like he does, particularly when the petitioner leaves his calling card and offers some sort of reciprocity. These demands, if they are not too earth-shaking, can be and are in reality decided by those who receive them, although formality requires that they be submitted to the judgment of higher officials. When the petitioner belongs to the lower class, he is received with a long list of "ifs," "buts," and formalistic steps (such as a properly written presentation) which force him to hire a middle-class intermediary or to give up.[33] It is

[32] See the treatment given to the May, 1967, teachers' strike by the pro-administration magazine *Oiga;* for instance, in its May 19, 1967, issue, pp. 4–7 and 30.

[33] The upper class seldom enters this picture; as has already been indicated, it has direct access to the top, and the decisions are formally or informally handed down to those responsible for carrying them out.

mostly in this type of situation that the salient characteristics of the Peruvian bureaucracy (legalism, formalism, multiplicity of agencies with jurisdiction over a given problem, inflexibility, and rigidity) come into play, with the evident design of giving the appearance of responding, while delaying a substantive action.[34]

Brief reference should be made to two special interest groups of middle-class origin: the military and the university students. The former have been placed in a special category and analyzed at length in Chapter 7. Suffice it to repeat here that they have concentrated on articulating their own immediate interests—those of the military establishment—and appear to have done little on behalf of other middle-class groups. The university students, on the other hand, by definition overwhelmingly members of the middle class, have often taken up causes not directly related to their activities as students and have provided an element of violence which the direct beneficiaries were either unwilling or unable to provide. The reasons for this behavior are complex and largely unexplored, mostly because Peruvian university students can be counted among the most unwilling subjects of political inquiry. However, studies carried out at the University of San Marcos and at the other institutions of higher education in the Lima area tend to confirm the general impression that the student body is dominated by the urban middle class: the figures indicate that more than 75 per cent of the students come from families who derive their income from small business, the professions, public service, and white-collar employment. Coincidentally, 81.7 per cent placed themselves in the middle class.[35] The profile of the student body and of the political role it plays could be better understood if it is remembered that the politically active students belong to highly structured, ver-

[34] These characteristics have been identified and analyzed by DeProspo in "The Peruvian Land Reform Program," pp. 41–46 and 215–19, and Hopkins in "The Government Executive," *passim.*

[35] The figures mentioned in this section were collected by the Institute of Sociological Research of San Marcos University, and are available there. Part of the data has been published in *Caretas* (Lima), July 9–22, 1965, pp. 10–13, and in José Mejía Valera's article, "Estudio Sociológico de la Juventud."

tically organized branches of the national political parties and are represented in their highest ruling councils. This is an important channel of access for a group which does not exceed 45,000 individuals, many of whom are students only in name.[36]

The importance of the students as interest articulators or, more precisely, as vehicles to articulate demands through various types of violence, is based on the fact that certain groups of students can be easily mobilized for almost any action which constitutes opposition to the political system and, quite often, to the government of the day. It is important to note that, although most of the students are ready and willing to engage in violent actions to emphasize their demands, this occurs only sporadically. More often, the students take to the streets of Lima to lend support to demands by other middle-class groups, and occasionally even to back up lower-class inputs. Thus, university (and sometimes even high school) students could be seen participating in and sometimes leading demonstrations and picketing for issues such as the eight-hour day for industrial workers and salary increases for elementary and high school teachers.[37] The university students' proclivity to demonstrate and resort to violence can probably be explained by their preference for political action, as opposed to the acquisition of political information, and by their perception of themselves as the vanguard of society, as well as their desire to "make a little noise." This eagerness to take to the streets and show their courage and strength is enhanced by the unwillingness of the coercive agencies to intervene, since relatives and friends may be among the unruly; it should not be forgotten that active political participation in

[36] There were 56,000 students registered in all Peruvian universities in 1965; how many students are full-time, or even bona fide part-time, is very difficult to ascertain, but it may be remembered that only 9 per cent of the freshman classes in the early 1960's graduated (Inter-American Development Bank, *Progreso Socio-Económico de América Latina: Fondo Fiduciario de Progreso Social, Sexto Informe Anual, 1966*, p. 371).

[37] On the question of the eight-hour day see Jorge Basadre, *Historia de la República del Perú*, VIII, 3906–8; and César Lévano, *La Verdadera Historia de las 8 Horas* . . . , pp. 30–34. Although the latter tries to downgrade the significance of student participation, it recognizes their involvement. On the teachers' strike, see Payne, *Labor and Politics*, pp. 248–49.

demonstrations and the like gives the students a sense of power and increases their prestige within peer groups.[38]

Peruvian students seem to make a clear distinction between their own situation and that of their society; 37.9 per cent of those interviewed indicated that the country's situation was bad, but only 13.7 per cent expressed varying degrees of dissatisfaction with their personal situation, and 41.8 per cent were satisfied with what they had. In spite of the seemingly important role played by the party organizations in university politics, only 13.8 per cent acknowledged membership, the majority in either Belaúnde Terry's Acción Popular or APRA. Direct observation of internal university politics (which elicit a great deal of interest among students) provides evidence of the students' general disregard for the articulation of immediate and feasible interests (middle-class or otherwise) and their involvement in matters of international politics or choices of ideological conceptions of which they have little knowledge and even less influence. Presented in those terms, the results of elections held by university student bodies have the limited usefulness of informing the political system and all interested citizens how that portion of the university community feels on matters such as the United States' landing of marines in the Dominican Republic, or which "ism" will save Peru.[39] Since in fact student party leaders are more flexible than their senior counterparts at making deals, their tickets reflect and often go beyond national party coalitions (for instance, temporary alliances between the Communists and Acción Popular in different schools of the same university or in different universities, to counteract the APRA-UNO coalition). While some individual students organized and led lower-class interest groups, these moves received no active support from the various student bodies as a whole, regardless of the

[38] The point is also made by Jacques Lambert in *América Latina: Estructuras Sociales e Instituciones Políticas*, pp. 337–42. The author can testify to the naïve involvement of some San Marcos students in the 1965 guerrilla actions. The details were being discussed in the special buses which ran from the old buildings to the new campus.

[39] This characteristic is also mentioned by Mercier Vega in *Mecanismos*, p. 65.

individual sympathy gained by the organizers. The significance of university students as interest articulators comes from their ability and willingness to add an element of violence to those causes which catch their fancy and that of their leaders. Because of students' volatile natures, other middle- and lower-class interest groups hope for and request their assistance, but they seldom count on it.

Lower-Class Interest Groups

In exploring the processes of interest articulation at the level of the lower class, the first observation that should be made is that homogeneity and unity are lacking. There are probably four identifiable sectors of this stratum: the members of urban workers' organizations, the marginal inhabitants of the urban areas, the unionized workers of the coastal plantations, and the peasants located mostly in the Sierra landholdings and communities.

Unionized Urban and Coastal Plantation Workers. As James Payne has pointed out, it is extremely difficult to ascertain the size of a Peruvian union's membership, and this is particularly true of lower-class unions.[40] Leaders are inclined to overstate their membership figures, and practically nobody seems to care about accuracy; thus every union has an "effective membership" (those who would tend to obey a strike order) and a dues-paying membership (50 to 60 per cent of these). In any case, if Payne's figures are accepted (and the writer has nothing better to offer), and middle-class unions are deducted from the total, there were approximately 263,000 unionized urban and coastal plantation workers in Peru in 1962. Taking into account the growth of industry and of the coastal and urban population, that figure may currently reach 280,000, or almost 6.9 per cent of the economically active population. Most of these unionized workers are concentrated in manufacturing establishments employing more than twenty workers and located in the capital city area; 70.4 per cent of a representative sample of blue-collar workers in that category claimed in 1962 to

[40] *Labor and Politics,* pp. 129–31.

belong to unions.[41] It is important to remember, as Payne has pointed out:

In this underdeveloped country the proportion of independent workers who are difficult to organize, such as shopkeepers, street vendors, artisans, domestic servants, is much higher than in the United States, where economic concentration has greatly reduced the number of self-employed or singly-employed workers. If one examines the degree of unionization in firms of over 50 workers, he discovers that in Peru practically all private firms of this size or larger are organized.[42]

But this reasoning does not change—indeed it reinforces—the fact that unionized urban workers are a privileged minority within the lower class and occupy the top of its economic ladder. This advantageous status can be demonstrated by comparing the wages on the textile industry (highly organized) with those of the garment industry (not organized): from near equality in 1939, the wages of textile workers grew to almost double the daily average wage of garment workers by 1959. Other industries show a similar trend. If the premise that this type of economic reward is important for a relatively undernourished and poorly-housed lower class is accepted, then the unionized urban workers seem to be effective in obtaining positive responses to the demands they place on the political system, when compared with the rest of the lower class. As with the middle-class interest groups, however, the question of whether their relative success is due to their power or to the moderation of their demands appears to be relevant.

The history of the Peruvian labor unions shows that since 1930 most of them have been the focal point in the political struggle between Apristas and Communists. This struggle has manifested itself at the leadership level, with varying reactions from the rank and file. In fact, most labor leaders have been activists of one of these parties as much as they have been workers' representatives. Often they have won or lost positions because of their party alle-

[41] Guillermo Briones and José Mejía Valera, *El Obrero Industrial: Aspectos Sociales del Desarrollo Económico en el Perú*, p. 53.

[42] Payne, *Labor and Politics*, p. 131.

giance, and on occasion they have subordinated union demands to over-all party strategy or redirected party strategy because of union demands. This interlocking directorate has brought both advantages and disadvantages to the lower-class unionized workers, but the latter appear to have outweighed the former. The most obvious disadvantage has been the subordination of the unions' interests to those of the party in terms of maintaining the party's position in national politics; an example is the refusal of the party, in whose ruling committees the labor representatives are outnumbered, to sanction a proposed strike because it may have damaging consequences on the national administration, which the party is supporting (it happened with APRA in the period 1956–62), or the decision of the party to call a strike for reasons not directly related to union matters (as happened with APRA immediately after the 1962 *coup d'état*). The Communists, less important in national politics and more dependent on the support of urban labor unions, have been more careful in subordinating labor organizations to party politics, but their labor leaders have not been above making "deals" with administrations that reflected the interests of the traditional upper class in order to improve their position in the organized labor movement vis-à-vis their Aprista competitors.[43]

This political involvement of organized urban labor has probably been related to some of its economic successes, particularly when the parties with which the unions were connected enjoyed good relations with those in control of the national government. Nevertheless, this relationship has often resulted in the toning down of the unions' objectives, circumscribing them to "bread-and-butter" matters for their members. This political allegiance has also had the consequence of weakening the power of urban labor organizations, not only by dividing one from the other, but by fostering disunity within the leadership and between the lead-

[43] This was the case during the first term served by Manuel Prado (1940–45), when the Apristas were persecuted and the Communist labor leader Juan P. Luna became secretary-general of the Confederation of Peruvian Workers. He again played an important role under Odría, when the Apristas were also persecuted.

ership and the rank and file.[44] This disunity was evidenced in the survey of industrial workers alluded to above, in which 53 per cent of all those interviewed had doubts about the commitment of the union leaders to the interests of the workers, as opposed to those of the parties to which they belong.

The history of the Peruvian lower-class labor unions and the available data tend to confirm the hypothesis advanced by Henry Landsberger (and before him by Lenin) that organized labor in Latin America supports the *status quo* more than some scholars think or are willing to admit. It appears to be true in Peru that "labor's basic aims are mundane ones: short-range, limited, economic, and not primarily the total reconstruction of society. In this sense, labor is neither 'ideologized' nor 'revolutionary.'"[45] This impression is reinforced by the evidence collected among Peruvian industrial workers; when asked to indicate what the main task of their union should be, they responded with various specific requests for wage increases, enforcement of work contracts, and other improvements of their immediate well-being. No one seemed to think that the union should have a political role. The surveyors concluded:

the workers . . . seem to think that the union is an organization which should engage exclusively in the defense of the interests related to their situation within the plant. With the exception of the answer "to teach the workers," only mentioned by 3.3 per cent, there are no other func-

[44] These by-products of the partisan involvement of labor leaders are discussed by Briones and Mejía Valera in *El Obrero Industrial,* p. 52, and in Payne's *Labor and Politics,* pp. 120–24 and 157.

[45] Henry A. Landsberger, "The Labor Elite: Is It Revolutionary?" in Lipset and Solari, *Elites,* p. 264. The view that Latin American labor is revolutionary has been unequivocally espoused by Robert Alexander; see, for instance, his *Organized Labor in Latin America,* especially ch. 1. Landsberger's view is also rejected, at least partially and in regard to Cuba, by Maurice Zeitlin in *Revolutionary Politics and the Cuban Working Class* and "Political Generations in the Cuban Working Class," in James Petras and Zeitlin (eds.), *Latin America: Reform or Revolution?,* pp. 264–88. Without getting into a discussion of Professor Zeitlin's views, it should be said here that he refers to a country where revolutionary elements are already in power. The fact is that organized labor gave very little support to Castro prior to his victory.

tions of a social or political type that the workers consider important tasks of the labor organizations.[46]

This lack of revolutionary zeal on the part of unionized urban labor is confirmed by other indicators: 57.4 per cent showed confidence that the situation was improving, 82.5 per cent showed satisfaction with their job, and only 27.7 per cent were willing to classify themselves as having a preference for the political Left—in spite of the fact that practically all parties which participated in the electoral campaigns of 1962 and 1963 placed themselves on the left of the political spectrum. It may be added that the Peruvian industrial workers exhibited some characteristics of the lower-class authoritarianism outlined by S. M. Lipset: only 38.7 per cent were interested in having two or more political parties in the country. Whether this general attitude is a consequence of the long-term influence of the Apristas and, to a lesser extent, of the Communists in the labor organizations or whether these parties have become influential because they have had these characteristics is a matter which warrants a study of its own. But the fact is that the goals of urban labor unions are limited and are backed by the rank and file; furthermore, most unionized workers are concentrated in the Lima-Callao area, a situation which increases their capability to mount demonstrations and engage in strikes to obtain positive responses to their limited demands. Therefore, it is not surprising that the political system, acting as arbiter, has sometimes gone along with the workers and forced reluctant industrialists to accept wage increases or greater job stability.[47] Thus, while the political system is not above using whatever coercion is necessary to handle union demands which get out of line,[48] it is inclined to go

[46] Briones and Mejía Valera, *El Obrero Industrial,* p. 51.

[47] In most of the Latin American countries, the government plays a much more important role in the settlement of disputes than it does in the United States. This fact seems to have been accepted by organized labor in Peru, a further indication of its acceptance of the *status quo.* For some of the reasons see Landsberger, "The Labor Elite," in Lipset and Solari, *Elites,* pp. 290–95.

[48] See, for instance, the reaction of the military junta to the demands of the mining union in December, 1962, described in Genaro Ledesma Izquieto, *Complot,* chs. 1–4.

along with settlements of labor disputes which at least partially accept organized labor's "moderate" goals, just like it accepts middle class ones, as long as these goals constitute adjustments to the *status quo* and do not threaten it. The fact that these settlements "may have no relation to the needs of the firm" [49] should come as no surprise, since the needs of a given *industrial* firm are not crucial to the Peruvian ruling class. On the other hand, industrial establishments have probably not been driven out of business as a consequence of government-imposed settlements.

The above statements can be extended to the relatively small number of agricultural workers from the northern coastal plantations who provide the core of the APRA-dominated National Federation of Peruvian Peasants. Most of the members work on the relatively modern cotton and sugar plantations, which produce for the export market and are usually in a better position to accept limited increases in wages and fringe benefits, particularly when the alternative is likely to be a disruption in production and the loss of foreign markets to producers from other countries. Furthermore, the recent apparent willingness of the plantation owners to go along with limited union demands should be tied to the "prudence" exercised by the Aprista union leaders and to the necessity of providing these leaders with "victories" which they could take back to their rank-and-file members, lest the Apristas be replaced by "extremists." This apparent agreement on certain "rules of the game" can be explained further by the importance of the unionized plantation workers to the Apristas at election time, when they provide an important part of the voting strength in the key party stronghold, the "solid North." This, in turn, was a prime consideration in APRA's decision to support the exemption of the coastal plantations from the provisions of the Agrarian Reform Act.

Here again, the demands articulated by the coastal workers have been allowed to enter the political system (in the last few years through the sizable number of Aprista representatives in Congress), and more often than not they have received responses which can be considered at least partially positive. But the de-

[49] Payne, *Labor and Politics*, p. 65.

mands have first been toned down by the same political party, and sometimes by the same Aprista politicians who act as mediators between the organized peasants and the political system. And, as has been said before, the mediators were instrumental in eliminating whatever prospects of structural change the Agrarian Reform Act had for them.

The Marginal Urban Dwellers. This significant group, already described in Chapter 5, can be easily identified by visiting the shantytowns and tenement houses found in all Peruvian cities and their environs. It is practically impossible to provide reliable figures on the size of the marginal population, but rough (and probably conservative) estimates indicate that more than 400,000 inhabitants of Lima (or approximately 25 per cent) live in shantytowns. The percentages increase in other urban centers such as Arequipa (40 per cent), Iquitos (65 per cent), Trujillo (35 per cent), and Chiclayo (36 per cent), and reach their peak in Chimbote (70 per cent).[50] All available information indicates that these shantytown dwellers tend to have little or no education and skills, hold temporary and part-time employment, mostly in unproductive services and nonunionized jobs, and show very little political involvement. Nevertheless, political necessity and the trials of living in the city have apparently taught them the difficulties of altering policies to suit themselves. The same thing applies to those who occupy the tenement houses located in the older parts of the largest urban centers, for whom figures cannot even be guessed.[51]

Unable to join the established lower-class interest groups and, what is perhaps more important, to benefit from their successes, these marginal dwellers have resorted to two types of organizations: the neighborhood association and the provincial club. The former can be found in most shantytowns, often under the name, "Association of Residents of ———"; many have joined a loose confederation known as Federation of Occupants of Public Lands

[50] José Matos Mar, "Consideraciones sobre la Situación Social del Perú," p. 66.

[51] For a first-hand description of some of Lima's tenement houses and the marginal city dwellers who inhabit them see Richard W. Patch, "La Parada, Lima's Market."

—a fitting name, since most of the shantytowns have been built on property owned by the municipalities or other governmental agencies.[52] These associations represent the community in its dealings with public agencies, petition on the community's behalf, and become responsible for whatever improvements are going to take place in the shantytown. Obviously, in so doing they procede to articulate the demands of the dwellers of that particular shantytown and, whenever possible, to negotiate the response with the decision-makers. While many of the associations are run by individuals chosen by those whom the associations represent, there are indications that in some cases the leadership comes from the outside, often from middle-class activists whose allegiance belongs to one of the political parties.[53] These cases seem to be examples of attempts by the various parties to take over the role of intermediary between the marginal urban dwellers and the political system, not only with the obvious purpose of capturing their votes, but also in order to tailor their demands to the party's goals and tactics and to make their demands more "realistic"—which means, in most countries and certainly in Peru, more conservative and limited.

The experiences of those who live in the shantytowns that surround the cities of Peru contribute to their acceptance of intermediaries and their withholding of demands which may cause a negative response from the political system. Most of them have not forgotten that they settled on land which does not belong to them and which they have occupied more or less forcibly, sometimes after pitched battles with the police. They also sense that the established residents of the cities, and particularly the unionized workers and the bureaucrats, despise and disdain them. The police

[52] The most comprehensive descriptions of the shantytowns which surround Lima can be found in Pablo Berckholtz Salinas, *Barrios Marginales: Aberración Social,* and in Esther Palacio de Habich, "Investigación Socio-económica y Etnolo-educacional de los Moradores de los Cerros Circunvecinos y Arrabales de la Ciudad de Lima." For a more general description see José Matos Mar, "Migration and Urbanization: The Barriadas of Lima—An Example of Integration into Urban Life," in Phillip M. Hauser (ed.), *Urbanization in Latin America,* pp. 170–90.

[53] At least one case is cited in Palacio de Habich, "Investigación," p. 84.

immediately place them in the category of "troublemakers" and harass them, without providing regular protective services within their communities; this treatment gives at least the appearance of a "law of the jungle" situation, thus increasing the poor reputation of the shantytown dwellers among the other urban residents. Their individual and collective attempts at contacting the bureaucracy are rebuffed and sometimes literally ignored; the petitioners are ordered (not asked) to "wait outside" day after day, until they realize the hopelessness of their situation.[54] It is not surprising therefore, that the marginal city dwellers tend to rely on intermediaries who can at least get through the "gatekeepers." More often than not, however, the inhabitants of shantytowns simply do not formulate the demands that they would like, and feel entitled, to formulate, on the assumption that they have no hope of getting a positive response. This move away from political involvement is reflected in Table 15 (p. 77) and Table 24 and confirms Bourricaud's view of the Lima shantytowns:

Political life is reduced to a series of high-level transactions between the agents of the candidate and his party and the more or less spontaneous leaders who place at the disposal of the politicians the votes of their friends, their relatives, and their *compadres*, who are quite willing to go along with what is required of them since this formality, the vote for a candidate, does not constitute a significant contribution vis-à-vis the substantial services the candidate has already performed.[55]

The second type of organization that tends to articulate the interests of the marginal urban dweller is the provincial or regional club. It differs from the neighborhood association in that its membership is based on area of origin and its functions are somewhat broader. There are hundreds of these clubs in Lima, and they also

[54] The writer has seen the poorly dressed mestizos waiting for whole days in the hallways of public offices, only to be told at the end of the day that they should return the following morning. Naturally, no petitioner or group of petitioners in this class can afford to miss work very long, and they soon realize that it is economically more convenient to rely on an intermediary or, more likely, to forget their demand and do without the government, if at all possible.

[55] François Bourricaud, "Lima en la Vida Política Peruana," p. 94.

Table 24. Responses to questions concerning reliance on the government in two shantytowns near Lima, 1965

| | Responses | |
Position	Pampa Seca (%)	El Espíritu (%)
Much or some help given by president	28	38
Much or some help given by municipality	34	22
Much or some help given by other officials	22	31
Much or some help given by a party	15	20
Unfairness in public housing selection process	66	82

Source: Prepared by the author from data provided by Daniel Goldrich, Raymond B. Pratt, and C. R. Schuller, in "The Political Integration of Lower Class Urban Settlements in Chile and Peru: A Provisional Inquiry."

exist in the other coastal cities that have received a large influx of migrants from the rural areas, particularly from the Sierra. The boundaries of each club vary widely: the members may come from a department, a district, a town, or even a certain parish; in many of them, membership criteria are not likely to be strictly enforced, although it would be unusual for an individual to wish to join a regional club not of his area. While the criteria for membership in the regional clubs apparently would make them quite different from the neighborhood associations, this is often not the case in practice: it has been found that 89 per cent of the heads of families living in the shantytowns of Lima had been born elsewhere.[56] Those joining the neighborhood associations then, probably also tend to constitute the core of the regional clubs, a fact confirmed by direct observation but which cannot be documented because of the impossibility of obtaining a comprehensive list of organizations, let alone membership rosters.

[56] Matos Mar, "Migration and Urbanization," in Hauser, *Urbanization,* p. 179.

Regional clubs often invite distinguished citizens such as professionals, civil servants, and legislators from back home to join, but these dignitaries are not likely to become active participants in the truly regional institutions; some of them do take an interest, however, in departmental clubs, which encompass the largest political subdivisions and often coordinate and supervise the activities of lesser clubs within their jurisdiction. In any case, these middle- and upper-middle-class individuals do not depend on these organizations to articulate their demands and find themselves in a minority. More often than not the active participation of middle-class members is the consequence of a direct political interest. In the words of one observer:

Various political parties like their members to be club leaders and often aspiring politicians are attracted. Some of the North Coast Clubs are Aprista clubs, at least one Ancash club is a Communist club, but the vast majority of clubs, although often having "political" officials, are not political clubs. Club office, however, is often a form of political mobility.

The political functions of the regional institutions are twofold: they are expected to articulate the interests of their members and to orient newcomers in all aspects of urban life; and, in the case of the clubs located in Lima, they are expected to formulate and press the demands of those who remained back home:

The club members often defend local interests in the various government ministries and are usually in the forefront of attempts to get new schools, roads, water systems, sewers, clinics, and other public services and advantages for the town or district. Since few towns can afford full-time lobbyists in Lima, and since these things can only be done in Lima and the delays are legendary, this function of the clubs is quite important for the towns.[57]

Many clubs seem to have become accomplished lobbyists; they use regional and family ties quite effectively in order to obtain the

[57] Both quotations are from William P. Mangin, "The Role of Regional Associations in the Adaptation of Rural Migrants to Cities in Peru," in Dwight B. Heath and Richard N. Adams (eds.), *Contemporary Cultures and Societies of Latin America*, p. 315.

neutrality, and sometimes even the sympathy, of the "gatekeepers," as well as the help of effective intermediaries and bureaucrats. They develop those intangible skills needed to get through the Peruvian bureaucratic maze and are able to enlist the help of legislators for their objectives. While they tend to claim that they are acting on behalf of the home town, contacts and skills are used to pursue the interests of the members, particularly in the case of those located in Lima, and more often than not the demands articulated are those which the urban members think their friends back home would or should wish to articulate, as a Peruvian novelist has described so well.[58]

Nevertheless, as with the neighborhood associations—and perhaps even more so—there are factors which deter the lower-class majority of most regional clubs from formulating demands that would cause stress in the political system. First, the "gatekeepers" and intermediaries may refuse to go along with them and may suspend further collaboration to advance those demands which are "possible." Second, the political system may react with harassment and even violence; most club members, like members of the neighborhood associations, are defenseless against sanctions, such as the loss of employment in a market where the supply of unskilled labor exceeds the demand, and against police abuses, such as beatings and unjustified detention.[59] Third, demands intended to alter the *status quo* would certainly elicit the reaction of those at whose expense the reforms would be carried out, and the members of these organizations seem to realize that, at the present time, those favoring the *status quo* carry much more political weight than they do. Fourth, most of those who belong to the marginal urban population are relative newcomers who are resented by the long-term residents for economic, social, and racial reasons; both in the shantytowns and in the tenement houses they suspect outsiders and even each other, and their general condition subjects them to

[58] José María Argüedas, *Yawar Fiesta, passim.*

[59] Although statistics on urban unemployment in Peru are meaningless, this situation has been reported by many observers. See, for instance, José Matos Mar, "Diagnóstico del Perú: Cambios en la Sociedad Peruana," and David Chaplin, "Industrial Labor Recruitment in Peru."

severe depressions—characteristics which make forceful political actions unlikely, even in the absence of other reasons.[60]

In conclusion, the marginal urban population could, under certain conditions, formulate demands which might threaten the political *status quo* and articulate them, if need be, through other than the regular channels. However, it has so far been prevented from doing so by the discouraging mechanisms developed by the political system, which appear to be most effective in the urban areas. The only somewhat successful forceful actions taken by the shantytown dwellers have been the occupation of government land and the resistance in a few instances to government eviction. On the whole, however, they have been unsuccessful even in obtaining basic public services (such as water, electricity, transportation, and police patrols) and low-rent housing (most of this type of housing seen around Lima was built during the Odría administration, which may explain the support for the former dictator among shantytown and tenement-house dwellers). Whether the Peruvian political system will be able to continue preventing the marginal urban population from articulating its demands, particularly in view of the example coming from the rural areas (to which many of these people are so closely tied), is an uncertain matter which will be discussed in Chapter 11.

The Peasants. The data provided in Chapters 4 and 5 show that the nonunionized peasants (living mostly in the Sierra) are those who, as a group, seem to be at the bottom of every social, political, and economic pyramid that one cares to outline. They appear to be as close to political weightlessness as human beings will ever be. Their cultural and educational isolation from the "legal country," in Basadre's words,[61] has led to a near impossibility on the

[60] This depressive state of mind has been reported by Mangin, among others, in "Mental Health and Migration to Cities: A Peruvian Case," in Heath and Adams, *Contemporary Cultures*, p. 551; and by Humberto Rotondo, "Psychological and Mental Health Problems of Urbanization Based on Case Studies in Peru," in Hauser, *Urbanization*, pp. 249–57. The effect of this mental state on political activities is discussed by Daniel Goldrich, Raymond B. Pratt, and C. R. Schuller in "The Political Integration of Lower Class Urban Settlements in Chile and Peru: A Provisional Inquiry."

[61] See Jorge Basadre, *La Multitud, La Ciudad y el Campo en la Historia de Perú*, p. 275.

part of most of them to articulate demands through the accepted channels. On those occasions when there have been attempts to do so outside the existing system—and there have been some in the last few decades—the system has reacted with untold ruthlessness and cruelty, forcing the Sierra peasants into submission and into the loss of whatever hope they entertained in the area of interest-articulation. At least one observer has flatly stated that this portion of the Peruvian population does not seem to belong to the nation.[62]

The peasants have tried to articulate their interests for a long time through what has been left of the old Indian communities developed under the Incas. As indicated in Chapter 5, a few communities have organized themselves to compete with the landowners, or at least to stop them from continuing their slow take-over of the communities. By and large, however, the communities have been ineffectual in stopping the abuses perpetrated by the traditional upper class in collusion with a portion of the dependent middle class. Furthermore, these communities could at best claim to be articulating the interests of their members, or approximately 40 per cent of the peasantry.[63] It is not surprising, then, that the "revolution of rising expectations" has led the peasants to search for new vehicles for articulating their demands and to develop more successful channels for doing so. They have resorted to regional peasant unions, although the word "union" (*sindicato* in Spanish) is somewhat misleading here, since the structure and objectives of the peasant organization had nothing to do with those traditionally found in unions.

These peasant unions, which were quite influential in the south-

[62] John Nathan Plank, "Peru: A Study in the Problems of Nation-Forming," pp. 248–49. There was a large peasant insurrection in the department of Ancash at the end of the nineteenth century; after some successes, it was wiped out by the Peruvian army. Other peasant rebellions took place in the departments of Puno in 1920 and Ayacucho in 1935; in the latter attempt the military executed every fifth prisoner.

[63] There is no precise figure on the total number of communities, since many of them have not registered, as the law requires. The total number of those living in communities has been estimated at 2,500,000, or approximately 40 per cent of those engaged in agriculture (Seoane, *Surcos de Paz,* pp. 130–37).

ern sector of the Sierra, although they cover most of rural Peru, were loosely linked by the Confederation of Peruvian Peasants and competed with the branches of the well-organized National Federation of Peruvian Peasants, which draws its membership from the workers of the coastal plantations and is controlled by APRA. The Confederation, on the other hand, groups the *de facto* serfs of the traditional landholdings, the owners of *minifundia*, the landless sharecroppers, and even some of those engaged in transporting goods between urban and rural areas and in selling them. Racially, the membership runs from the nearly pure Indian to the light mestizo, although the latter tends to occupy most leadership positions. Yet there is substantial diversity at the top, both ideologically and racially: Emiliano Huamantica, member of the Communist party, was considered an Indian by some, or at least a very dark mestizo; Hugo Blanco, the unchallenged leader of the Cuzco Peasants' Federation, was white and intellectually close to the National Liberation Front; Vladimiro Valer, also from Cuzco, was a university student and a member of a landowning family. This diversity is reproduced in the other regional unions.

One characteristic that stands out among the peasant organizations, both independent and affiliated with the Federation, is the limited control which the leadership is able to exercise over the members. This aspect of the new peasant unions became apparent in the various episodes which led to the occupation of large landholdings throughout the Sierra, and particularly in the La Convención and Lares valleys, under the jurisdiction of the Cuzco Peasants' Federation. As Aníbal Quijano Obregón points out:

The land invasion process . . . having begun under the influence and the direct action of political groups of urban origin and defined party allegiance, their nation-wide generalization took place in a relatively spontaneous manner; that is to say, by the peasants' own actions, and, for the most part, independent of all direct political or partisan influence.[64]

[64] "El Movimiento Campesino del Perú y sus Líderes," p. 48. The account of Hugo Neira, *Cuzco: Tierra y Muerte,* confirms this assertion.

Consequently, although most of the urban leaders who provided the original impetus for the peasant unions clearly represented the left-of-center parties and subscribed to Marxism (through rather personal interpretations), the demands articulated by the organizations unquestionably originated in the long-held grievances and represented the genuine interests perceived by the rural lower class as their own. In fact, as has already been emphasized, the most often performed role of the leadership appears to have been that of trying, many times with little success, to tone down the demands of the peasants and their inclination to resort to the land invasion procedure.[65] Even Hugo Blanco, the man who probably enjoys the most effective rapport with the peasantry, emphasizes the importance of organization, structuralization, and the formation of a political party which would unify the various left-of-center factions. At the same time, it is apparent that the rank and file are interested in the immediate formulation of specific demands related to their main source of income, agricultural land, and to its seizure if positive responses are not forthcoming.[66]

The demands being formulated by the peasants through the unions are unquestionably revolutionary, since they call for the immediate and effective transfer of most of the productive land to peasant communities and to individuals—an action which would take away the political power and the social prestige which the traditional upper class still enjoys. If one discounts the passage of the Agrarian Reform Act, the demands formulated by the peasant unions since the late 1950's have received a consistently negative response from the political system; this has occurred in spite of the fact that the demands were reinforced by land invasions, which, according to some reports, still take place from time to time. Token steps, such as the announcement of a pilot land reform program by the military junta in 1963 in La Convención Valley (coupled with persecution of the peasant leadership) cannot be considered serious responses, except in the sense that the answer of the political system is negative. This "tokenism" has not deceived the

[65] Neira, *Cuzco,* pp. 43–47.
[66] See Hugo Blanco, *El Camino de Nuestra Revolución, passim.*

peasantry, which remains as miserable as it has always been, or worse.[67] The continuing flow of unsatisfied demands places added stress on the Peruvian political system: this friction will likely accumulate since the growing (but by no means universal) politization of the peasants can be said to come from "an increasingly widespread belief that the conditions of life are not inevitably fixed, that they can be altered through human action." [68]

This stress is directed toward what Almond and Powell call the "distributive capability" of the political system: controlled by the traditional upper class, the political system is not (and cannot be expected to be) able to satisfy the growing demands by redistributing that which has served as the key source of economic, social, and political power to its most important members. But whether its leaders realize it or not, the constantly increasing demands of the rural lower class are already hindering what the same authors have identified as the "extractive," "regulative," and "symbolic" capabilities. This development may very well damage the "responsive" capability, an event which will be felt by other groups, sectors, or classes in direct relationship to the degree of positive responsiveness which the system has shown toward them.

[67] The point is clearly made by Oscar Delgado in his article, "Revolución, Reforma y Conservatismo: Tipos de Políticas Agrarias en Latinoamérica."

[68] Almond and Powell, *Comparative Politics,* p. 94.

10. External Factors Influencing Peruvian Politics

In the last few years the literature of political science seems to have discovered (or rediscovered) the role played within a society by elements who are not members of that society and who, according to traditional thinking, should not be involved in that society's politics. In a recent essay, James N. Rosenau brought forth the concept of a "penetrated political system" by which he identified a situation "in which non-members of a national society participated directly and authoritatively through actions taken jointly with the society's members, in either the allocation of its values or the mobilization of support on behalf of its goals." [1] If this concept were strictly applied we would have to say that in this interdependent world all political systems are penetrated, since none of them seem to be able to claim total inmunity from actions taken by outsiders. Under this strict interpretation the world would be made up of states which influence each other's domestic, as well as international, politics; in other words, a world of mutually penetrated politics.

It is not necessary to subscribe to such an extreme interpretation of political penetration or to engage in an extremely close scrutiny of political reality to discover that all the Latin American political systems have been and are subject to varying degrees of penetration, mostly by the United States, but also by European countries and, in some cases, by other Latin American countries. This penetration is quite evident in the economic sphere, where crucial in-

[1] "Pre-theories and Theories of Foreign Policy," in R. Barry Farrell (ed.), *Approaches to Comparative and International Politics*, p. 65.

vestments in important sectors of the economy are dominated by one or more outside investors (such as the chemical and automobile industries throughout the area). Penetration is also apparent in the military establishments of most of the Latin American countries which rely on outside missions, training centers, and manufacturers for their equipment and technical preparation.

Cuba constitutes a very interesting special case, but it does not alter the situation just described. The country shifted from being very highly penetrated by the United States to being now penetrated, although substantially less so as recent events demonstrated, by the Soviet Union. It should be pointed out, however, that this is not a case in which the penetrators have determined basic political changes, but a situation in which changes in the social order and in the dominant groups have altered the source of penetration.[2]

It is apparent that most of the penetration of the Latin American political systems, at least since World War II, has been carried out by the United States. What has sometimes confused the picture has been the fact that the nonmembers participating directly or authoritatively, or causing that participation, have not always been American diplomats. In most cases, United States investors have provided the energy for and have been the main beneficiaries of penetration, sometimes *at the expense* of their country's long-range foreign policy objectives. The United States involvement in a 1962 proposed land reform law in Honduras, in which some American senators prodded the State Department into action at the request of the United Fruit Company, provides an enlightening example of the nature and mechanics of this penetration. The events which took place in Guatemala in the 1950's and culminated with the overthrow of the reformist Arbenz administration by an invasion force sponsored by the CIA constitute another example of penetration.[3]

---

[2] The point is clearly made, in regard to Cuban foreign policy, by Vernon V. Aspaturian, "Internal Politics and Foreign Policy in the Soviet System," in Farrell, *Approaches*, p. 218.

[3] For details of the events in Honduras see Marvin D. Bernstein (ed.), *Foreign Investments in Latin America*, pp. 186–208. For details of the

These obvious cases of flagrant penetration appear to be confined to the countries of Central America and the Caribbean, an area which, publicly or privately, is considered within the immediate sphere of influence and the security perimeter of the United States. The countries of South America appear to have been subjected to a more subtle type of penetration, with the United States becoming the main actor only since World War II, often to the detriment of European countries which had played this role earlier. In these countries penetration seems to have been achieved through the close rapport developed between the United States military and its South American counterparts; this rapport is reflected in the mutual defense agreements and the military assistance programs. One Latin American commentator on these agreements has written:

The other party, our country, is the receiver of those services and equipment as a depository, who will have the right to have them but not to use them except in such a manner as established by the agreement (determined by an American law), who must allow the control —by citizens of the other party—of the use to which said equipment and services are put, who should pay the expenses of those who perform such control, who should protect the equipment and services and return them to the other side.[4]

Peru fits this general description quite well. During the nineteenth and early twentieth centuries the country was not a first-priority target of the European nations then actively engaged in penetration. More often, the relationship was of an economic nature and initiated by whomever was in power in Peru. Various Pe-

---

episode in Guatemala see David Wise and Thomas B. Ross, *The Invisible Government*, pp. 165–83, and Gregorio Selser, *El Guatemalazo, passim.* For a general discussion of this point see Aspaturian, "Revolutionary Change and the Strategy of the Status Quo," in Laurence W. Martin (ed.), *Neutralism and Nonalignment: The New States in World Affairs*, pp. 165–95.

[4] Horacio Luis Veneroni, *La Asistencia Militar de los Estados Unidos,* p. 39. The recent proposals for a permanent Inter-American Military Force appear to be an attempt to institutionalize this military penetration and provide it with a multinational facade; for a well-researched discussion see Veneroni's *Fuerza Militar Interamericana.*

ruvian administrations tried to sell bonds in the money markets of London and Paris in order to raise capital for different projects. On many occasions the capital thus raised (usually a small percentage of the bonds floated) ended up in the pockets of those in power. After their removal, the succeeding administration showed little disposition to repay these sums, claiming collusion between foreign bankers and those officials requesting the loan and lack of revenue; both arguments tended to be true, although of little value in the field of international law, particularly then.

The direct political consequences of the poorly negotiated, unpaid, and unserviced international loans were the exercise of direct pressure by the diplomatic representatives of the countries whose investors had borne the burden of the loan, the exaction of further payments from the administration being pressured, and a new default after a few payments. This sequence often led to a direct take-over of key Peruvian revenue-collecting agencies by outsiders who, through "better administration," tried to make it possible for the bondholders to collect. An example of this type of procedure was the contract signed with the Grace Corporation in 1887 but effective two years later. The agreement in essence turned over to British bondholders control of all Peruvian railroads for sixty-six years, plus all the guano not used domestically; consequently, in London the bondholders organized the Peruvian Corporation, Ltd., which exercised control not only over the railroads and guano but, in the words of one observer, "also over the country's entire range of fiscal activities." [5] British investments continued to flow into Peru, and by the end of 1915 they were estimated to have reached the figure of $121,000,000, as against $1,000,000 for France and $58,000,000 for the United States.[6] French influence seems to have been exercised at a different level and may not be accurately reflected by this figure. In 1896 a French military mission took over the reorganization and training of the Peruvian Army. During the first decade of this century a French officer served as Army Chief

[5] Fredrick B. Pike, *The Modern History of Peru,* p. 154.

[6] United Nations Economic Commission for Latin America, *External Financing in Latin America,* p. 17.

of Staff. This mission undoubtedly exercised some influence over those it was training; the French officers appeared to have determined the army's lack of involvement in the coup against Leguía which took place on May 29, 1909.[7]

After World War I Peru's foreign investment situation changed radically. Significant United States investments had begun moving into Peru at the turn of the century. The Cerro de Pasco Copper Corporation, formed by J. P. Morgan, Sr., and other well-known American financial figures, entered the Peruvian mining picture in 1901 with a $10,000,000 investment. The Grace enterprises, which started in the 1850's as a Peruvian corporation founded by a British subject, had become incorporated in the United States and moved their headquarters to Boston, thus acquiring American status. Since 1903 American diplomats in Peru had dedicated a great deal of their time to furthering the interests of these two corporations and a few other investors. During the first administration of President Leguía (1908–12), the government showed particular receptiveness to the representations made by the United States State Department on behalf of foreign investors. One observer has noted:

Leguía, who had been Minister of Finance in the cabinet of President Candamo in 1903, admired North American customs and manners more than did other presidents before him. Peru thus shifted her attention from Europe, and during the period 1908 to 1919 came to depend much more upon the United States.[8]

This dependency during the first Leguía administration was demonstrated not only by the preference shown to American investors, but also by appointment of American citizens to key positions in the Ministry of Education, thus placing the educational process in U.S. hands. Leguía's inclination toward the United States may not have been purely sentimental, however. During his commercial life he had been general manager of the New York Life

[7] For an account of this bizarre episode see Jorge Basadre, *Historia de la República del Perú*, VIII, 3558–64.

[8] James C. Carey, *Peru and the United States, 1900–1962*, pp. 23–24.

Insurance Company in his country, Ecuador, and Bolivia. Furthermore, after his first term in office ended and he ran into difficulties with his successor, the United States diplomatic personnel in Peru and Panama looked after him, and the State Department assisted him in the United States.

But the penetration of American capital in Peru really increased during the second Leguía administration (1919–30). By 1924, direct United States investments had grown to $140,500,000, and near the end of the *oncenio,* in 1929, they were estimated at $161,500,000; in addition, at least $105,000,000 in portfolio investments materialized during this period.[9] It should be noted here that the preponderance of American economic influence in Peru did not bring about the type of financial rivalry with European, and particularly British, investors which later on took place in the Plata River region. In fact, Leguía seems to have been on as good terms with the British as he was with the Americans. He had managed the British Sugar Company, Ltd., in Peru and had developed close contacts with British business leaders—contacts which were reinforced during his exile in London between his two administrations.

In view of this background, it is worth mentioning that Leguía stopped in New York and Washington on his way back to Peru to run in the 1919 elections. At that time, he seems to have contacted investors and made plans for his second term. These contacts included conversations with the president of the National City Bank of New York, to whom he promised substantial business, and officials of the Electric Boat Company, whose role in the growing American penetration of Peru will be discussed later. He also met with high United States government officials, although those meetings have remained secret.

Leguía seized power by a *coup d'état* on July 4, 1919. It has been maintained that certain military officers closely connected

---

[9] Data on direct investments are from U.N. Economic Commission for Latin America, *External Financing*, p. 17; the figure for the portfolio investments were estimated by the author from data provided in Basadre, *Historia*, IX, 4113–23.

with United States weapons manufacturers and with the American Embassy played an extremely important role in Leguía's success.[10] Be that as it may, it is a matter of record that following the coup the American representative encouraged his government to recognize and support Leguía and that in doing so he was articulating the interest of the American business colony in Peru.[11]

The American penetration of Peru was not limited to the economic sphere during the second Leguía administration. The Peruvian President continued his policy of appointing United States citizens to important governmental positions, including Air Force chief, director of commercial aviation, customs chief, director of education, and other regional and national positions in the field of education. Furthermore, shortly after his take-over, Leguía requested and received a United States naval mission, which was extremely influential in the Peruvian Navy and in governmental circles until the President's overthrow.

The naval mission was useful to the Electric Boat Company of New York, which was engaged in the production of submarines. This manufacturer had been trying to sell its product throughout Latin America but it had limited success, except in Peru. With the assistance of the American naval mission and bribes paid to Peruvian officials, it was able to sell four submarines to Peru between 1924 and 1926. When the boundary disputes with Chile were partially settled with active State Department participation, the vice-president of the Electric Boat Company complained that the accord reduced the possibility of new orders from Peru.[12]

If Leguía was extremely receptive to American desires, the United States government and investors were quite grateful. American diplomats defended Leguía both in Peru and in the United States, and one of them nominated the dictator as a candidate for

[10] A naval officer, Luis Aubry, showed up as a Peruvian naval attaché in Washington in 1920; by 1923 he was the Electric Boat Company representative in Peru. For his role see United States Senate, *Munitions Industry: Hearings before the Special Committee Investigating the Munitions Industry*, pp. 376–79. For an account of the coup see Basadre, *Historia*, VIII, 3936–46.

[11] On this point see Carey, *Peru and the U.S.*, pp. 36–40.

[12] *Ibid.*, p. 94.

the Nobel Peace Prize. Furthermore, American authorities made things difficult for the Aprista leader Haya de la Torre when he was exiled from Peru and prohibited his landing in Panama. American investors showed their appreciation by bribing the dictator's son, Juan Leguía, who is known to have received more than $600,000, although there is no evidence that any of it went to his father. However, when Leguía was overthrown by Colonel Sánchez Cerro (see Chapter 7), the State Department decided to do nothing to assist its former ally under the advice of American investors and of the naval mission.

Although members of the traditional upper class at first resented the American penetration, they soon found that the progress brought about by the newcomers and the roads built with some of the loans increased the value of their landholdings. Those who owned real estate near Lima soon found themselves within the growing metropolitan area and were able to sell their land at prices which would have been unthinkable a few years earlier. Others acted as advisors or partners of the American investors and profited substantially from this relationship. Consequently, when Leguía was overthrown, there was relatively little antiforeign and anti-American feeling among those who replaced him, although such sentiments undoubtedly existed among the middle and urban lower classes.

Leguía's successors respected the agreements made with those foreign investors who were already in the country but did not encourage new ones; the depression and World War II caused a reduction of American investment. However, the virtual disappearance of European investments increased American dominance of the foreign investment field. During the 1930's American businessmen practically monopolized the production of minerals, external financing, and international communications and transportation. A consequence of their presence was the constant growth of the American share of Peru's foreign trade: in the late 1930's one-third of the country's imports came from the United States, and one-fourth of its exports went to the American market.[13] The naval

[13] See Ronald J. Owens, *Peru,* p. 165.

mission was withdrawn in 1933 (it had been too closely associated with the Leguía regime), but it returned, together with an Army mission, just before World War II. To complete the American supervision of the military establishment, an Air Force mission was added in 1946.

Military Penetration: The Case of the Cuban Documents

The penetration of a military establishment by a foreign power has become quite sophisticated; evidence is extremely difficult to come by and the documentation usually demanded by the academic community is nearly always unavailable and often nonexistent. This is particularly true of the Latin American countries, where nationalism is so prevalent. Thus, Latin American military establishments go out of their way to make it appear that the decisions they make are, in fact, theirs, and not dictated by outsiders. Furthermore, political as well as other decisions are sometimes made under the influence of a roll of dollar bills, an argument which can be easily dismissed by those not faced with the situation; but a bribe carries substantial weight when offered in secrecy by one who is known to be able to deliver. Consequently, penetration of a military establishment has to be deduced from the limited circumstantial evidence which sometimes reaches the researcher. The following episode provides such evidence.[14]

On March 15, 1963, a regularly scheduled Bolivian airliner of the Lloyd Aereo Boliviano, flying from northern Chile to Bolivia, went down in Peruvian territory, near the Chilean and Bolivian

[14] The information that follows has been collected by the author from *Expreso* (Lima), March 16, p. 6; March 17, p. 1; March 18, p. 1; March 19, p. 3; March 20, p. 1; March 21, pp. 3, 6; March 22, p. 3; March 23, p. 4; and March 26, p. 7 (all in 1963). Also *La Prensa* (Lima), March 16, pp. 1, 6; March 17, p. 1; March 18, p. 1; March 19, pp. 1, 5; March 20, pp. 1, 2; March 21, p. 1; March 22, p. 1; March 24, p. 1; March 26, p. 1; March 28, p. 10; and March 29, p. 1. A brief article also appeared in *La Prensa's Suplemento Dominical, Siete Días del Perú y del Mundo*, March 24, 1963, p. 3. Information was also collected from Peruvian officials familiar with the operation. It is interesting that APRA's official newspaper, *La Tribuna*, played down the American role and practically ignored the episode (see March 19, p. 2 and March 21, p. 1).

boundaries. Two Cuban couriers were aboard the plane, and apparently they were carrying diplomatic pouches with documents which appeared to be of interest to the United States government. At the time of the accident, Peru had already broken diplomatic relations with the Cuban regime, while Chile and Bolivia had not. News of the accident was delayed, and many details were withheld by the Peruvian police and army. But it soon became apparent that the rescue operation was being conducted by American military personnel and CIA representatives, with the Peruvians acting as escorts.

The Tacna airport in southern Peru became the operations center, and, according to one observer, "it looked like a United States base." Two large Air Force transport planes arrived, apparently from their base in South Carolina, bringing a variety of rescue equipment, including two large helicopters which were rapidly assembled in Tacna. American military personnel from the missions to Peru and Bolivia flew to the area, and Colonel Robert Wiemer, apparently the United States military attaché in Bolivia, took charge of the operation. The United States military personnel also installed a very powerful radio transmitter, giving them direct communication with the Panama Canal Zone and the continental United States.

The first members of the rescue party that reached the scene of the accident were overwhelmingly American, with only token Peruvian representation; the group included, among others, three United States Army colonels, a Navy captain, and a CIA representative. From the very beginning, the Peruvian police and military limited themselves to keeping newspapermen and others away from the accident site. The bodies of crash victims, mostly Chileans and Bolivians, apparently lay around for some time while the American party searched the area for the documents carried by the Cuban diplomats. They finally found microfilm, secret files, and one or two submachine guns. On March 19 the United States Air Force attaché in Lima announced to newspapermen that the operations to retrieve the bodies would begin the following day and that they would cost $500,000. Colonel Weimer personally carried the documents to Tacna in a United States helicopter and on to Lima in a United States Air Force plane. At the Lima airport, under heavy custody by Peruvian police, he turned over the weapons to a Peruvian officer and left with what apparently were the documents.

The Peruvian government tried to play down both the American involvement and the significance of the whole episode. The Ministers of Government and Foreign Affairs stated that neither weapons nor documents existed. Later on, they stated that the documents were being studied by the Peruvian intelligence service and that American military personnel had participated in the search and rescue for "no important reason." The desperate efforts made shortly after the accident by the Cuban ambassador to Bolivia and the second secretary of the Cuban Embassy in Chile to reach the crash site before the Americans further contradict these assertions. The former's request to enter Peruvian territory was denied, and he had to remain at the border; the latter was caught trying to enter Peru with forged documents and was later expelled from Chile.

This episode clearly shows the high degree to which the United States military-intelligence combination was able to penetrate its Peruvian counterpart. The role of the United States Military Mission, supported by a Special Action Force, in the 1965 fight against guerrilla bands (see Chapter 7) supports this evidence. Although the details of the American involvement have not been made public, it is known that the United States provided advisors, equipment, and air transportation, including Hercules-130 planes and helicopters. It has also been suggested that the advisors in fact planned and directed the military operations. In addition, for a number of years the United States government had been training Peruvian police and military personnel both in the United States Army School of the Americas in the Panama Canal Zone and in the Agency for International Development Police Academy in Washington, D.C., where political indoctrination is a very important part of the curriculum. In view of the political role played by the military establishment and, to a lesser extent, by the police

forces, the influence thus acquired by the United States government and, more specifically, by the American military, over Peruvian politics cannot be ignored or dismissed. It is remarkable, for
instance, that the writer has been unable to find a significant foreign policy disagreement between any of the regimes which held
power in Peru and the United States in the course of this century.

Economic Penetration: The International Petroleum Company

Toward the end of the nineteenth century, British explorers decided that the northern region of Peru offered good possibilities
for oil production; the concessions obtained ended up in the hands
of a British firm, the London and Pacific Petroleum Company. In
1916 Standard Oil of New Jersey created a subsidiary, the International Petroleum Company, to take over the British operation, beginning with the La Brea and Pariñas oil fields. The purchase was
completed in 1924, after the British firm had obtained privileged
treatment and sizable tax concessions, plus a confirmation of its
dubious rights. Most of these advantages were granted by the
second Leguía administration, which also went along with the
transfer to the International Petroleum Company.

The new company increased production, and shortly thereafter
it became responsible for more than 80 per cent of all Peruvian oil
and 90 per cent of the country's natural gas. In 1946 it was
granted extensive concessions in the Sechura area, which had been
heretofore reserved for the State Oil Company. One student of Peruvian affairs has observed:

Apristas warmly backed the agreement, known as the Sechura Contract, when it came before Congress for approval, even claiming credit
for having conceived it. Undoubtedly *aprismo's* friendly attitude to-
wards the IPC helped account for the fact that at this time the United
States Department of State began to regard the APRA as its favourite
Peruvian political party, a policy it would maintain at least through
the mid-1960's.[15]

_____

[15] Pike, *Modern History of Peru*, p. 285. For background information on the
La Brea and Pariñas oil fields see Basadre, *Historia,* VIII, 3774–75, and IX,
4010–13; Alfonso Benavides Correa, *Oro Negro del Perú, passim;* José

In 1952, under the Odría regime, the International Petroleum Company and other American corporations received further concessions. By 1957, the IPC completed its control over Peruvian oil by taking over the Lobitos oil fields, held until that time by a British firm. During the 1960's approximately 98 per cent of all Peruvian oil production, as well as most of the refining done in the country, which is handled at the huge Talara refinery, has been in the hands of the IPC.[16] In addition, the International Petroleum Company has enjoyed duty exemptions for the importation of some types of oil not produced in the country.

The way in which the La Brea and Pariñas oil concessions were originally obtained and later confirmed, plus the overwhelming presence of the International Petroleum Company in the production, refining, and distribution of oil products, soon made this matter a significant political issue. Although in principle representatives of all sectors claim to be in favor of the recovery of the La Brea and Pariñas oil fields and of stringent taxation of the International Petroleum Company, in practice no Peruvian administration has actually acted to achieve either end. At the same time, the parliamentary majorities, which articulate the interests of the traditional upper class (see Chapter 4), have not only shown reluctance to deal with this matter, but have in fact obstructed the growth of the State Petroleum Company, thus supporting the argument that the latter is not prepared to take over the oil fields. This has been done by reducing the State Oil Company appropriations, by eliminating its fleet of oil tankers, by authorizing the International Petroleum Company to develop its own chain of service stations, which then forced independent retailers out of business, and by granting new concessions to companies such as the Peruvian Pacific Petroleum Corporation, which appears to have been an IPC front. But the traditional upper class was not alone in this enterprise. One of the few legislators who actually acted against the International Petroleum Company made the following observation:

Macedo Mendoza, *¡Nacionalicemos el Petroleo!, passim;* and Owens, *Peru,* pp. 151–53.

[16] Carey, *Peru and the U.S.,* pp. 169–72.

There are coincidences which are not accidental and which should be pointed out. One of them is that, among the most forceful accusers of suspected poor management of the State Oil Company and demanders of investigations, one finds the stronger defenders of the Sechura Contract in favor of the International Petroleum Company: the Apristas. Their parliamentary group in the Chamber of Deputies, disguised or acting under the "independent" label, was the source of the accusations, in the same way that it defended the price increases and said nothing in the debate over the Arbitral Decision. . . . The investigation—which has lasted three years—has fulfilled until the present time its unannounced objective: to paralyze the development of the State Oil Company.[17]

The mention of price increases refers to Prime Minister Pedro Beltrán's decision in 1959 to authorize sizable increases in the price of oil products sold in Peru. The justification was that the government needed extra revenue; since the government received a share of IPC profits, the authorized price increases would raise the company profits, which in turn would raise government revenues.[18] Naturally, the real objective was to make it possible for the oil monopoly to increase its profits. It has been said that Mr. Beltrán owns IPC stock and that he participates in a corporation which has received exploratory rights near the present oil fields.

The Penetrators and the Ruling Class

While Peru's traditional upper class, and particularly its coastal sector, tended to reject the American investors—especially since they came in under Leguía, whom the traditional upper class did not trust—they soon learned to live with the Americans. The economic penetrators gave some members of the traditional upper class an opportunity to share in the benefits, either as stockholders or as highly paid advisors. What is perhaps more important, the United States increased further its dominant position in regard to

[17] Macedo Mendoza, *Nacionalicemos,* pp. 134–35.

[18] Pike, *Modern History of Peru,* p. 298. Apparently the IPC was pressuring the Prado administration both through American diplomatic channels and, more directly, by reducing domestic oil production. Once the price increases were authorized, production went up.

Peru's international trade; during the 1960's, approximately 45 per cent of Peru's imports have come from the U.S., and 35 per cent of its exports have gone to the American market.[19] Cotton, sugar, and fish products depend heavily on American buyers. Members of the Peruvian traditional upper class soon discovered that United States investors have access to both the executive and legislative branches of the United States government and that both have been ready and willing to exercise effective retaliatory action. Thus, a sort of *modus vivendi* appears to have developed, with the American investors in almost exclusive control of mining, certain industries, and international transportation, and the traditional upper class in control of urban and rural real estate and its products. Both share in the important banking business, but American banks have so far been very careful to follow the lead of the financial institutions controlled by the traditional upper class.

Occasionally, this relationship is reinforced by marriages, such as one reported a few years ago in the society pages of the New York *Times* between the great-grandson of former President Pardo (and nephew of Cardinal Landazuri) and the daughter of a distinguished New York family.[20] It is also interesting to notice that practically all nondiplomatic foreign names found in the roster of the Jockey Club—fifty-seven—are Anglo-Saxon, and some of them are listed as representing the large American corporations operating in the country. Furthermore, the laissez-faire economic philosophy favored by the traditional upper class and modified only when it suits their immediate interests has found and finds a great deal of support from the economic penetrators. Even at the social level, the income of the managers and executives of most American enterprises almost forces them to interact solely with the Peruvian upper class, since the other segments of society would be extremely reluctant to associate with the foreign executives because of income limitations.

In terms of governmental penetration it seems apparent that the

[19] Owens, *Peru*, pp. 164–70, and U.N. Economic Commission for Latin America, *Economic Survey of Latin America, 1965*, pp. 248–51.
[20] June 25, 1967, p. 60.

American government, and particularly its military establishment, shares the anti-Communist tendencies shown by the Peruvian ruling class and, as Vernon Aspaturian has clearly stated, also exhibits the latter's interest in stability and the *status quo*.[21] Support of mild reforms, such as those in the area of land ownership, at the expense of the traditional upper class has been countered with threats to nationalize the holdings of some of the large American corporations. These corporations, in turn, have utilized their direct access to the United States foreign policy-makers and the American Congress to have those reformist policies watered down or eliminated; such action has relieved the pressure on their own investments. When the pressure was not relieved, the economic assistance granted by the United States and by international agencies in which the United States has a preponderant voice was reduced or delayed until the necessary guarantees were given.[22]

This is not to say that the *modus vivendi* always operates with equal smoothness. The 1968 refusal of the American government to make certain tanks and supersonic fighter planes available to the Peruvian military and the latter's decision to buy them in Europe exemplifies one type of disagreement. The complaints of members of the traditional upper class against the American policy of selling cotton on the international market below the internal support price or against reductions of the Peruvian sugar quota are another type. But neither one has threatened to alter the *modus vivendi* just described or seems powerful enough to do so in the future.[23]

Some Peruvian writers have recently claimed that Peru's ruling class is only a shadow of the United States and of American investors. One has gone so far as to state that what is at stake in the question of the La Brea and Pariñas oil fields is whether or not

[21] "Revolutionary Change," *passim,* in Martin, *Neutralism and Nonalignment.*

[22] An example of this type of conflict was reported in the New York *Times,* August 13, 1967, p. 31.

[23] The first disagreement was partially reported in the New York *Times,* May 17, 1968, p. 1. Regarding the second see, for instance, Julio de la Piedra, "Acto Inamistoso de la Administración de Estados Unidos, contra el Perú."

Peru is in fact a nation or a province of the International Petroleum Company.[24] These claims seem to be exaggerations and, in some cases, appear to be an attempt to lighten whatever responsibility the traditional upper class may have for the country's present state of affairs; if the premises advanced by these writers are accepted, then the real responsibility for Peru's problems lies with the penetrators and not with the native ruling class. This view, however, appears to be groundless. The writer is under the impression that, because of Peru's size and location, the penetrators could do very little if faced with a common front formed against them by the military establishment and the traditional upper class; such a front could easily obtain middle- and lower-class support because of its chauvinistic appeal. But it has been in the interest of the military and the traditional upper class, as they perceive it, not to form such a front, and in its absence the penetrators have had a share, and only a share, of internal political power. Up to this time, that share of power has been employed to maintain the *status quo* and to charter a foreign policy of adherence to American views. The writer is unable to foresee any immediate change in the use of the penetrators' share of power.

[24] The issue is raised by Benavides Correa in *Oro Negro*, pp. 7–23. The idea of the Peruvian ruling class as an agent of foreign investors has been presented by Jorge Bravo Bresani in his article "Mito y Realidad de la Oligarquía Peruana." The same concept is intimated by Carlos Delgado, "Notas sobre Mobilidad Social en el Perú," p. 20. However, Mr. Bravo Bresani did not seem to hold those views in his contribution to *Breve Introducción al Estudio de la Realidad Nacional*, pp. 100–174. Recently, after long negotiations with IPC, the Belaúnde administration fulfilled its 1963 promise and, under the authority of a law passed in 1967, moved toward the transfer of the La Brea and Pariñas oil fields to the state; the company is to be compensated by other concessions. This action may be intended to reinforce Acción Popular's position in the 1969 presidential election.

11. The Possibility and Source of Political Change: Revolution from Above or Below?

It is apparent that the previous chapters give a somewhat static view of the Peruvian political system. Daily changes at the individual, group, class, or national level are easy to point out. Somebody from the lower class rises to the middle class, a member of the latter enters the upper class (through marriage or other means), a landlord sells his estate to the peasants, a new mine goes into production, the gross national product increases, the Christian Democratic party splits, and cabinet members resign or are dismissed. Changes of this type constantly occur in every society, but they have no meaning unless they are seen within the nation's political context. Observation indicates that in Peru the essential features of the political system as they have been described are dominant. Changes of the type mentioned above constitute only adjustments to the *status quo;* if they are not sporadic events, then, as in the case of the gross national product, the beneficial effects reinforce the position of those already on top. On the other hand, a leading Peruvian intellectual tells us:

There exists in Peru the widely-held conviction that the country has entered into a defining moment of its historical evolution. It would seem that today hidden forces have awakened and are ringing forcefully in our ears. We know that we are living at a great turn in our route and we are aware of the uneasiness which those brusque changes of direction toward still unknown goals are causing.[1]

[1] Jorge Guillermo Llosa P., *En Busca del Perú,* p. 5.

Is the writer speaking of internal modifications or adjustments which do not alter the essence of the distribution of power and societal rewards in Peru, or is he referring to revolutionary change —that is, a substantial redistribution of power and social rewards? Let it not be forgotten that latent demands for change have long existed in Peru; the problem is that such demands came from individuals who lacked the willingness or the power to act. And yet, as has been indicated in previous chapters, the power elites are not monolithic, although they have, so far, been able to present a united front in their dealings with less privileged groups and classes. A few reformists have appeared in the Catholic Church, and if the example of other Latin American countries is transferable, more are bound to come into public view. The existence of reformist military elements has already been pointed out, not only at the Center of Higher Military Studies but in the 1962 military junta as well; although they were ousted then, there are indications that many of them still remain in active service. Within the upper class, the incipient differentiation between the now-powerful landowning sector and the new industrial elements may tend to increase, and if it does, the contradictory interests of foreign markets in raw materials versus protection for domestic products will intensify (as is the case in the more advanced Latin American countries, such as Argentina). This cleavage is likely to be compounded by the diverse positions of the coastal and Sierra sectors within the traditional upper class.

The picture is further clouded by certain events now taking place which are enlarging the potential for change but which cannot by themselves crystalize it. One such factor is urban migration, discussed in Chapter 5. The most obvious consequence of this move is the reduction in the size of the rural lower class, particularly in the Sierra, and the growth of the marginal urban lower class; if this trend continues—and all indications are that it will—a shortage of rural laborers may very well develop, and the Sierra landlords will be the principal victims. Furthermore, this reduction of the population of the Sierra will diminish the very sector over which the Sierra landlords exercise direct influence; in other

words, they may end up controlling large landholdings but relatively few people, although this will take a number of years. Because of their relative economic weakness, their inability to sell
outside the country, and their economic backwardness, it is unlikely that the landlords will be in a position to mechanize in order
to compensate for the migrating peasants. The long-run result,
therefore, may very well be the further impoverishing of this sector of the traditional upper class and its final disappearance into
the other identifiable social groups. Such a development will probably create a "revolutionary situation," as well as the personnel
able and willing, because of their frustration, to set it in motion,
and so will affect all the other classes.

The effect of the migration on the middle and lower classes will
be significant. The strength of the rural lower class now pressing
demands which carry true revolutionary implications (see Chapter
9) will tend to be diminished, since it is likely that those elements
which are most active in pressing the demands for land will be the
ones with enough initiative to move to the cities if they see no
prospects of success in the country. As has been seen, the migration itself does not increase the political effectiveness of the lower
class in Peru; it is obvious that migration moves these individuals
closer to the means of increasing their political weight through
some of the methods actually or potentially available to the urban
lower class. Furthermore, since a significant percentage migrate to
Lima, whatever actions they eventually decide to take are going to
be felt in the country's political center. Finally, in regard to the
middle classes, the migration may diminish the usefulness of the
few representatives of this stratum located in the Sierra and force
them to migrate to the larger urban centers; this move and the
added pressure of the newly arrived lower-class migrants will tend
to increase middle-class insecurity, at least in the short run.

Another potential element which may tend to alter the *status
quo* is the growth of the industrial sector, a possibility more con-
ceivable because of the migration of the peasantry to the urban
areas. The presence of the marginal urban lower class is an important factor in keeping wages low, at least in the unskilled and semi-

skilled categories; even the supply of skilled workers could be enlarged in a relatively short period of time if salaries were to move upward rapidly enough to justify a crash training program. Furthermore, it is likely that at least a portion of the newcomers will become consumers of some manufactured goods, thus increasing the demand. Consequently, other things being equal, the urban migration will accelerate industrial growth primarily at the expense of the highland landholdings but eventually also at the expense of the coastal plantations and even of the mining enclaves. This situation will not, per se, insure the development of an independent industrial upper class interested in a protected domestic market (even with the threat of retaliation which will be borne by the coastal plantations) as well as in low-priced foodstuffs. But the control of the financial institutions now exercised by the coastal sector of the traditional upper class could be easily upset by powerful external sources such as the large automobile producers or United States banks (but see Chapter 10). If this type of situation were to develop, the industrial upper class would be in a position to contribute to the development of a crisis situation in the upper stratum, which would lead to a fundamental alteration of the distribution of power.[2]

Pressures for essential change could also come from within the armed forces, although a true revolution has yet to originate from within the Latin American military. On the other hand, there have been some indications in other countries of the existence of revolutionary groups of military officers (such as some of those who put Perón in power in Argentina and those who backed Arbenz in Guatemala). Pressure for change from within the Peruvian armed forces is likely to be directed toward a strengthening of the national society against internal and external threats to its security rather than toward an abstract desire for a more equitable distribution of

[2] See the welcome extended by the reformist magazine *Oiga* (July 16, 1965, pp. 15–17) to the establishment of a General Motors automobile assembly plant, which it tied to the appearance of the social classes of the twentieth century. See also Vernon V. Aspaturian, "The Challenge of Soviet Foreign Policy," in Morton A. Kaplan (ed.), *The Revolution in World Politics*, pp. 209–32.

social rewards. But the military may conclude, as social scientists have done, that legitimacy through performance is perhaps the most effective way to combat subversion and to present a unified and solid front in the face of real or imaginary foreign menaces. This intellectual conversion, which surfaced in some of CAEM's papers, would be made painless by the fact that the overwhelming majority of the officer corps appears to come from the middle class (see Chapter 7) and would not be likely to suffer economically by a redistribution of rewards, particularly one conducted by them. The examples of Fidel Castro and, to a certain extent, the Mexican and Bolivian revolutions constitute powerful motivational forces for individuals who would prefer to maintain their privileges at the expense of the rest of those who benefit from the *status quo.*

The other power elite, the Catholic Church, has not really shown the same signs of change which have appeared in the military establishment. With the exception of Father Bolo Hidalgo, who has decided to work from a political party rather than from the Church, those who have abetted profound changes have been few and mostly foreign-born. But, as elsewhere in Latin America, with some encouragement from the Holy See, more sponsors of structural change are likely to appear, particularly among the younger priests who are in direct contact with the lower-class faithful. This is only natural; one of the main functions of the clergy, of course, is to maintain and increase the number of believers. At the lower-class level (and even at the lower-middle-class level) the priests who minister to the parishioners are the symbol of the Catholic Church; the "revolution of rising expectations" has fostered the idea that the economic situation of those at the bottom of the pyramid need not remain as it is forever, and left-of-center ideologies not only confirm this belief but provide the methodology to achieve it. This "revolution of rising expectations" is in direct conflict with the ideology transmitted by the Peruvian clergy. While concrete data has not been disclosed by the Church, all indications are that the Church is losing out in the confrontations. It will not take very long for many of those priests who work with the lower class to reach the conclusion that the only way to retain their following is to offer a Catholic ideology of change, able to compete successfully with the atheistic or agnostic left-of-center philosophies now luring individuals away from the ranks of the faithful. The situation is further complicated by the fact that even if the Peruvian hierarchy had access to coercive measures, they would only be effective in stopping activities the Church disliked and would be useless in converting those who have abandoned the Catholic faith.

What makes a basic modification of Catholic political ideology (as interpreted by the Peruvian clergy) likely is the sense of change on temporal matters which has been coming from the highest Catholic councils. The post–World War II encyclicals and the decisions made by Vatican II provide extremely valid sources on which to base a Catholic political ideology of change in a country such as Peru—a fact which is supported by the systematic disregard of such pronouncements among the conservative Church hierarchies still in control in most of the Latin American countries, including Peru. But such a turnabout would have traumatic consequences, particularly in the short run, for the relationship between the Catholic Church and the upper and most of the middle classes of Peru (described in Chapter 8); in short, it would take the ideological rug out from under their feet. The perception of the importance of this shift, which has begun to take place in areas such as northeastern Brazil, is reflected in the violent and almost instantaneous reaction by the upper class and often by the Church leadership to silence "unorthodox" interpretations by members of the clergy.[3]

Finally, those parties and groups committed to change should

[3] See, as only one example, the report which appeared in the New York *Times*, April 21, 1968, p. 62. According to it, attempts by a few Argentine and foreign priests to live closer to the lower class and to guide it in its search for improvements resulted in charges of communism from the traditional upper class. It is interesting that at the same time powerful American businessmen asked Pope Paul VI for a "clarification" of recent pronouncements, and particularly of his encyclical *Populorum Progressio*. The report made absolutely clear that the businessmen were particularly worried about the effect of the encyclical in Latin America, particularly the possibility of its upsetting the established system (New York *Times*, April 21, 1968, p. F11).

not be forgotten: they include the left-of-center groups identified in Chapter 6, and the Communist party. In regard to the latter, it is true that since the 1950's it has acted within the political system, more or less as the "left-wing legal opposition," [4] but its objectives are still reformist, and it seems unwarranted to entertain doubts regarding the policies it would put into effect if it were able to take power. Naturally, the choice of the legal way, apparently under Moscow's directives, makes this possibility quite remote. It has often been pointed out that parties or movements which espouse profound reforms will never be allowed to win power within the system; thus the charge of having renounced change is leveled against the Peruvian Communists. The fact is, however, that the prospects of the other proreform organizations do not appear to be any better as long as the same elites which block a Communist take-over oppose them. The failure of the guerrilla groups which went into action in 1965 (see Chapter 7) and their inability to elicit any significant support from the peasants tend to confirm this assertion. An observer sympathetic to the guerrillas puts it as follows:

The Peruvian peasant, mostly Indian, has his own style of life, his way of understanding things, his tradition, and the burden of his servile status. Between the university conception of the revolution and the attitude of the peasantry vis-à-vis change there is an unlimited distance. An intermediate, but fundamental process, has not taken place. The guerrilla fighter is a stranger to the peasant.[5]

With this background in mind, the chances for profound structural changes in Peruvian society can now be contemplated.

The Possibility of Revolution from Above

The concept of "revolution from above" conveys the idea of profound political, economic, and social changes carried out by the ruling class or a sector thereof. Literally, all revolutions take place

[4] The expression is Alberto Ciria's (*Cambio y Estancamiento en América Latina*, p. 69).

[5] Jaime Ortiz, "Izquierda Peruana y Guerrilleros," *Marcha*, January 28, 1966, quoted by Ciria, *Cambio y Estancamiento*, p. 86.

"from above," in that the implied changes cannot be carried out unless the revolutionaries are in control of the governmental machinery. In another sense, however, it could be claimed that pure revolutions from above do not occur: it is likely that a sizable portion of any ruling class will oppose what in fact amounts to at least a partial surrender of its power and privileges; thus, the group carrying out the revolution may be considered as making a "deal" with other groups and strata in order to insure its political, economic, social, and even physical survival at the expense of the rest of its peers. In spite of its lack of absolute precision, this concept is nevertheless useful in identifying processes of profound change formally initiated by the ruling class, or a segment of it, without irresistible coercion from the rest of the national society or from abroad.

The traditional examples of revolutions from above are the Bismarckian changes in Imperial Germany (1826–90) and the Meiji Restoration and Revolution in Japan (1867–71), whose details are well known. To these could be added the changes being carried out by the present Shah of Iran, although there the process has by no means been completed.[6] These classic examples may serve as general references, but there are at least two specific models in Latin America—partially successful attempts at revolution from above to which the specialists have paid little attention. One was the voluntary surrender of political power by the Argentine traditional upper class to the middle class they had been instrumental in forming; this culminated in the democratization of the electoral system through the Saenz-Peña Act in 1912. Attempts by another sector of the traditional upper class to regain power in 1930 were only temporarily and partially successful, and it is realistic to say that the Argentine traditional upper class has never regained the power it held prior to the second decade of this century.[7]

[6] A good account of these revolutions from above can be found in James A. Bill, "Social Structure and Political Power in Iran," ch. 7.

[7] This period of Argentine political history has been studied by numerous writers. Comprehensive and well-documented analyses can be found in Darío Cantón, *El Parlamento Argentino en Épocas de Cambio: 1890, 1916 y 1946;* Carlos S. Fayt, "La Organización Interna de los Partidos y los Métodos

The other Latin American example of a revolution from above is the one which occurred in Uruguay, essentially similar to the Argentine experience, except that the traditional upper class never really tried to regain its position. The reforms were led by different members of the distinguished Battle family, and particularly by José Battle y Ordóñez, who carried out his reforms in the first twenty years of this century. The net result was to transfer political power from the traditional upper class to the urban middle class, concentrated in the capital city of Montevideo.[8] In both cases the middle class was enlarged and diversified by the immigrants who entered Argentina and Uruguay beginning in the 1870's; these European immigrants were sponsored and actually encouraged by those in power, who facilitated their migration both legally and economically. It was this urban middle class that requested (more or less forcefully) a share of political power and of the social and economic rewards that accompany it. In Argentina an enlightened group within the ruling traditional upper class decided to act favorably on the demand for a more democratic franchise (which gave power to the middle-class Radical party in the following general election); in Uruguay, progressive members of the traditional upper class enacted the key middle-class demands (and enforced the resulting laws), opened both major parties first to the middle class and later to all citizens, and aggregated and articulated the interests of their new constituencies. In doing so, the traditional upper class of both countries has been

---

Políticos en la Argentina," in José S. Campobassi and others, *Los Partidos Políticos: Estructura y Vigencia en la Argentina*, pp. 33–52; José Luis de Imaz, *Los que Mandan;* Delbert C. Miller, Eva Chamorro Greco, and Juan Carlos Agulla, *De la Industria al Poder;* and Gino Germani, *Política y Sociedad en una Época de Transición: De la Sociedad Tradicional a la Sociedad de Masas,* chs. 7–10.

[8] The revolution from above in Uruguay has been analyzed and documented by Aldo E. Solari, *Estudios sobre la Sociedad Uruguaya;* Oscar Bruschera, *Los Partidos Tradicionales en el Uruguay;* Carlos M. Rama, *Sociologia del Uruguay,* chs. 4 and 6, and *Ensayo de Sociología Uruguaya,* ch. 13; Carlos Real de Azua, *El Patriciado Uruguayo;* Russell H. Fitzgibbon, *Uruguay: Portrait of a Democracy;* and Instituto de Estudios Políticos para América Latina, *Uruguay: Un País sin Problemas en Crisis.*

able to maintain its sources of wealth, although its returns have undoubtedly been diminished by the enactment of middle- and lower-class demands.

Does the Peruvian political scene show any indication of a similar process? The writer has not perceived any. As indicated earlier, immigration to Peru has been negligible. The only officially sponsored program attracted Chinese coolies, who provided the labor needed to exploit the guano; their effect on the social structure of Peru can be considered negligible. A survey of four different groups of Peruvian public servants (clearly middle-class) found that from 92 to 98 per cent of the sample was at least second-generation Peruvian, a fact which partially confirms the absence of immigration in this century.[9] What is perhaps more important is that this study has not uncovered any upper-class faction which has shown willingness to carry out profound reforms in order to keep its sources of income and its social prestige essentially intact. It is true that there is a certain willingness on the part of the coastal sector to sacrifice its Sierra counterpart, but so far it has not done that; on the other hand, even the sacrifice of the Sierra upper class is likely to be too little and too late. Finally, the demands for basic changes have not, up to now, come from the middle class—as was the case in both Argentina and Uruguay—but from the rural lower class. In fact, particularly in the urban centers near the areas of unrest, the demands were received with hostility by the bulk of the middle class. Needless to say, all these factors are subject to change, but at this time the elements needed to effect a revolution from above simply do not appear to be present in Peru.

The Possibility of Revolution from Below

Revolution from below can be identified as the replacement of the old ruling class by a new governing stratum; in all actual cases, the new rulers have come from the middle class (as in the Soviet Revolution) or from one of the power elites (such as in

[9] Jack Walker Hopkins, "The Government Executive of Modern Peru," pp. 62–64.

Turkey and Egypt). Here again, however, it is not necessary to go outside Latin America in search of guiding examples, for there have been three relatively successful revolutions from below in the region. In chronological order, Latin America has seen the Mexican Revolution (which started in 1910), the Bolivian Revolution of 1952 (apparently suspended by the military coup of 1964), and the Cuban Revolution.[10] It may perhaps be too early to analyze the latter, but the first two have been led by middle-class elements who had obtained the support of the lower class and who retained that support by carrying out profound structural reforms, including land redistribution and nationalization of the most important industries. The net result has been the political disappearance of the traditional upper class as a power elite and a substantial reduction of its wealth, the downgrading of the armed forces and the Catholic Church *as political actors* (not always permanently), and the growth and enrichment of the revolutionary middle class.[11]

[10] The Mexican Revolution has been widely studied. See, for instance, Frank Brandenburg, *The Making of Modern Mexico;* Robert E. Scott, *Mexican Government in Transition;* L. Vincent Padgett, *The Mexican Political System;* Pablo González Casanova, *La Democracia en México;* and Stanley R. Ross (ed.), *Is the Mexican Revolution Dead?* The materials on the Bolivian Revolution, on the other hand, are quite limited. See Robert E. Hunter, "Bolivia," in Ben G. Burnett and Kenneth F. Johnson (eds.), *Political Forces in Latin America: Dimensions of the Quest for Stability,* pp. 313–36; Mario Rolón Anaya, *Política y Partidos en Bolivia;* Richard W. Patch, "Peasantry and National Revolution: Bolivia," in Kalman H. Silvert (ed.), *Expectant Peoples: Nationalism and Development,* pp. 95–126, and "Bolivia: The Restrained Revolution"; and Arthur P. Whitaker and David C. Jordan, *Nationalism in Contemporary Latin America,* ch. 8, which also includes Cuba. On the latter, the best evidence of the profound changes can be obtained from the mostly upper-class and dependent middle-class Cuban refugees; also see Hugh Thomas, "Middle Class Politics and the Cuban Revolution," in Claudio Véliz (ed.), *The Politics of Conformity in Latin America,* pp. 249–77; Boris Goldenberg, "The Cuban Revolution—A New Type of Revolution"; Dudley Seers (ed.), *Cuba: The Economic and Social Revolution;* and Michel Chartrand, Vernel Olson, and John Riddell, *The Real Cuba as Three Canadians Saw It.*

[11] The downgrading of the Bolivian military was only temporary; when President Paz Estenssoro discovered that the miners' militia was as willing to use its weapons to advance its interest as the military had been, he decided to upgrade the armed forces and received enthusiastic American assistance; finally, the military overthrew him and defeated the miners. Castro

Present evidence tends to indicate that the Cuban process is not very different, although its commitment to communism, its relationship with the Soviet Union, and Castro's charisma are factors which were not present in the other two cases.

This study has identified some potential sources of revolution from below in Peru, although the potential revolutionaries' ability to obtain a positive response to their revolutionary demands has so far been largely nominal. It has already been indicated that the strongest revolutionary potential can be found in the demands formulated by the peasant organizations which are strong in the Sierra; their most important objective is the effective redistribution of land, a demand which, if carried out, will take away the most important source of wealth of the traditional upper class. The leaders of the peasant organizations recognize that

the national popular revolution is a necessary condition for the change of the agrarian structure, and inversely the persistence in power of the traditional elites is a sufficient condition to block the relevant change of the agrarian structure. . . . The hypothesis is, then, that the agrarian structure changes after a *popular* revolution (the revolutions of independence were not of that type), and does not change before that popular revolution takes place.[12]

To maintain that the peasant organizations, with the sometimes lukewarm backing of the left-of-center parties, have a realistic chance of carrying out the popular revolution which will permit them to obtain their objective does not seem warranted. The 1965 attempt at guerrilla warfare (which some of their leaders announced as the actual conversion of the Andes into the *Sierra Maestra* of Peru) ended in failure, and it appears unlikely that a more successful attempt can be made in the near future. It is also naïve to believe that the traditional upper class will suddenly give in on the question of land reform, particularly on the coastal plan-

replaced the Batista military establishment with a popular militia; he then proceeded to build his own armed forces, with Soviet help, and when this was done the militia was downgraded.

[12] Oscar Delgado, "Revolución, Reforma y Conservatismo: Tipos de Políticas Agrarias en Latinoamérica," p. 173.

tations, without a real fight. It seems evident, therefore, that the Sierra peasant organizations do not have the power to effectuate a revolution from below which will make it possible for them to obtain a positive response to their demands. The question is, are there other groups which can and would be likely to provide assistance?

Two groups come immediately to mind: the reformist officers in the armed forces (sometimes called "Nasserites") and the priests who are receptive to the new interpretations of Catholic philosophy originating in the Holy See and in CELAM. It is quite difficult to determine the strength of the military men who have been pushed together through CAEM, but they do not seem to constitute a large group. They came closest to power when General Bossio became Minister of Government during the first months of the 1962–63 military junta. But he and his followers were promptly displaced and have not shown significant influence since then. In any case, the reformist spirit of many of these officers is likely to fall far short of the expectations of the organized peasantry and its leaders, and it may be further dampened by the apparent middle-class Sierra origin of many officers (see Chapter 7). Furthermore, it should be pointed out that no military establishment in Latin America has carried out a true land redistribution program; the Castro example and the intelligent use of the asserted association between land reform and communism propagandized by the traditional upper class make it doubtful that the Peruvian military will take the lead in this matter.

The progressive Catholic clergy is in a less comfortable position; regardless of the sincerity of their desire for fundamental reforms, which the writer does not question, these progressive clergymen are seeing the lower-class faithful drift away from a religion which is not offering them a viable solution to their material problems. Furthermore, if the members of the lower class do not make the move on their own, the political ideologies of change are there to offer them not only a vision of the society they want, but of the methods to attain it; and they can point to believable examples:

Cuba, far away, and Bolivia, next door.[13] But this group is a very small minority of the Catholic clergy of Peru, and so far they have been rapidly identified and rendered harmless by the hierarchy, which has not shown any inclination to back radical alterations of the economic, social, and political *status quo*. Nevertheless, it may very well be that this group will grow in number and influence, as it has in neighboring Colombia (with the example of Father Camilo Torres) and more recently in Guatemala. If this happens, the clergy will provide ideological respectability, as well as leadership, to those who are seeking structural reforms; by protecting them from charges of communism, the progressive Catholic clergy may attract to its side other groups who would like to see many of the reforms carried out, but who fear a "Communist take-over."

Finally, a third group which may be interested in backing the demands of the organized Sierra peasants is the new middle class (see Chapters 4 and 9), particularly if special attention is given to industrial development, either under domestic private ownership or under governmental control. It has become clear to many of the members of the middle class that the changes being sought will increase their role in Peruvian society, as well as their sources of employment and probably their political power, particularly if the new industries are owned by the government, thus making their managers and technicians part of it. The technocrats, relatively underpaid by the standards of the more developed countries and aware of it, have much to gain by bringing the peasantry of the Sierra and the marginal urban population fully into the money economy, and the repetition of what they may consider wanton acts on the part of the power elites could convince them that the advantages of drastic changes far outweigh the risks involved. But other factors counterbalance this alternative; inasmuch as the Peruvian new middle class, besides being extremely small, lacks a

[13] The reforms carried out in Bolivia in the 1950's are widely known throughout Peru, and particularly in the southern region, where the peasants have a common origin, speak the same languages, and were in the same situation prior to 1952.

solid economic base, its attempts to modify the *status quo* will un-doubtedly have to take place through exclusively political means. But, in order to employ such means, this sector of the middle class will have to exhibit a clear will to take over and exercise political power to its ultimate consequences. As many observers have pointed out, this will has not yet been exercised, and indications of its existence are few.[14]

Political studies are bound to analyze that which exists, and they may venture into what could be, but that which ought to be is best left to the philosophers. In the absence of a catalyst which can push these potential or actual revolutionary forces together and into action (this catalyst may very well be a charismatic leader, but none has appeared so far) informed observers have to conclude from the available evidence that the net effect of the var-ious existing forces on the Peruvian political system will be the maintenance of what amounts to a "non-consensual structure of passive [and sometimes active] coercion."[15] What characterizes Peruvian politics is the presence of some relatively integrated power elites in the midst of an unintegrated national community, with the power elites showing no intention of promoting national integration.[16] The country's political institutions have been created to maintain the *status quo* and to settle disagreements among those individuals and groups who own shares of power. This ownership is not static, but adjustments take place only from time to time, and even then they are of a mild nature; as tends to

[14] The point is made by Jorge Graciarena, *Poder y Clases Sociales en el Desarrollo de América Latina,* p. 176; see also César Guardia Mayorga, *La Reforma Agraria en el Perú,* pp. 187–92, and the lecture by Jorge Bravo Bresani reproduced in *Breve Introducción al Estudio de la Realidad Nacional,* pp. 100–174.

[15] Vernon V. Aspaturian, "Internal Politics and Foreign Policy in the Soviet System," in R. Barry Farrell (ed.), *Approaches to Comparative and International Politics,* p. 215.

[16] On this aspect, see John Nathan Plank, "Peru: a Study in the Problems of Nation-Forming," pp. 248–49, and José Matos Mar, "Consideraciones sobre la Situación Social del Perú," p. 58. On the permanency of the present system, see François Bourricaud, "Remarques sur l'Oligarchie Peruvienne," and "Les Règles du Jeu en Situation d'Anomie: Le Cas Péruvien."

happen in all walks of life, these adjustments do not usually include those who are not shareholders.

In the absence of a popular uprising of gigantic proportions, which in 1968 does not seem feasible in view of the new means of coercion developed by modern technology, the present distribution of power in Peru shows a remarkable tendency to remain essentially as it is, and as it has been for a long time. Distasteful as this finding may be to those who have perceived the inequities of Peruvian society, it should be recognized that all available political indicators point to a continuation of the present nonconsensual structure, with the likelihood of increasing recourse to active coercion. Neither revolution from above nor revolution from below seems to be around the corner.

12. Postscript: The *Coup d'État* of October 3, 1968

After this manuscript had been completed and delivered to the publisher, the Peruvian military overthrew the administration of President Fernando Belaúnde Terry more than five years after it had taken office and less than a year before a new constitutional president was to have been popularly chosen. A brief description and analysis of this new overt political involvement by the Peruvian military establishment may shed further light on its political role and its current relationship with the other actors already identified in this study.

Immediate Background of the Coup d'État

A high degree of certainty regarding the events and causes of the military take-over is necessary in order to make any assumptions regarding the true motivations and goals of those who carried it out. At the time of this writing (December, 1968), nobody seems to have that certainty. The customary proclamation of the military junta mentioned different subjects with varying degrees of generality. They included corruption, the heavy economic dependency on outside sources, the maldistribution of wealth, and the agreement reached between the Belaúnde administration and the International Petroleum Company regarding the La Brea and Pariñas oil fields. Present in the minds of many Peruvians was the split within the ranks of the President's party, Acción Popular, which opened the doors to an almost certain victory by APRA in the 1969 presidential elections.

The Schism of Acción Popular. The selection of First Vice-President Edgardo Seoane as Acción Popular's presidential candidate for the 1969 elections had been a rebuke to President Belaúnde by the majority of the delegates attending his party's convention (see Chapter 6). During the few months following that decision, Belaúnde gave the impression of accepting the verdict, but it is apparent that during the second half of 1968 he decided, or was forced by his more conservative supporters, to fight back. Thus a clear split developed between those backing Seoane, known as *termocéfalos,* and those who preferred Belaúnde and wanted the party to stand on his record. The division culminated in the forcible take-over of the party's national headquarters by pro-Belaúnde elements, with some police assistance, and the physical expulsion of its pro-Seoane defenders, who had been in control of the party's machinery.[1]

President Belaúnde confirmed his involvement in the forcible attempt to wrest control of the party machinery from the *termocéfalos* by annulling the candidacy of Seoane and, as its leader, ordering the "reorganization" of Acción Popular, which undoubtedly meant a purge of pro-Seoane elements. As the open break between the two factions drew near, and perhaps in order to protect his administration from the forthcoming struggle for party control, Belaúnde reached an understanding with APRA. This understanding required him to appoint a "technical" cabinet in exchange for a delegation of congressional authority; the "technical" cabinet in fact appeared to articulate the interest of the coastal sector of the traditional upper class and of economic penetrators. Its most important actions seem to have included a greater degree of economic orthodoxy and the granting of further advantages to foreign investors in areas such as oil and banking.

The Agreement with the International Petroleum Company. Congress had granted the executive broad authority to settle the question of the La Brea and Pariñas oil fields. This congressional action threw this "extremely hot potato" back in Belaúnde's hands. Nevertheless, faced with the unpleasant reality and re-

---

[1] The events have been described in *Oiga,* September 27, 1968, pp. 8 ff., and by *Primera Plana* (Buenos Aires), October 1, 1968, pp. 26–27.

minded of his electoral promises, Belaúnde and his cabinet proceeded to negotiate an agreement whereby the International Petroleum Company returned to Peru the oil fields under dispute in exchange for other concessions, including a virtual monopoly in the area of refining.[2] The agreement was rejected by most of those familiar with the issue, and Belaúnde's prestige was further damaged by the denunciation of irregularities, which included the alleged disappearance of the last page of the agreement signed between the International Petroleum Company and the State Oil Company in the early hours of the morning of August 13, 1968.

The political implications of this issue became apparent approximately one week before the *coup d'état,* when the Army reported to the Joint Command that it opposed the agreement in question. It is significant, however, that neither the Navy nor the Air Force had taken a position on the matter.[3] Since public opinion appears to have been overwhelmingly against the pact signed by the Belaúnde administration, it could be concluded that this delay reflected a very strong feeling in these two services in favor of the agreement or, at least, of the Belaúnde administration.

Finally, the role played by part of the Peruvian press cannot be ignored. The newspaper *El Comercio,* long an articulator of antiforeign sentiment, particularly in regard to investors, and on occasions the voice of the incipient industrial upper class, attacked bitterly the agreement in the pact and denounced the apparent irregularities connected with it. Less sanguine, but perhaps more effective, was the magazine *Oiga,* which had supported Belaúnde at the beginning of his administration but slowly turned against him during the last two years and finally backed the pro-Seoane faction of Acción Popular. It has been widely rumored in Peru that *El Comercio* played a very important role in the military move; some maintained that it triggered the *coup d'état* with its sensational-

[2] For a description of the agreement, see *Oiga,* September 20, 1968, pp. 8–11.

[3] The position of the military services was reported by *Oiga,* September 27, 1968, pp. 11 and 34.

istic treatment of the irregularities denounced after the conclusion of the pact with the International Petroleum Company. Although it is doubtful that it forced the military to do something they were not prepared to do, it seems apparent that *El Comercio* was very important in molding public opinion against Belaúnde and in favor of an alternative, which could only come from a *coup d'état*.

Progressive Indebtedness of Peru. The programs carried out by the Belaúnde Terry administration, particularly the building of roads and other infrastructure, and its inability to reform the tax system forced the regime to borrow, mostly from abroad. The foreign debt has been put at more than $742 million, complicated by deteriorations in international trade and massive capital flights since 1967. The "technical" cabinet appointed by Belaúnde Terry and given special economic powers with Aprista concurrence was heavily influenced by individuals who had been instrumental in negotiating the foreign loans. They were led by Manuel Ulloa, the Finance Minister, who had been an officer of the Deltec Banking Corporation, one of the creditor institutions which had made short- and intermediate-term loans at 8.5 to 9 per cent interest.

While Mr. Ulloa occupied the position of finance minister he negotiated new operations with the Deltec Banking Corporation, such as the one approved by decree 291-68-HC of August 9, 1968. These new loans were broadly authorized by the refinancing authority granted by Congress as part of the special economic powers. Under the same authority and within a few days, Mr. Ulloa issued a decree (297-68-HC) which reversed previous legislation and opened the door for foreign banks to take over the private banking system. This action, which was overshadowed by the division of the ruling party and by the agreement with the International Petroleum Company, may not have been ignored by the members of the traditional upper class who control Peru's private banks. It is not unlikely that they suspected a strong desire on the part of foreign bankers, to whom Finance Minister Ulloa was very close, to attempt a take-over of the financial institutions the traditional upper class has heretofore controlled.

The Unfolding of the Coup d'État

Vague threats of forthcoming *coups d'état,* or at least rumors to that effect, had been widespread in Peru as early as 1965, when the guerrilla bands went into action. They intensified both in number and in believability during 1967 and 1968. Most of the time the rumors centered on the Army and, within it, on the intermediate ranks of the officer corps. Besides the political preferences of the colonels and their view of the Belaúnde regime, two factors seem to have annoyed them. In the first place, military promotions were actually subject to some congressional control, thus forcing military officers to deal with legislators, and particularly with the Apristas. It is no accident that Colonel Gonzalo Briceño, who led the takeover of the presidential palace in the 1962 *coup d'état* (see Chapter 7), was still a colonel when he led a remarkably similar operation on October 3, 1968.

The second contributing factor, as so many times before, was the military share of the national budget—perhaps it would be more accurate to say the distribution of the military share of the budget among the three services. In fact, the armed forces were receiving approximately 23 per cent of the national budget, a figure which normally would place a civilian government safely above the danger mark. However, the apportionment of the military budget was being questioned because the 23 per cent was being divided as follows: the Army, with more than 70 per cent of all men in uniform, received 9 per cent of the national budget; the Air Force received the same percentage; and the Navy was allocated 5 per cent of the total government expenditures.[4] Needless to say, this type of distribution was considered detrimental by most Army officers, while Air Force and Navy personnel felt satisfied and unwilling to act against the Belaúnde Terry administration.

[4] The percentage of men in the Peruvian army comes from Irving Louis Horowitz, "The Military Elites," in Seymour Martin Lipset and Aldo Solari, (eds.), *Elites in Latin America,* p. 154. The budgetary breakdown, which refers to the 1968 budget, appeared in *La Prensa* (Lima), October 29, 1968, p. 2. The matter of promotions is mentioned in *Oiga,* October 25, 1968, p. 8.

The plotting was reported to have been conducted by a generally unidentified group of colonels, who in the early hours of the morning of October 3 met at Lima's International Airport to settle the final details and a few hours later pulled Belaúnde out of bed, took him to the headquarters of the tank division and from there to the airport, where he was put aboard a Peruvian Airline jet which had been commandeered during the colonels' earlier visit to the airport. These events have led to widespread speculation regarding the possibility of the coup's being engineered and spearheaded by the dissatisfied Army colonels with the passive acceptance of the senior officers. If this version is correct, the senior Army officers actively joined the coup and took over leadership of the government when it became evident that they could not prevent it from taking place.

On the other hand, it is clear that such pressure was not present within the Air Force and Navy; neither service participated in the overthrow. On the contrary, General Gagliardi, Air Force Minister, joined the other members of the last cabinet named by Belaúnde in a show of defiance after the civilian government's overthrow; the Navy Minister, Vice-Admiral Luna Ferrecio, was reported to have joined "the naval forces which were loyal to the Belaúnde government." [5] The existence of disagreements between the Army and the other two services became apparent when the military cabinet was announced: the Army received the presidency and five ministries, including the premiership; the Navy was awarded two seats and the Air Force three. The new ministries created almost two months later added two more Navy representatives and another Army officer. This distribution is substantially different from that which took place after the 1962 coup, in which the three services shared the presidency. Finally, it has been widely reported that the swearing-in ceremony, held approximately fifteen hours after Belaúnde was overthrown, was attended almost exclu-

[5] *Siete Días de Perú y del Mundo* (supplement of *La Prensa*), October 6, 1968, p. 14. The events and the role of the colonels have been described in *Oiga,* October 4, 1968, pp. 4–6; *La Prensa,* October 3, 1968, pp. 1–4, and October 4, 1968, pp. 1–5; *Primera Plana,* October 8, 1968, pp. 25–27; and *El Comercio,* October 3, 1968, p. 1, and October 4, 1968, p. 1.

sively by Army officers, with only two or three Navy and Air Force officers present. *La Prensa* observed:

> Only at noon Wednesday did the high commands of the Navy and the Air Force join the coup, after tense deliberations. A number of high Air Force officers are said to have backed the constitutionalist attitude of the Air Force Minister José Gagliardi. And in the Navy, where a cordial feeling toward Belaúnde was always visible, agreement was obtained after some hours of debate.[6]

The disputes between the services have not ceased. The Navy Chief of Staff, Vice-Admiral Mario Castro de Mendoza, was ignored in the appointment of the new service minister, despite the fact that, according to the proclamation of the leaders of the revolt, he was entitled to that position. Two days later his resignation was announced, without indicating his reasons. Another unexplained resignation made public shortly after the new government took office was that of the Army Chief of Staff, General Alejandro Sánchez Salazar, who at the end of October flew to Spain to take up the position of military attaché. Again, no reasons were given, although his son-in-law acknowledged the existence of disagreements.[7] Another significant change occurred three weeks after the military government was installed: the Chief of Staff of the Air Force, who also served as Air Force Minister, Lt. General Alberto López Causillas, resigned without explanation and was temporarily replaced by another Air Force officer already serving as Minister of Public Health. Three other officers of higher rank in active service were thus ignored.[8] The new military leadership seems to be willing to pay a relatively high price to achieve the consensus so easily developed in the "institutional" coup of 1962.

[6] *Siete Días de Perú y del Mundo* (*La Prensa*), October 6, 1968, p. 5.

[7] See *La Prensa*, October 31, 1968, p. 2.

[8] See *La Prensa*, October 27, 1968, p. 1; and *Primera Plana*, October 29, 1968, p. 28. It had been rumored that the resignation of López Causillas was the consequence of disagreements with President Velasco Alvarado over promotions in the Air Force, based on the desire of each of them to promote those officers whom he considers loyal to him; see *Siete Días del Perú y del Mundo* (*La Prensa*), October 27, 1968, p. 7.

Policies and Performance of the Military Government

If the researcher accepts the hypothesis that he is dealing in this case with a *coup d'état* inspired and executed by the Army, and if he remembers that, in a survey of thirty-six generals, twenty-nine rejected the agreement reached with the International Petroleum Company, then it is easy to predict that the first important action of the military government would concern this matter. Furthermore, the new government was faced with the opposition of most political parties and almost total apathy on the part of the population. It was clear that it needed an issue which could rally most Peruvians to the new government. For a long time the question of the La Brea and Pariñas oil fields has been such an issue, deeply felt not only by the middle and lower classes, but by the nationalist military officers as well. Consequently, within a week of the coup, its leader and President of Peru, General Juan Velasco Alvarado, announced the military take-over of the oil fields in question and of the Talara refinery, while Army troops occupied the facilities. The government also cancelled the agreement reached by the Belaúnde administration two months earlier. Two sympathetic observers put it quite well:

With the full reinvidication of La Brea and Pariñas, with the authentic recuperation of our Talara oil, the overthrow of a government which did not know how to respond to the requirements of its historic moment is thus justified.

And the starting point of the great embrace between the People and the Armed Forces, united in an exalted nationalistic and revolutionary ideal, has been the expropriation of the oil wealth which, against all reason, in violation of our sovereignty and in outrage to our national dignity, was held by rapacious foreign enterprises.[9]

The desired effect appears to have been achieved. After the spectacular seizure it was difficult to find Peruvians who were willing to express reservations about it. Approval came from such con-

[9] Francisco Igartúa and Francisco Bendezu in *Oiga,* October 11, 1968, pp. 3 and 8, respectively.

tradictory sources as Cardinal Landazurri and the National Liberation Front; and it was not difficult for the military government to convert support for the take-over of the disputed oil fields into a legitimation of its existence. Riding on the popularity gained by the swift action, it closed newspapers, magazines, and radio stations which had been critical of the military.[10] The new government suddenly enjoyed the approval of every political party in Peru.

In reality the original seizure, though spectacular, was limited. It did not include the other oil fields exploited by the IPC or its distribution services. It has also been announced that all concessions granted, both to extract oil and to refine it, will be respected. What caught the writer's attention was the extremely mild reaction on the part of the company and of the United States government; the former in fact almost collaborated with the military government, by asking its staff to continue working, which they did. The United States recognized the new regime within a short time and made only mild representations regarding adequate compensation. It would appear that the take-over of the La Brea and Pariñas oil fields has been considered by all interested parties as a necessary move, in order to strengthen and popularize the new authorities, as well as to satisfy the demands of the supposedly "Nasserite" colonels who are credited with setting events in motion. In view of the parallels which many observers see between the Peruvian military leaders and their Argentine counterparts, who took over that government in 1966, the writer wonders if this is not another attempt at creating a nationalistic facade for domestic consumption, while at the same time maintaining and increasing American penetration under the protection of just such a facade.

Three months after the military overthrew Belaúnde, their reformist zeal had not yet been demonstrated domestically. In the area of agrarian reform, the policy statements made by the members of the cabinet do not seem to forecast radical changes. The Minister of Agriculture is General Oscar Benavides, Jr. (see Chapter 7), who has said:

[10] See, *Oiga,* November 4, 1968, pp. 8–10 and 36; and *La Prensa,* November 1, 1968, pp. 1–2.

It is understandable that the difficulties met in the process of Agrarian Reform be natural and explainable owing to the matter's complexity and the limited experience in it. In accordance with reality based on the fiscal possibilities, it is the intention of the Revolutionary Government to define the actions which it is going to carry out in the process of Agrarian Reform, in order to clear up the uncertainty of those affected and benefited by it, and to dedicate the greatest effort of the Public Agrarian Sector to the technical and economic assistance of the small farmers. In spite of the restrictions imposed by the scarcity of financial resources, the Government wishes to make the Agrarian Reform process more agile.[11]

In the area of taxation, the government has announced that it is forced to utilize existing taxes in view of the economic situation, thus postponing whatever tax changes it plans to make. In fact, in outlining priorities the military government stated that its efforts would be directed toward refinancing Peru's foreign debt, guaranteeing the existing foreign exchange system, and balancing the budget.[12] To negotiate the refinancing of the foreign debt the military selected Fernando Berckemeyer, one of the most distinguished members of the traditional upper class. The choice was lauded in international financial circles, although not among Peruvian nationalists. Mr. Berckemeyer appears to have been successful in his mission: a month after his appointment, the International Monetary Fund approved the stand-by credit arrangement badly needed by the new Peruvian authorities.[13]

[11] *La Prensa*, November 4, 1968, p. 4. General Benavides also announced that the government was going to proceed with the expropriation of the cattle ranches of the Cerro de Pasco Corporation, a step already decreed by the Belaúnde administration but whose implementation had been delayed, apparently for lack of funds. It should be pointed out that the mining corporation had indicated its willingness to divest itself of the land. It has also been reported that the corporation was awarded an oil concession in the Selva covering 53 million acres; see *El Comercio* (Lima), November 12, 1968, p. 1, quoting the *Washington Post* of November 10, 1968.

[12] See Communique No. 10 of the military government, reproduced by *La Prensa*, October 6, 1968, p. 1.

[13] International Monetary Fund Press Release No. 708, dated November 8, 1968, and reproduced in *International Financial News Survey*, 20:381 (November 15, 1968).

Nothing seems to have changed in the treatment of peasants who engage in disputes with landlords. An alleged attempt to invade a landholding in the Sierra was prevented by the police and the landlord, who killed seven peasants and injured fifteen others; according to the peasants, the landlord also burned fifty of their huts, and, as a magazine relatively friendly to the new government points out, "the government reported the event repeating the same impassive, cold, insensitive arguments used by all the previous governments." [14] This episode seems to confirm reports of increasingly close contacts between the military government and members of the traditional upper class. The picture is also clarified by the appointment of followers of former dictator Odría and individuals close to Pedro Beltrán to important positions. These moves may explain the attitude of *La Prensa* which, after indicating its disagreement with the route taken by the Army officers, quoted from its own editorial commenting on the 1962 *coup d'état* and went on to subscribe to most of the objectives made public by the military leaders.[15]

It is also interesting to point out that such reliable (from the point of view of the traditional upper class) sources as Odría and some of the interest groups that supported his regime have come out in favor of the military take-over. Furthermore, the list of requests presented by the Secretary-General of the Confederation of Peruvian Workers two days after Belaúnde was replaced has received no reply from the new regime; the petitioner was called in by the military officer in charge of the city of Lima, a colonel, a few days after he made the presentation and was apparently told in no uncertain terms that nothing would be done in the immediate future. It is not surprising that three days after the coup *La Prensa* editorialists began considering Belaúnde responsible for his own overthrow and three weeks later the same newspaper applauded the economic and fiscal policy announced by the Minister of Commerce and Finance, General Angel Valdivia Morriberón.[16]

[14] *Oiga,* November 4, 1968, p. 36. The events were also reported by *La Prensa,* October 31, 1968, p. 1.

[15] *La Prensa,* October 4, 1968, p. 11.

[16] *La Prensa,* October 6, 1968, p. 15, and October 27, 1968, p. 13.

Those originally in favor of the *coup d'état* were prompt to point out the presence of representatives of the traditional upper class in the presidential palace, the existence of pressures that were blunting the reformist zeal of the new authorities, the close ties between individuals close to former President Prado and some members of the government, and the lack of direct reference to the problem of the distribution of wealth.[17]

Finally, the "moralizing campaign," which promised to denounce and prosecute those who had profited illegally while holding public office, bogged down to a general denunciation of legislators for taking junkets at public expense and putting relatives on the government's payroll. The findings of a committee that had investigated smuggling were not fully utilized when it became evident that some high-ranking military officers could be involved. The most recent reference to this campaign was made when opposition newspapers, radios, and magazines were closed; the actions were justified under this label.[18]

In conclusion, the author believes that the reformist Army officers identified in the study were involved in the *coup d'état* which overthrew the same administration that some of them had helped into power when they revolted against the Prado regime and annulled the 1962 elections. And again, as in 1962, they are apparently being superseded and dominated by the traditional upper class. The opportunities for action by these true revolutionaries are being further reduced by the opposition of the Navy and Air Force. The writer feels that the Peruvian political system should be able to survive the present coup without going through a redistribution of power or of societal rewards. It is even possible that the influence of the penetrators will be reduced, thus enhancing the position of the traditional upper class.

[17] *Oiga*, October 11, 1968, p. 6, October 18, 1968, p. 6, October 25, 1968, p. 16, and November 29, 1968, p. 9.
[18] See section 3 of Communique No. 14, reproduced by *La Prensa*, November 1, 1968, p. 1.

Bibliography

Adams, Richard N. "A Change from Caste to Class in a Peruvian *Sierra* Town," *Social Forces*, 31:238–44 (1953).

——. *A Community in the Andes: Problems and Progress in Muquiyauyo*. Seattle: University of Washington Press, 1959.

——. *The Second Sowing: Power and Secondary Development in Latin America*. San Francisco: Chandler Publishing Company, 1967.

Aguilar Grimaldi, Antonio. "Organización del Ejército del Perú," *Revista del Ejército y de la Marina* (Mexico City) April, 1934, pp. 99–108.

Aguirre Gamio, Hernando. *Liquidación Histórica del Apra y del Colonialismo Neoliberal*. Lima: Ediciones Debate, 1962.

Alarco, Eugenio. *De las "Elites" en el Perú*. Lima: Insula, 1959.

Albornoz, Santiago F. *Reivindicatorio para la Historia del Perú*. Buenos Aires: Cagnasso y Cía., 1960.

Alers-Montalvo, Manuel. "Social System Analysis of Supervised Agricultural Credit in an Andean Community," *Rural Sociology*, 25:51–64 (1960).

Alexander, Robert J. "The Latin American *Aprista* Parties," *Political Quarterly*, 20:236–47 (1949).

——. "Nationalism: Latin America's Predominant Ideology," *Journal of International Affairs*, 15:108–14 (1961).

——. *Organized Labor in Latin America*. New York: Free Press of Glencoe, 1965.

——. *Today's Latin America*. Garden City, N.Y.: Doubleday, 1962.

Allred, Wells Merrill. *System of Government in Peru*. Ithaca, N.Y.: Cornell University Press, 1959.

——. "System of Government in Peru," *Philippine Journal of Public Administration*, 4:46–60 (1960).

Almond, Gabriel A., and James S. Coleman (eds.). *The Politics of the*

Developing Areas. Princeton, N.J.: Princeton University Press, 1960.

Almond, Gabriel A., and G. Bingham Powell, Jr. *Comparative Politics: A Developmental Approach.* Boston: Little, Brown, 1966.

Alva Orlandini, Hernán (ed.). *Biblioteca Hombres del Perú.* 10 vols. Lima: Tipográfica Peruana, 1964.

Álvarez Natale, Hugo E. *Contribución al Estudio de los Grupos de Interés.* Buenos Aires: Ed. Abeledo-Perrot, 1960.

Álvarez Romero, J. M. "Lis Partidos Demócratas de Izquierda en Iberoamérica," *Revista de Política Internacional,* July–October, 1961, pp. 139–59.

Alzamora Valdés, Mario. *La Educación Peruana—Crisis y Perspectivas: Errores de una Política Educativa.* Lima: Editorial Universitaria, 1960.

Ames González, Edmundo. *Hacia el Estado de Derecho Auténtico por la Educación Democrática Integral.* Lima: Universidad Nacional Mayor de San Marcos, 1961.

Andreski, S. "Conservatism and Radicalism of the Military," *Archives Européennes de Sociologie,* 2:23–61 (1961).

Andrzejewski, Stanislaw. *Military Organization and Society.* London: Routledge & Kegan Paul, 1954.

Angulo A., Jorge M. *El Contrato de Yanaconaje en el Perú.* Trujillo, Peru: Gráfica Trujillo, 1962.

Añi Castillo, Gonzalo. *Historia Secreta de las Guerrillas.* Lima: Ediciones "Más Allá," 1967.

Arciniegas, Germán. "Perú bajo la Dictadura," *Bohemia* (Havana), April 5, 1953, pp. 22–23, 95–99.

Argüedas, José María. "Las Comunidades de Castilla y el Perú: Estructura Social del Grupo," *Revista del Museo Nacional,* 32:81–88, (1963).

——. "Mesa Redonda y Seminario de Ciencias Sociales," *Etnología y Arqueología,* 1:237–88 (1960).

——. *Yawar Fiesta.* Lima: J. Mejía Baca, 1958.

Arias Larreta, Abraham. "Indios y Cholos," *América,* 47:36–50, (1947).

Armestar V., Miguel A. *La Tierra y el Hombre: Visión Panorámica del Problema Agrario-Social del Periú y su Estrecha Relación con el Capital.* Lima: Imprenta y Litografía Saleciana, 1963.

Arriola Grande, F. M. *Discurso a la Nación Peruana.* Buenos Aires: Editorial Pueblo Continente, 1959.

Arroyo O. F. M., Luis. *Comisarios Generales del Perú.* Madrid: Consejo Superior de Investigaciones Científicas, Instituto Santo Toribio de Modrovejo, 1950.

Aspaturian, Vernon V. "Social Structure and Political Power in the Soviet System." Mimeo. Paper delivered at the Annual Meeting of the American Political Science Association, New York, September 4–7, 1963.

———. "Strategies of the Status Quo and Revolutionary Change in Underdeveloped Countries." Mimeo. Pennsylvania State University, 1962.

Astiz, Carlos Alberto. "The Changing Face of Latin American Higher Education," *Bulletin of the Atomic Scientists,* February, 1967, pp. 4–8.

———. "Integration, Legitimation, and Institutionalization in a Latin American Country: The Peruvian Case." Mimeo. Paper presented at the Seventh World Congress of the International Political Science Association, Brussels, Belgium, September 18–23, 1967.

———. "La Universidad Latinoamericana," *Facetas,* 1:48–54 (1968).

Baeza Flores, Alberto. *Las Cadenas Vienen de Lejos: Cuba, América Latina y la Libertad.* Mexico City: Editorial Letras, 1960.

———. *Haya de la Torre y la Revolución Constructiva de las Américas.* Buenos Aires: Editorial Claridad, 1962.

Bagú, Sergio. *Acusación y Defensa del Intelectual.* Buenos Aires: Editorial Perrot, 1959.

Banco Central de Reserva del Perú. *Programación del Desarrollo.* 2 vols. Lima: El Banco, 1963.

———. *Renta Nacional del Perú.* Lima: Imprenta Casa Nacional de Moneda, 1958, 1960.

Banco de Crédito del Perú. *Vademecum del Inversionista.* Lima: El Banco, various issues (1954–55, 1956–57, 1961–62).

Barents, J. "La Democracia y los Países Subdesarrollados," *Revista de Estudios Políticos,* 1961, pp. 83–88.

Barra, Felipe de la. *El Indio Peruano en las Etapas de la Conquista y Frente a la República: Ensayo Histórico-Militar-Sociológico y con Proposiciones para la Solución del Problema Indio Peruano.* Lima: Talleres Gráficos del Servicio de Prensa, Propaganda y Publicaciones Militares, 1948.

———. *Por la Gran Ruta del Chinchaysuyo: Panorama Histórico-Geográfico-Militar del Incanato a la República.* Lima: N.pub., 1960.

Barrientos Casós, Luis Felipe. *Los Tres Sindicalismos: Sindicalismo Proletario, Sindicalismo Patronal, Sindicalismo Político.* Lima: Ediciones Continente, 1958.

Barros, Oscar C. *Asunto Brea y Pariñas.* Second edition. Lima: Imprenta "Minerva," 1960.

Basadre, Jorge. "La Aristocracia y las Clases Medias Civiles en el Perú Republicano," *Mercurio Peruano.* 44:461–71 (1963).

———. *Historia de la República del Perú.* 10 vols. Lima: Ediciones "Historia," 1961–64.

———. *La Multitud, la Ciudad y el Campo en la Historia de Perú.* Second Edition. Lima: Editorial Huascarán, 1947.

———. *Perú—Problema y Posibilidad: Ensayo de una Síntesis de la Evolución Histórica del Perú.* Lima: F. y E. Rosay, 1931.

———. *La Promesa de la Vida Peruana.* Lima: Librería-Editorial Juan Mejía Baca, 1958.

——— and Rómulo A. Ferrero. *Historia de la Cámara de Comercio de Lima.* Lima: Santiago Valverde, 1963.

Basadre y Chocano, Modesto. *Diez Años de Historia Política del Perú.* Lima: Editorial Huascarán, 1953.

Baudin, Louis. *A Socialist Empire: The Incas of Peru.* New York: Van Nostrand, 1961.

Baudouin, Julio. *El Pueblo Debe Saber: Candentes Temas del Momento Político Actual.* Lima: Ediciones Pacífico Sur, 1967.

Bauer, Peter Tomas, and Basil S. Yamey. *The Economies of Underdeveloped Countries.* Chicago: University of Chicago Press, 1957.

Beals, Ralph L. "Social Stratification in Latin America," *American Journal of Sociology,* 58:327–39 (1953).

Belaúnde, César H. *Problemas de Política Social.* Second edition. Buenos Aires: Troquel, 1964.

———. *Reforma de Estructuras.* Buenos Aires: Ediciones Esnaola, 1965.

Belaúnde, Víctor Andrés. *Arequipa de mi Infancia.* Lima: Imprenta Lumen, 1960.

———. *Meditaciones Peruanas.* Second edition. Lima: N.pub., 1963.

———. *Mi Generación en la Universidad.* Lima: Imprenta Lumen, 1961.

———. "Mi Posición ante las Elecciones de 1963," *Mercurio Peruano,* 44:145–53 (1963).

———. *Peruanidad.* Second edition. Lima: Ediciones Librería Studium, 1957.

———. *Planteamiento del Problema Nacional.* Lima: N.pub., 1962.

——. *La Realidad Nacional.* Third edition. Lima: Talleres Gráficos Villanueva, 1964.

Belaúnde Terry, Fernando. *La Conquista del Perú por los Peruanos.* Lima: Ediciones Tawantinsuyu, 1959. (There is an English version: *Peru's Own Conquest,* translated and with an introduction by David A. Robinson. Lima: American Studies Press, 1965.)

Beltrán, Pedro G. "Foreign Loans and Politics in Latin America," *Foreign Affairs,* 34:297–304 (1956).

Benavides Correa, Alfonso. "Esquema para una Interpretación Geopolítica (Antiguo y Nuevo Perú)," *Revista de América,* July–August, 1948, pp. 115–23.

——. *Interpelación a la Cancillería.* Lima: N.pub., 1958.

——. *Oro Negro del Perú.* Lima: "El Escritorio," 1963.

——. *El Petróleo Peruano, o la Autópsia de un Clan.* Lima: N.pub., 1961.

——. *Rumbos Contemporáneos del Pensamiento Político: Ensayo de Interpretación sobre las Corrientes Ideológicas y Regímenes Políticos en su Perfil Teórico y Operancia Real.* Lima: Librería Internacional del Perú, 1957.

Berckholtz Salinas, Pablo. *Barrios Marginales: Aberración Social.* Lima: N. pub., 1963.

Bernstein, Marvin D. (ed.). *Foreign Investments in Latin America.* New York: Alfred A. Knopf, 1966.

Betancourt, Rómulo. "Derrotada Electoralmente la Dictadura en el Perú y Afirmada la Revolución en Bolivia," *Bohemia* (Havana), July 8, 1956, pp. 44–45, 98–99.

Beteta B., A. Eduardo. *Apuntes Socio-Económicos del Perú y Latino-América.* Lima: La Confianza, 1959.

Bidart Campos, Germán José. *Grupos de Presión y Factores de Poder.* Buenos Aires: Editorial A. Peña Lillo, 1961.

Bill, James A. "Social Structure and Political Power in Iran." M.A. thesis, Pennsylvania State University, 1963.

Bingham, Hiram. *Inca Land.* Boston: Houghton Mifflin, 1922.

Blanco, Hugo. *El Camino de Nuestra Revolución.* Lima: Ediciones Revolución Peruana, 1964.

Blanksten, George I. "Political Groups in Latin America," *American Political Science Review,* 53:106–27 (1959).

Bolo Hidalgo, Salomón. *Cartas de Mi Refugio.* Lima: Imprenta Gráfica T. Scheuch, 1963.

——. *Cristianismo y Liberación Nacional.* Lima: Ediciones Liberación, 1962.

Bourricaud, François. "Algunas Características Originales de la Cultura Mestiza en el Perú Contemporáneo," *Revista del Museo Nacional,* 23:162–73 (1954).

——. "Castas y Clases en Puno," *Revista del Museo Nacional,* 32:308–21 (1963).

——. *Ideología y Desarrollo: El Caso del Partido Aprista Peruano.* Mexico City: El Colegio de México, 1966.

——. "Lima en la Vida Política del Perú," *América Latina,* 7:89–95 (1964).

——. "El Ocaso de las Oligarquías y la Sobrevivencia del Hombre Oligárquico," *Aportes,* April, 1967, pp. 4–23.

——. *Poder y Sociedad en el Perú Contemporáneo.* Buenos Aires: Editorial Sur, 1967.

——. "Les Regles du Jeu en Situation d'Anomie: Le Cas Peruvien," *Sociologie du Travail,* 9:329–51 (1967).

——. "Remarques sur l'Oligarchie Peruvienne," *Revue Française de Science Politique,* 14:675–708 (1964).

——. "Structure and Functions of the Peruvian Oligarchy," *Studies in Comparative International Development,* 2:17–36 (1966).

——. "Sur le Regime Constitutionnel du Perou," *Revue Française de Science Politique,* 5:92–109 (1955).

——. "Syndicalisme et Politique: Le Cas Peruvien," *Sociologie du Travail,* 3:33–49 (1961).

Brandenburg, Frank. *The Making of Modern Mexico.* Englewood Cliffs, N.J.: Prentice-Hall, 1964.

Bravo Bresani, Jorge. "Mito y Realidad de la Oligarquía Peruana," *Revista de Sociología,* 3:43–71 (1966).

Breve Introducción al Estudio de la Realidad Nacional. Lima: Universidad Nacional Mayor de San Marcos, 1963.

Briones, Guillermo, and José Mejía Valera. *El Obrero Industrial: Aspectos Sociales del Desarrollo Económico en el Perú.* Lima: Universidad Nacional Mayor de San Marcos, 1964.

Brundage, Burr Cartwright. *Empire of the Incas.* Norman: University of Oklahoma Press, 1963.

Bruschera, Oscar. *Los Partidos Tradicionales en el Uruguay.* Montevideo: Ediciones del Río de la Plata, 1966.

Bueno Ortiz, Armendo. "Algunos Aspectos Geopolíticos del Perú y la

Defensa Nacional," *Revista de Marina* (Lima), September–October, 1947, pp. 370–78.

Bueno Tovar, Oscar. *Las Fuerzas Armadas y el APRA: Exposición Televisada.* Lima: I.M.P., 1963.

Bunge Guerrico, Hugo. *Perú.* Buenos Aires: Talleres Gráficos San Pablo, 1956.

Burgess, Eugene Willard, and Frederick H. Harbison. *Casa Grace in Peru.* Washington, D.C.: National Planning Association, 1954.

Burnett, Ben G., and Kenneth F. Johnson, (eds.). *Political Forces in Latin America: Dimensions of the Quest for Stability.* Belmont, Calif.: Wadsworth Publishing Company, 1968.

Busey, James L. *Latin America: Political Institutions and Processes.* New York: Random House, 1964.

Bustamante y Rivero, José Luis. *Mensaje al Perú y Perú, Estructura Social.* Lima: Editorial Universitaria, 1960.

——. *Tres Años de Lucha por la Democracia en el Perú.* Buenos Aires: Bartolomé U. Chiesino, 1949.

——. *Una Visión del Perú y Elogio de Arequipa.* Lima: Talleres Gráficos P. L. Villanueva, 1960.

Cabrera Charún, Eloy. "Sinopsis de la Economía Nacional," *Revista de la Facultad de Ciencias Económicas y Comerciales,* 59:254–57 (1958).

Cáceres, José Raúl. *El Pasmo de una Insurgencia.* Lima: Editorial Perú, 1934.

Calderón M., José P. "El Comandante y la Comunidad," *Revista Militar del Perú,* May–June, 1962, pp. 33–35.

Campobassi, José S., and others. *Los Partidos Políticos: Estructura y Vigencia en la Argentina.* Buenos Aires: Cooperadora de Derecho y Ciencias Sociales, 1963.

Camprubi Alcazar, Carlos. *El Banco de la Emancipación.* Lima: Talleres Gráficos P. L. Villanueva, 1960.

——. *Historia de los Bancos en el Perú.* Lima: Editorial Lumen, 1957.

Cantón, Darío. *El Parlamento Argentino en Épocas de Cambio: 1890, 1916 y 1946.* Buenos Aires: Editorial del Instituto, 1966.

Caravedo, Baltazar, Humberto Rotondo, and Javier Mariátegui. *Estudios de Psiquiatría Social en el Perú.* Lima: Ediciones del Sol, 1963.

Cardoso de Oliveira, R. "Bases para una Política Indigenista," *Revista Brasileira de Estudos Políticos,* 10:130–59 (1961).

Carey, James C. *Peru and the United States, 1900–1962.* Notre Dame, Ind.: University of Notre Dame Press, 1964.

Carneiro, Mario Afonso. "Opinião Militar," *Cadernos Brasileiros,* 8:17–28 (November–December, 1966).

Carrera Vergara, Eudocio. *La Lima Criolla de 1900.* Lima: N.pub., 1964.

Carta Pastoral del Episcopado Peruano sobre algunos Aspectos de la Cuestión Social en el Perú. Lima: N.pub., 1958.

Carta Pastoral de Pedro Pascual Farfán con Motivo de la Próxima Festividad de Santa Rosa de Lima. Lima: N.pub., 1937.

Casas Grieve, Luis Felipe de las. *Liberalismo Económico: Mito y Realidad de una Doctrina.* Lima: Secretariado Nacional de Propaganda del Partido Aprista Peruano, 1959.

———. *Plan y Gobierno: Fundamentos de la Planificación Aprista.* Lima: Partido Aprista Peruano, 1961.

———. *Unidad Económica Indoamericana.* Lima: Ediciones "Páginas Libres," 1946.

Castro Arenas, Mario. *La Novela Peruana y la Evolución Social.* Lima: Ediciones Cultura y Libertad, n.d.

Castro Bastos, Leónidas. *Geohistoria del Perú: Ensayo Económico, Político, Social.* Lima: Editorial Librería e Imprenta "D. Miranda," 1962.

———. *¡Golpismo!* Lima: Editorial Librería e Imprenta "D. Miranda," 1964.

Los Católicos y la Política: Carta Pastoral del Episcopado del Perú a los Sacerdotes y Fieles. Lima: N.pub., 1961.

Cavero Bendezú, José. "El Ejército en las Democracias Hispanoamericanas," *Revista de la Escuela Militar de Chorrillos,* September, 1944, pp. 701–7.

Chang-Rodríguez, Eugenio. "Chinese Labor Migration into Latin America in the Nineteenth Century," *Revista de Historia de América,* 46:375–99 (1958).

———. "Cosas y Gentes," *Cuadernos,* May–June, 1956, pp. 19–22.

———. *La Literatura Política de González Prada, Mariátegui y Haya de la Torre.* Mexico City: Ediciones de Andrea, 1957.

Chaplin, David. "A Discussion of Major Issues Arising in the Recruitment of Industrial Labor in Peru." Mimeo. The Land Tenure Center, University of Wisconsin, 1966.

———. "Industrial Labor Recruitment in Peru," *América Latina*, 9:22–39 (October–December, 1966).

Chartrand, Michel, Vernel Olson, and John Riddell. *The Real Cuba as Three Canadians Saw It.* Toronto: Fair Play for Cuba Committee, 1964.

Chirinos Lorentzen, Hector. *Perú, el Bienestar o el Caos.* Lima: N.pub., 1965.

Chirinos Soto, Enrique. *Actores en el Drama del Perú y del Mundo.* Lima: Ediciones de Divulgación Popular, 1961.

———. *Cuenta y Balance de las Elecciones de 1962.* Lima: Ediciones Perú, 1962.

———. *El Perú Frente a Junio de 1962.* Lima: Ediciones del Sol, 1962.

Cieza de León, Pedro de. *The Incas.* Norman: University of Oklahoma Press, 1959.

Ciria, Alberto. *Cambio y Estancamiento en América Latina.* Buenos Aires: Editorial Jorge Álvarez, 1967.

——— and Horacio Sanguinetti. *Universidad y Estudiantes: Testimonio Juvenil.* Buenos Aires: Ediciones Depalma, 1962.

Cohen, Alvin. "Societal Structure, Agrarian Reform, and Economic Development in Peru," *Inter-American Economic Affairs*, 18:45–59 (1964).

Conduruna, Silvestre. *Las Experiencias de la Última Etapa de las Luchas Revolucionarias en el Perú.* Lima: Editorial Vanguardia Revolucionaria, 1966.

Confederación de Trabajadores del Perú. *Posición Democrática del Sindicalismo Peruano: Notas Polémicas contra la Penetración Comunista.* Lima: Empresa Editorial EETSA, n.d.

Cordero Torres, J. M. "La América Dependiente," *Revista de Política Internacional,* July–October, 1961, pp. 373–85.

Cornejo, Cirilo A. *Visión Objetiva del Problema Indígena: Planteamiento y Solución Inmediata.* Lima: Ediciones Continente, 1959.

Cornejo Bouroncle, Jorge. *Monografías de Geografía Humana del Perú.* Cuzco: Universidad Nacional del Cuzco, 1964.

———. *Situación Económica de la Región del Cuzco.* Cuzco: Editorial H. G. Rozas, 1952.

———. *Tierras Ajenas: Estampas de la Vida Andina.* Cuzco: Ediciones Inca, 1959.

———.*Tupac Amaru: La Revolución Precursora de la Emancipación*

Continental. Second edition. Cuzco: Universidad Nacional del Cuzco, 1963.

Cornejo Chávez, Hector. *Nuevos Principios para un Nuevo Perú.* Lima: Juventud Demócrata Cristiana, 1960.

Cossio del Pomar, Felipe. "Oligarquía y Militarismo en el Perú," *Cuadernos,* February, 1962, pp. 27–31.

———. *Víctor Raúl: Biografía de Haya de la Torre.* Mexico City: Editorial Cultura, 1961.

Costa Villavicencio, Lázaro. *Monografía de la Provincia Litoral y Constitucional del Callao.* Lima: N.pub., 1956.

———. *Monografía del Departamento de Ica.* Lima: Crédito Editorial Victory, 1954.

Cotler, Julio. "La Mecánica de la Dominación Interna y del Cambio Social en el Perú." Mimeo. Instituto de Estudios Peruanos, 1967.

Cuadros y Villena, Carlos Ferdinand. *Análisis Crítico de la Legislación Peruana Tutelar del Indio.* Lima: Revista del Foro, 1957.

Cúneo, Dardo. *Comportamiento y Crisis de la Clase Empresarial.* Buenos Aires: Editorial Pleamar, 1967.

Dávalos y Lisson, Pedro. *La Primera Centuria: Causas Geográficas, Políticas y Económicas que han Detenido el Progreso Moral y Material del Perú en el Primer Siglo de su Vida Independiente.* 4 vols. Lima: Librería e Imprenta Gil, 1919–26.

De'Angeli, Giorgio. "Revolución Industrial en el Perú," *Mercurio Peruano,* 31:133–37 (1950).

Debuyst, Federico. *Las Clases Sociales en América Latina.* Bogotá: Oficina Internacional de Investigaciones de FERES, 1962.

Delgado, Carlos. "Notas sobre Movilidad Social en el Perú." Mimeo. Instituto de Estudios Peruanos, 1967.

———. "Panorama Político Peruano," *Combate,* 4:23–30 (May–June, 1962).

Delgado, Luis Humberto. *Drama del Perú.* Lima: Ariel Editores, 1963.

Delgado, Oscar. "Revolución, Reforma y Conservatismo: Tipos de Políticas Agrarias en Latinoamérica," *Revista Brasileira de Ciencias Sociais,* July, 1963, pp. 172–251.

DeProspo, Ernest R., Jr. "The Administration of the Peruvian Land Reform Program." Ph.D. dissertation, Pennsylvania State University, 1967.

Derteano Urrutia, Carlos. "Importancia e Influencia de la Agricultura en la Economía Nacional," *Mercurio Peruano*, 34:440–60 (1953).

Deustua P., Carlos. "Sobre la Burguesía Peruana en el Siglo XVIII," *Mercurio Peruano*, 44:481–90 (1963).

Diez Canseco, Octavio. *De Espaldas al Desarrollo Agrario Peruano.* Lima: Imprenta Americana, 1960.

———. *La Falsa Reforma Agraria.* Lima: Imprenta "Minerva," 1961.

Dobyns, Henry F., and Mario C. Vásquez, (eds.). *Migración e Integración en el Perú.* Lima: Editorial Estudios Andinos, 1963.

Doce Aportes a la Tarea del Desarrollo en el Perú. Lima: Biblioteca de Acción para el Desarrollo, 1963.

Donahue, F. "Students in Latin American Politics," *Antioch Review*, 26:91–106 (1966).

Easton, David. *A Framework for Political Analysis.* Englewood Cliffs, N.J.: Prentice Hall, 1965.

Echenique, José Rufino. *Memorias para la Historia del Perú.* Lima: Editorial Huascarán, 1952.

Edelmann, Alexander T. *Latin American Government and Politics.* Homewood, Ill.: Dorsey Press, 1965.

Edinger, Lewis J., and Donald D. Searing. "Social Background in Elite Analysis: A Methodological Inquiry," *American Political Science Review*, 61:428–45 (1967).

Eggers Lan, Conrado. *Cristianismo, Marxismo y Revolución Social.* Buenos Aires: Jorge Álvarez Editor, 1964.

Egner, Erich. *El Crecimiento Económico del Perú y sus Obstáculos.* Estudios del Instituto de Investigaciones Económicas No. 3. Lima: Universidad Nacional Mayor de San Marcos, 1963.

———. "El Crecimiento Económico del Perú y sus Obstáculos," *Revista de la Facultad de Ciencias Económicas y Comerciales*, 66:18–20 (1963).

Eguiguren, Luis Antonio. *Hojas para la Historia de la Emancipación del Perú.* 2 vols. Lima: N.pub., 1959–61.

Einaudi, Luigi. "Changing Contexts of Revolution in Latin America." Mimeo. Paper delivered at the Annual Meeting of the American Political Science Association, New York, September 6–10, 1966.

Episcopado del Perú. *Los Católicos y la Política: Carta pastoral del Episcopado del Perú a los Sacerdotes y Fieles.* Lima: Tipográfica Sesator, 1961.

Erickson, Edwin E., and others. *U.S. Army Area Handbook for Peru.*

Washington, D.C.: Special Operations Research Office, American University, 1965.

Escobar M., Gabriel. *Organización Social y Cultural del Sur del Perú*. Mexico City: Instituto Indigenista Interamericano, 1967.

Esteva Fabregat, Claudio. "El Indigenismo en la Política Hispanoamericana," *Revista de Política Internacional*, July–October, 1961, pp. 49–63.

Farrell, R. Barry (ed.). *Approaches to Comparative and International Politics*. Evanston, Ill.: Northwestern University Press, 1966.

Fayt, Carlos S. *Teoría de la Política*. Buenos Aires: Ed. Abeledo-Perrot, 1959.

Ferrero, Raúl. *Derecho Constitucional*. Lima: Ediciones Librería Studium, 1963.

——. *El Liberalismo Peruano: Contribución a una Historia de las Ideas*. Lima: Tipografia Peruana, 1958.

Ferrero, Rómulo, and Arthur J. Altmeyer. *Estudio Económico de la Legislación Social Peruana y Sugerencias para su Mejoramiento*. Lima: N.pub., 1957.

Finer, S. E. *The Man on Horseback*. New York: Frederick A. Praeger, 1962.

Fitchett, Delbert Arthur. "Agricultural Land Tenure Arrangements on the Northern Coast of Peru," *Inter-American Economic Affairs*, 20: 65–86 (Summer, 1966).

——. "Defects in the Agrarian Structure as Obstacles to Economic Development: A Study of the Northern Coast of Peru." Ph.D. dissertation, University of California at Berkeley, 1963.

Fitzgibbon, Russell H. *Uruguay: Portrait of a Democracy*. New Brunswick, N.J.: Rutgers University Press, 1954.

——. "What Price Latin American Armies?" *Virginia Quarterly Review*, 36:517–32 (1960).

—— and K. F. Johnson. "Measurement of Latin American Political Change," *American Political Science Review*, 55:515–26 (1961).

Ford, Thomas Robert. *Man and Land in Peru*. Gainesville: University of Florida Press, 1962.

Form, William H., and Albert A. Blum, (eds.). *Industrial Relations and Social Change in Latin America*. Gainesville: University of Florida Press, 1965.

"Forum sobre Economía Nacional, Organizado por la Facultad de

Ciencias Económicas," *Anales de la Universidad Nacional Mayor de San Marcos,* 9:84–166 (1958).

Fraga Iribarne, Manuel. "El Sindicalismo como Fuerza Política," *Revista de Estudios Políticos,* January–February, 1961, pp. 5–39.

———. "Tendencias Estructurales del Constitucionalismo Peruano," *Mercurio Peruano,* 44:419–33 (1963).

Frias, Ismael. *La Revolución Peruana.* Lima: N.pub., n.d.

Fuentes Álvarez, Enrique. *La Realidad Política del Pueblo Peruano: Neonacionalismo de los Pueblos Oprimidos.* Lima: N.pub., 1968.

Galarreta González, Julio. *Pasión y Rumbo de una Juventud.* Lima: Ediciones Stampa, 1959.

Gall, Norman. "Letter from Peru," *Commentary,* June, 1964, p. 64.

Galván, Luis Enrique. *Reflexiones sobre una Pedagogía Universitaria Aplicable al Peru.* Lima: T. Scheuch, 1958.

Gálvez, José. *Una Lima que se Va.* . . . Lima: Editorial Universitaria, 1965.

Gamarra, Abelardo M. *Cien Años de Vida Perdularia.* Lima: Casa de la Cultura del Perú, 1963.

Ganoza Bustamante, Jorge. *La Verdad sobre la Crisis Pesquera.* Lima: Editora Italperú, 1967.

García Calderón, Francisco. *En Torno al Perú y América.* Lima: Juan Mejía Baca & P. L. Villanueva, 1954.

Garrigos, P. A. "La Iglesia Católica en Hispanoamérica," *Revista de Política Internacional,* July–October, 1961, pp. 65–100.

Germani, Gino. "Démocratie Représentative et Classes Populaires en Amérique Latine," *Sociologie du Travail,* 3:96–113 (1961).

———. *Política y Sociedad en una Epoca de Transición: De la Sociedad Tradicional a la Sociedad de Masas.* Buenos Aires: Editorial Paidos, 1962.

——— and Kalman H. Silvert. "Politics, Social Structure and Military Intervention in Latin America," *Archives Européennes de Sociologie,* 2:62–81 (1961).

Girard, Rafael. *Indios Selváticos de la Amazonia Peruana.* Mexico City: Libro Mex Editores, 1958.

Goldenberg, Boris. "The Cuban Revolution—A New Type of Revolution," *Europa Archiv,* 17:805–14 (1962).

Goldrich, Daniel, Raymond B. Pratt, and C. R. Schuller. "The Political Integration of Lower Class Urban Settlements in Chile and Peru: A Provisional Inquiry." Mimeo. Paper delivered at the Annual Meeting of the American Political Science Association, New York, September 6–10, 1966.

Golembiewski, Robert T. "The Group Basis of Politics: Notes on Analysis and Development," *American Political Science Review*, 54:962–71 (1960).

Gómez, R. A. *Government and Politics in Latin America.* New York: Random House, 1963.

González Casanova, Pablo. *La Democracia en México.* Mexico City: Ediciones ERA, 1965.

González Prada, Adriana de (ed.). *Horas de Lucha.* Second edition. Callao: Tipográfica Lux, 1924.

González Prada, Manuel. *Anarquía.* Lima: P.T.C.M., 1948.

——. *Figuras y Figurones.* Paris: Tipografía de Louis Bellenand et Fils, 1938.

——. *Nuevas Páginas Libres.* Santiago, Chile: Editorial Ercilla, 1937.

——. *Páginas Libres. Second* edition. Madrid: Editorial América, 1915.

——. *Propaganda y Ataque.* Buenos Aires: Editorial Imán, 1939.

——. *Prosa Menuda.* Buenos Aires: Editorial Imán, 1941.

González Tafur, Oswaldo B. *La Agricultura Peruana: Problemas y Posibilidades.* Lima: Editorial-Imprenta Amauta, 1964.

——. *Fundamentos de la Prosperidad Nacional (Perú Agropecuario).* Lima: Mejía Baca, 1959.

González Vigil, Francisco de Paula. *Opúsculo de la Libertad de Cultos, con Religión del Estado.* Tacna: N.pub., 1861.

Grace, J. P. "United States Business Responds," *Annals*, 334:143–47 (1961).

Graciarena, Jorge. *Poder y Clases Sociales en el Desarrollo de América Latina.* Buenos Aires: Editorial Paidos, 1967.

Guardia Mayorga, César. *La Reforma Agraria en el Perú.* Second edition. Lima: Ed. Minerva, 1962.

Guerra Carreño, Vicente. "La Reforma Agraria en el Perú." Thesis, Universidad Nacional Mayor de San Marcos, 1961.

Las Guerrillas en el Perú y su Represión. Lima: Ministerio de Guerra, 1966.

Guevara, J. Guillermo. *La Rebelión de los Provincianos.* Lima: Editorial Folklore, 1959.

Guevara Velasco, Agustín. *Apuntes sobre mi Patria: Volumen del Departamento de Puno.* Cuzco: Editorial H. G. Rozas, 1954–55.

Guillén, Pedro. "Militarismo y Golpes de Estado en América Latina," *Cuadernos Americanos*, 24:7–19 (May–June, 1965).

Hall, M. Françoise. "Birth Control in Lima, Peru," *Milbank Fund Memorial Quarterly*, 43:409–38 (1965).

Hammel, Eugene A. *Wealth, Authority, and Prestige in the Ica Valley, Perú*. Albuquerque: University of New Mexico Press, 1962.

Harbron, John D. "The Dilemma of an Elite Group: The Industrialist in Latin America," *Inter-American Economic Affairs*, 19:43–62 (Autumn, 1965).

Harris, Walter D., and others. *La Vivienda en el Perú*. Washington, D.C.: Pan American Union, 1963.

Hauser, Phillip M. (ed.). *Urbanization in Latin America*. Paris: UNESCO, 1961.

Haya de la Torre, Víctor Raúl. *¿A Dónde va Indoamérica?* Santiago de Chile: Edit. Ercilla, 1935.

——. *El Antiimperialismo y el Apra*. Santiago de Chile: Ediciones Ercilla, 1936.

——. *Aprismo y Filosofía*. Lima: Ediciones Pueblo, 1961.

——. *Construyendo el Aprismo*. Buenos Aires: Colección Claridad, 1933.

——. *La Defensa Continental*. Third edition. Buenos Aires: Ediciones Problemas de América, 1945.

——. *Indoamérica*. Lima: Ediciones Pueblo, 1961.

——. "My Five-Year Exile in My Own Country," *Life*, 36:152–56 (May 3, 1954).

——. *Pensamiento Político*. 5 vols. Lima: Ediciones Pueblo, 1961.

——. *Política Aprista*. Lima: Editorial Cooperativa Aprista Atahualpa, 1933.

——. *Treinta Años de Aprismo*. Mexico City: Fondo de Cultura Económica, 1956.

Heath, Dwight B., and Richard N. Adams (eds.). *Contemporary Cultures and Societies of Latin America*. New York: Random House, 1965.

Hernández Urbina, Alfredo. *Compendio de Sociología Peruana*. Lima: Ediciones Raíz, 1963.

——. *Nueva Política Nacional*. Trujillo, Perú: Ediciones Raíz, 1962.

——. *Los Partidos y la Crisis del Apra*. Lima: Editorial Raíz, 1956.

——. "La Seguridad Social y el Drama del Hombre en el Agro Peruano," *Cuadernos Americanos*, 23:21–27 (March–April, 1964).

Heysen, Luis E. *Enfoques Económico-Agrarios.* Lima: Facultad de Ciencias Económicas, 1962.

———. *Fundamentos Sociológicos del Desarrollo Regional.* Lima: Editorial Nuevo Día, 1964.

Hidalgo Morey, V. "Miseria y Posibilidades de la Región Amazónica Peruana," *Informaciones Comerciales* (Lima), 9:16–19 (September, 1958).

Homberg, Allan. "From Paternalism to Democracy: The Cornell-Peru Project," *Human Organization,* 15:15–18 (Fall, 1956).

———. "Land Tenure and Planned Social Change: A Case from Vicos, Peru," *Human Organization,* 18:7–10 (Spring, 1959).

Hopkins, Jack W. "The Government Executive of Modern Peru." Ph.D. dissertation, University of Florida, 1966.

Horowitz, Irving Louis. *Three Worlds of Development: The Theory and Practice of International Stratification.* New York: Oxford University Press, 1966.

Hoyos Osores, Guillermo. "Crisis de la Democracia en el Perú: Causas de su Quebranto y Condiciones para su Recuperación," *Cuadernos Americanos,* 28:7–31 (January–February, 1969).

Huayimaca Saldívar, Teófilo. "Estado de Derecho y Estado Democrático en el Perú," *Combate,* 2:62–66 (1960).

Icaza Tigerino, J. "Idea Política de Hispanoamérica," *Revista de Política Internacional,* July–October, 1961, pp. 3–20.

Imaz, José Luis de. *Los que Mandan.* Buenos Aires: Editorial Universitaria de Buenos Aires, 1964.

Indice Perú. Lima: Editora Latinoamericana, 1962.

Institute for the Comparative Study of Political Systems. *Peru Election Memoranda.* Washington, D.C.: The Institute, 1963.

Instituto de Estudios Políticos para América Latina. *Perú.* Montevideo: El Instituto, 1964.

———. *Uruguay; un País sin Problemas en Crisis.* Montevideo: N.pub., 1965.

Inter-American Development Bank. *Progreso Socio-Económico de América Latina: Fondo Fiduciario de Progreso Social, Sexto Informe Anual, 1966.* Washington, D.C.: N.pub., 1967.

Irie, Toraji. "History of Japanese Migration to Perú," *Hispanic American Historical Review,* 31:437–52, 648–64 (1951); 32:73–82 (1952).

Ismodes, Aníbal. "La Conducta Política de los Militares," *Panoramas* (Mexico) March–April, 1963, pp. 61–70.

Jaguaribe, Helio. *Desenvolvimento Econômico e Desenvolvimento Político*. Rio de Janeiro: Editora Fundo de Cultura, 1962.

——. *O Nacionalismo na Atualidade Brasileira*. Rio de Janeiro: Instituto Superior de Estudos Brasileiros, 1958.

——. "Política de Clientela e Política Ideológica," *Digesto Econômico*, 6:41–62 (July, 1950).

Jara Palomino, Fidel. "Rol de la Banca Privada en la Economía Peruana." Thesis, Universidad Nacional Mayor de San Marcos, 1963.

Jockey Club del Perú. *Memoria Correspondiente al Año 1963*. Lima: Empresa Editorial Peruana, [1964?].

Johnson, John J. *The Military and Society in Latin America*. Stanford, Calif.: Stanford University Press, 1964.

——. *Political Change in Latin America: The Emergence of the Middle Sectors*. Stanford, Calif.: Stanford University Press, 1958.

——. "The Political Role of the Latin American Middle Sectors," *Annals*, 334:20–29 (March, 1961).

Kantor, Harry. *El Movimiento Aprista Peruano*. Buenos Aires: Ediciones Pleamar, 1964. (Originally published as *The Ideology and Program of the Peruvian Aprista Movement*. Berkeley: University of California Press, 1953.)

Kaplan, Morton A. (ed.). *The Revolution in World Politics*. New York: John Wiley & Sons, 1962.

Kauffmann Doig, Federico. *Origen de la Cultura Peruana*. Lima: Sociedad Académica de Estudios Americanos, 1963.

——. *El Perú Arqueológico*. Lima: N.pub., 1963.

Kling, Merle. "Toward a Theory of Power and Political Instability in Latin America," *Western Political Quarterly*, 9:21–35 (1956).

Koch, Roberto. *Algunos Problemas de la Educación Nacional*. Lima: Universidad Nacional Mayor de San Marcos, Facultad de Educación, 1955.

Lambert, Jacques. *América Latina: Estructuras Sociales e Instituciones Políticas*. Barcelona: Ediciones Ariel, 1964.

Larraín Errázuriz, Manuel. *Desarrollo: Éxito o Fracaso en América Latina*. Santiago, Chile: Editorial de la Universidad Católica, 1965.

Ledesma Izquieta, Genaro. *Complot*. Lima: Talleres, Tipográficos Editorial "Thesis," 1964.

Leguía, Jorge Guillermo. *Estudios Históricos*. Santiago, Chile: Editorial Ercilla, 1939.

Lelong, Bernard. *The Stars Weep*. London: Hutchinson, 1956.

Letts Colmenares, Ricardo. *Reforma Agraria: Conferencia y Debate.* Lima: Compañía de Impresiones y Publicidad, 1962.

———. *Reforma Agraria Peruana: Justificación Económica y Política.* Lima: Ediciones Tierra, 1964.

Lévano, César. "Por la Nacionalización del Petroleo," *Tareas del Pensamiento Peruano,* 1:50–83 (May–June, 1960).

———. *La Verdadera Historia de las 8 Horas: Una Epopeya Heróica de la Clase Obrera Peruana.* Lima: N.pub., n.d.

Li Pun, Jorge Víctor. "La Inmigración China en el Perú y su Contribución al Progreso de Nuestras Actividades." Thesis, Universidad Nacional Mayor de San Marcos, 1962.

Lieuwen, Edwin. *Arms and Politics in Latin America.* Revised edition. New York: Frederick A. Praeger, 1961.

———. *Generals vs. Presidents: Neomilitarism in Latin America.* New York: Frederick A. Praeger, 1964.

Lipset, Seymour Martin. *Political Man: The Social Bases of Politics.* Garden City, N.Y.: Doubleday, 1960.

——— and Aldo Solari (eds.). *Elites in Latin America.* New York: Oxford University Press, 1967.

Lizarraga Robio, Raúl. "Poblaciones Marginales." Thesis, Universidad Nacional Mayor de San Marcos, 1962.

Llosa P., Jorge Guillermo. *En Busca del Perú.* Lima: Ediciones del Sol, 1962.

———. *Visión Sintética del Perú.* Lima: Ediciones Tawantinsuyu, 1959.

Luna Vegas, Emilio. *El Perú Invadido.* Lima: Ediciones Tawantinsuyu, 1962.

Luna Victoria, Romeo. *Ciencia y Práctica de la Revolución.* Lima: Editorial Studium, 1966.

———. *El Problema Indígena y la Tenencia de Tierras en el Perú.* Trujillo, Perú: Cosmos, 1964.

McAlister, Lyle N. "Civil-Military Relations in Latin America," *Journal of Inter-American Studies,* 3:341–50 (1961).

McCoy, Terry L. "The Politics of Agrarian Reform in Peru." Mimeo. University of Wisconsin, 1965.

Macedo Mendoza, José. *¡Nacionalicemos el Petroleo!* Lima: Ediciones Hora del Hombre, 1960.

MacLean y Estenós, Percy. *Historia de una Revolución.* Buenos Aires: Editorial EAPAL, 1953.

MacLean y Estenós, Roberto. *La Crisis Universitaria en Hispano-*

américa. Mexico City: Instituto de Investigaciones Sociales, 1956.

———. "Economía y Trabajo de los Aborígenes del Perú," *Revista Mexicana de Sociología*, 20:385–412 (1958).

———. *Sociología del Perú*. Mexico City: Universidad Nacional Autónoma de México, 1959.

———. "El Trabajo en las Comunidades Indígenas del Perú," *Revista Mexicana de Sociología*, 23:797–837 (1961).

McNicoll, Robert E. "Recent Political Developments in Peru," *Inter-American Economic Affairs*, 18:77–86 (Summer, 1964).

Maier, Joseph, and Richard W. Weatherhead (eds.). *Politics of Change in Latin America*. New York: Frederick A. Praeger, 1964.

Malpica, Carlos. *Los Dueños del Perú*. Lima: Fondo de Cultura Popular, n.d.

———. *Guerra a Muerte al Latifundio*. Lima: Ediciones "Voz Rebelde," n.d.

Mangin, William O., and Jerome Cohen. "Cultural and Psychological Characteristics of Mountain Migrants to Lima, Peru," *Sociologus* (Berlin), 14:81–88 (1964).

Mangin, William P. "The Role of Regional Associations in the Adaptation of Rural Migrants to Cities in Peru," *Sociologus* (Berlin), 9:23–36 (1959).

Mariátegui, José Carlos. *La Escena Contemporánea*. Second edition. Lima: Empresa Editora Amauta, 1959.

———. *Siete Ensayos de Interpretación de la Realidad Peruana*. Ninth edition. Lima: Empresa Editora Amauta, 1964.

Mariátegui Oliva, Ricardo. *Historia del Rotary Club de Lima (1920–1955)*. Lima: Talleres Gráficos Cecil, 1956.

Marquina, Leónidas A. *¿A Dónde Vamos Nosotros? Pensamientos Peruanos*. Lima: Taller de Linotipia, 1948.

Marsal, Juan F. *Cambio Social en América Latina: Crítica de Algunas Interpretaciones Dominantes en las Ciencias Sociales*. Buenos Aires: Solar Hachette, 1967.

Marta, Víctor Graciano. *Política Agraria*. Lima: Librería y Editorial Mario Campos y Campos, 1963.

Martelli, Juan C. "La Iglesia ya no Quiere que Soben a los Santos," *Caretas*, May 29–June 9, 1967, pp. 24A–24D.

Marthans Garro, Hércules. "El Centro de Altos Estudios Militares y la Planificación Nacional." Thesis, Universidad Nacional Mayor de San Marcos, 1963.

Martin, Laurence W. (ed.). *Neutralism and Nonalignment: The New States in World Affairs.* New York: Frederick A. Praeger, 1962.

Martin Saunders, César. *Dichos y Hechos de la Política Peruana.* Lima: Tipografía Santa Rosa, 1963.

Martínez de la Torre, Ricardo. *Apuntes para una Interpretación Marxista de Historia Social del Perú.* 2 vols. Lima: Empresa Editora Peruana, 1947.

Martínez Herrera, Miguel. "El Ejército como Factor de Producción." Thesis, Universidad Nacional Mayor de San Marcos, 1955.

Martz, John D. "Dilemmas in the Study of Latin American Political Parties," *Journal of Politics,* 26:509–31 (1964).

—— (ed.). *The Dynamics of Change in Latin American Politics.* Englewood Cliffs, N.J.: Prentice-Hall, 1965.

Matos Mar, José. "Consideraciones sobre la Situación Social del Perú," *América Latina,* 7:57–70 (1964).

——. "Diagnóstico del Perú: Cambios en la Sociedad Peruana," *Revista del Museo Nacional,* 32:294–307 (1963).

Maynaud, Jean. "Les Militaires et le Pouvoir," *Revue Française de Sociologie,* 2:75–87 (1961).

Medina, Carlos Alberto de. *A Favela e o Demagogo.* São Paulo: Livraria Martins Editora, 1964.

Mejía Valera, José. "La Estratificación Social en el Perú," *Cuadernos Americanos,* 23:107–17 (March–April, 1964).

——. "Estudio Sociológico de la Juventud," *Revista de Sociología* (Lima), 2:5–43 (1965).

Mejía Zagastizábal, Lisandro. "Acción Cívica en el Campo Laboral," *Revista Militar del Perú,* January–February, 1964, pp. 100–111.

Memorias de los Virreyes que han Gobernado el Perú durante el Tiempo del Coloniaje Español. Callao: Librería Central de Felipe Bailly, 1859.

Mendoza Acosta, Lorenzo. *Un Paso hacia la Liberación.* Lima: Empresa Gráfica T. Scheuch, 1962.

Mercado, Rogger. *Las Guerrillas del Perú—El MIR: De la Prédica Ideológica a la Acción Armada.* Lima: Fondo de Cultura Popular, 1967.

Mercier Vega, Luis. *Mecanismos del Poder en América Latina.* Buenos Aires: Editorial Sur, 1967.

Merino de Zela, E. Mildred. "El Cerro San Cosme." Thesis, Universidad Nacional Mayor de San Marcos, 1958.

Merton, Robert K. *Social Theory and Social Structure*. Glencoe, Ill.: Free Press, 1957.

Miller, Delbert C., Eva Chamorro Greco, and Juan Carlos Agulla. *De la Industria al Poder*. Buenos Aires: Ediciones Libera, 1966.

Millones, Luis. "Introducción al Estudio de las Idolatrías: Análisis del Proceso de Aculturación Religiosa en el Área Andina," *Aportes*, April, 1967, pp. 47–82.

Miró Quesada Cantaturias, Francisco. *Las Estructuras Sociales*. Lima: Tipográfica Santa Rosa, 1961.

———. *La Ideología de Acción Popular*. Lima: Tipográfica Santa Rosa, 1964.

Miró Quesada Laos, Carlos. *Autopsia de los Partidos Políticos*. Lima: Ediciones Páginas Peruanas, 1961.

———. *Historia del Periodismo Peruano*. Lima: N.pub., 1957.

———. *Radiografía de la Política Peruana*. Lima: Ediciones Páginas Peruanas, 1959.

———. *Sánchez Cerro y su Tiempo*. Buenos Aires: Editorial el Ateneo, 1947.

Miró Quesada S., Aurelio. *Costa, Sierra y Montaña*. Third edition. Lima: Talleres Gráficos P. L. Villanueva, 1964.

Moll, Bruno. *¿Hay Justicia en la Economía?* Buenos Aires: Selcón, 1959.

———. *El Problema Monetario Actual del Perú*. Lima: Ediciones Librería Studium, 1964.

———. "Las Tres Opiniones sobre el Desarrollo del Perú," *Revista de la Facultad de Ciencias Económicas y Comerciales*, 67:69–76 (1963).

Montero Bernales, Manuel. *Crisis en el Perú*. Lima: Imprenta "Minerva," 1961.

Montoya Rojas, Rodrigo. "La Migración Interna en el Perú: Un Caso Concreto," *América Latina*, 10:83–107 (October–December, 1967).

More, Federico. *Una Multitud contra un Pueblo*. Lima: Editorial "Todo el Mundo," n.d.

Moreno Mendiguren, Alfredo (ed.). *Repertorio de Noticias Breves sobre Personajes Peruanos*. Madrid: N.pub., 1956.

Movimiento de Izquierda Revolucionaria. *Bases Doctrinarias y Programáticas*. Lima: Ediciones Voz Rebelde, 1963.

Muñoz, Luis. *La Constitución Política del Perú Comentada*. Lima: Ediciones Juris, 1956.

Needler, Martin C. "Cabinet Responsibility in a Presidential System: The Case of Peru," *Parliamentary Affairs,* 18:156–61 (1965).

——. *Latin American Politics in Perspective.* Princeton, N.J.: Van Nostrand, 1963.

——. "Peru since the Coup d'État," *World Today,* 19:77–83 (1963).

—— (ed.). *Political Systems of Latin America.* Princeton: Van Nostrand, 1964.

Neira, Hugo. *Cuzco: Tierra y Muerte.* Lima: Problemas de Hoy, 1964.

Nieves Ayala, Arturo. *Los Extranjeros ante la Ley Peruana.* Lima: N.pub., 1960.

——. *Legislación sobre Compañías e Instituciones Extranjeras.* Lima: La Confianza, 1962.

North, Liisa. *Civil-Military Relations in Argentina, Chile, and Peru.* Berkeley: University of California, 1966.

Nun, José. "Los Paradigmas de la Ciencia Política: Un Intento de Conceptualización," *Revista Latinoamericana de Sociología,* 2:67–96 (1966).

Nuñez Anavitarte, Carlos. *Mariátegui y el Descentralismo.* Cuzco: Editorial "Garcilaso," 1958.

Obelson, William. *Funerales del Apra: El Fraude Electoral y Fiscal.* Lima: N.pub., 1962.

Oficina de Estudios para la Colaboración Económica Internacional. *Perú: Síntesis Económica y Financiera.* Buenos Aires: La Oficina, 1962.

Otero, Gustavo Adolfo. "Las Clases Sociales en la América Latina," *Filosofía, Letras, y Ciencias de la Educación,* (Quito, Ecuador), 11:163–95 (1958).

Owens, Ronald Jerome. *Peru.* London: Oxford University Press, 1963.

Padgett, L. Vincent. *The Mexican Political System.* Boston: Houghton Mifflin, 1966.

"El Palacete del Club Nacional," *Ciudad y Campo,* No. 45, pp. 12–21 (1929).

Palacio de Habich, Esther. "Investigación Socio-económica y Etnolo-educacional de los Moradores de los Cerros Circunvecinos y Arrabales de la Ciudad de Lima," *Revista del Servicio Social* (Lima), 7:56–94 (December, 1949).

Palacio Pimentel, H. Gustavo. "Relaciones de Trabajo entre el Patrón y los Colonos de los Fundos de la Provincia de Paucartambo," *Revista Universitaria del Cuzco,* 49:145–63 (1960); 50:67–140 (1961).

Palacios, Leoncio Miguel. "Encuesta sobre Condiciones de Vida de las Familias de Trabajadores en Arequipa," *Revista de la Facultad de Ciencias Económicas y Comerciales*, 61:154–64 (1960).

Pareja Paz-Soldán, José. *Las Constituciones del Perú*. Madrid: Ediciones Cultura Hispánica, 1954.

―― (ed.). *Biblioteca de Cultura Peruana Contemporánea*. Vol. I, *Sociología*. Lima: Ediciones del Sol, 1963.

―― and others. *Visión del Perú en el Siglo XX*. 2 vols. Lima: Ediciones Librería Studium, 1962–63.

Parodi, Ezio. "Clases Sociales y Comunidad Peruana," *Mercurio Peruano*, 41:86–94 (1960)

Parra del Riego, Manuel. *Síntesis Monográfica del Perú*. Lima: Fábrica Nacional de Tejidos de Santa Catalina, 1945.

Patch, Richard W. "Bolivia: The Restrained Revolution," *Annals*, 334:123–32 (March, 1961).

――. "La Parada, Lima's Market" (3 parts), *American Universities Field Staff Service Reports*, West Coast South America Series, Vol. XIV, Nos. 1, 2, and 3 (February, 1967).

――. "The Peruvian Elections of 1962 and their Annulment," *American Universities Field Staff Service Reports*, West Coast South America Series, Vol. IX, No. 2 (September, 1962).

――. "The Peruvian Elections of 1963," *American Universities Field Staff Service Reports*, West Coast South America Series, Vol. X, No. 1 (July, 1963).

Patrón Faura, Pedro. *Legislación Peruana sobre Empleados Públicos*. Lima: Imprenta Colegio Militar Leoncio Prado, 1964.

Payne, Arnold. "Latin America's Silent Revolution," *Inter-American Economic Affairs*, 20:69–78 (Winter, 1966).

――. *The Peruvian Coup D'État of 1962: The Overthrow of Manuel Prado*. Washington, D.C.: Institute for the Comparative Study of Political Systems, 1968.

Payne, James L. *Labor and Politics in Peru: The System of Political Bargaining*. New Haven, Conn.: Yale University Press, 1965.

――. "Peru: The Politics of Structured Violence," *Journal of Politics*, 27:362–74 (1965).

Paz-Soldán, Juan Pedro. *Diccionario Biográfico de Peruanos Contemporáneos*. Lima: Librería e Imprenta Gil, 1917.

Pequeño Diccionario Biográfico del Perú. Lima: Field Ediciones, 1961.

Perú, Armed Forces. *La Fuerza Armada y el Proceso Electoral de 1962.* Lima: Imprentas de la Fuerza Armada, 1963.

Perú, Comisión Para la Reforma Agraria y la Vivienda. *La Reforma Agraria en el Perú.* Documentos. 2 vols. Lima: N.pub., 1961.

——. *La Reforma Agraria en el Perú: Exposición de Motivos y Proyecto de Ley.* Lima: N.pub., 1960.

Perú, Departamento de Nutrición del Ministerio de Salud Pública y Asistencia Social. *La Familia Peruana: Suma y Resta de su Nutrición.* Lima: N.pub., 1954.

Perú, Dirección del Presupuesto. *Presupuesto Funcional de la República para 1964.* Lima: Imprenta del Ministerio de Hacienda y Comercio, 1964.

Perú, Dirección Nacional de Estadística y Censos. *Encuesta de Inmigración: Lima Metropolitana.* Lima: N.pub., 1968.

——. *Sexto Censo Nacional de Población y Primero de Vivienda.* 6 vols. Lima: N.pub., 1966.

Perú, Instituto Nacional de Promoción Industrial [and] Banco Industrial del Perú. *Situación de la Industria Peruana en 1964.* Lima: N.pub., 1965.

Perú, Ministerio de Agricultura. Dirección de Aguas de Regadío. *Padrones de Regantes de Todos los Valles del Perú.* Lima: N.pub., n.d.

Perú, Ministerio de Salud Pública. *La Alimentación y el Estado de la Nutrición en el Perú.* Lima: N.pub., 1960.

Perú, Partido Aprista Peruano. *¿De Qué Vive Haya de la Torre?* Lima: Empresa Editorial EETSA, 1960.

Peru, Senate. *El Perú y la International Petroleum Company: La Verdad sobre el Negociado de la "Brea y Pariñas."* Lima: N.pub., 1963.

——. *Presidentes del Senado, Comisiones Directivas y Señores Senadores, 1829–1960.* Lima: Talleres Gráficos del Senado, 1961.

Perú, Unión Nacional Odriista. *Plan de Gobierno.* Lima: N.pub., 1963.

Perú, Universidad Agraria. *Estadística Agraria, 1963.* Lima: Convenio de Cooperación Técnica, 1963.

Peterson, Robert L. "Social Structure and the Political Process in Latin America: A Methodological Re-examination," *Western Political Quarterly,* 16:885–96 (1963).

Petras, James, and Maurice Zeitlin (eds.). *Latin America: Reform or Revolution?* New York: Fawcet Publications, 1968.

Pflücker, Germán E. *Algunos Conceptos sobre el Desarrollo Económico del Perú*. Lima: Editorial Minerva, 1964.

Piedra, Julio de la. "Acto Inamistoso de la Administración de Estados Unidos, contra el Perú," *Conferencias*, no. 1 (1955), pp. 169–72.

Pierson, William W., and Federico G. Gil. *Governments of Latin America*. New York: McGraw-Hill, 1957.

Pike, Fredrick B. "The Catholic Church and Modernization in Peru and Chile," *Journal of International Affairs*, 20:272–88 (1966).

——. *The Modern History of Peru*. New York: Frederick A. Praeger, 1967.

——. "The Modernized Church in Peru: Two Aspects," *Review of Politics*, 26:307–18 (1964).

——. "The Old and the New APRA in Peru: Myth and Reality," *Inter-American Economic Affairs*, 18:3–45 (Autumn, 1964).

—— (ed.). *The Conflict between Church and State in Latin America*. New York: Alfred A. Knopf, 1964.

Plank, John Nathan. "Peru: A Study in the Problems of Nation-Forming." Ph.D. dissertation, Harvard University, 1959.

Porras Barrenechea, Raúl. *Fuentes Históricas Peruanas*. Lima: Universidad Nacional Mayor de San Marcos, 1963.

Prado, Jorge del. "Mariátegui: Un Hombre con una Filiación y una Fé," *Tareas del Pensamiento Peruano*, 1:27–45 (May–June, 1960).

La Profecía del Ché. Buenos Aires: Escorpión, 1964.

de la Puente Uceda, Luis F. "The Peruvian Revolution: Concepts and Perspectives," *Monthly Review*, 17:12–28 (1965).

Puga, Mario. *Los Incas (Sociedad y Estado)*. Mexico: Centauro, 1955.

Pumaruna, Américo. "Perú: Revolución, Insurrección, Guerrillas," *Cuadernos de Ruedo Ibérico*, April–May, 1966, pp. 62–86.

Pye, Lucian W. "The Non-Western Political Process," *Journal of Politics*, 20:468–86 (1958).

¿Qué es la Reforma Agraria? Lima: Centro de Documentación Económico-Social, 1963.

Quijano Obregón, Aníbal. "El Movimiento Campesino del Perú y sus Líderes," *América Latina* (Rio de Janeiro), 8:43–64 (1965).

Quintanilla Paulet, Antonio. "El Problema del Indio en el Perú," *Mercurio Peruano*, 27:107–21 (1956).

Rama, Carlos M. *Ensayo de Sociología Uruguaya*. Montevideo: Editorial Medina, 1957.

———. *Sociología del Uruguay.* Buenos Aires: Editorial Universitaria de Buenos Aires, 1965.

Ramírez Gastón, J. M. *Medio Siglo de la Política Económica y Financiera del Perú, 1915–64.* Lima: La Confianza, 1964.

Ramírez Novoa, Ezequiel. *Escándalo en Punta del Este: Alianza para el Retroceso.* Lima: Ediciones "28 de Julio," 1962.

———. *La Política Yanqui en América Latina.* 2 vols. Lima: Ediciones "28 de Julio," 1962–63.

———. *El Proceso de una gran Epopeya: La Revolución Cubana y el Imperialismo Yanqui.* Lima: Ediciones "28 de Julio," 1960.

———. *Recuperación de la Brea y Pariñas: Soberanía Nacional y Desarrollo Económico.* Lima: Ediciones "28 de Julio," 1964.

Ramírez y Berrios, M. Guillermo, *Examen Espectral de las Elecciones del 9 de Junio de 1963.* Lima: N.pub., 1963.

———. *Grandezas y Miserias de un Proceso Electoral.* Lima: Editorial Centenario, 1957.

Real de Azua, Carlos. *El Patriciado Uruguayo.* Montevideo: Ediciones Asir, 1961.

Recavarren, Jorge Luis. "De la Frustración a la Acción," *Panoramas,* (Mexico City), January–February, 1964, pp. 37–51.

Reinaga, César Augusto. *La Fisonomía Económica del Perú.* Cuzco: Editorial Garcilaso, 1957.

———. *El Indio y la Tierra en Mariátegui.* Cuzco: Editorial H. G. Rozas, 1959.

———. *Renta Nacional y Desarrollo Integral.* Cuzco: N.pub., 1964.

Riva Agüero, José de la. *Afirmación del Perú.* 2 vols. Lima: Instituto Riva Agüero, Pontificia Universidad Católica del Perú, 1960.

Rivera Serna, Raúl. *Los Guerrilleros del Centro en la Emancipación Peruana.* P. L. Villanueva, Lima, 1958.

Robinson, David A. *Peru in Four Dimensions.* Lima: American Studies Press, 1964.

Roca Sánchez, Pedro Erasmo. *El Nacionalismo Económico y la Justicia Social.* Lima: Universidad Nacional Mayor de San Marcos, 1961.

Rodríguez Araujo, Octavio. "Católicos Contra el Capitalismo," *Cuadernos Americanos,* 27:16–23 (January–February, 1968).

Roel Pineda, Virgilio. *La Economía Agraria Peruana: Hacia la Reforma de Nuestro Agro.* Second edition. 2 vols. Lima: Grafcolor, 1961.

———. *La Planificación Económica: Sus Técnicas y Problemas.* Lima: N.pub., 1963.

Rojas Cieza, Franco Alberto. "Encuesta sobre Condiciones de Vida de Familias de Trabajadores en Chisca y Vitarte." Thesis, Universidad Nacional Mayor de San Marcos, 1961.

Rojas Vidal, Floriano. "Estudio Geo-económico y Social de las Comunidades Indígenas del Canípaco de las Provincias de Huancayo y Huancavélica." Thesis, Universidad Nacional Mayor de San Marcos, 1964.

Rolón Anaya, Mario. *Política y Partidos en Bolivia.* La Paz: Librería Editorial "Juventud," 1966.

Romero, César Enrique. "Crisis del Gobierno Civil en América Latina," *Revista de Estudios Políticos,* March–April, 1962, pp. 227–32.

Romero, Emilio. *Geografía Económica del Perú.* Third edition. Lima: N.pub., 1961.

———. *Historia Económica del Perú.* Buenos Aires: Editorial Sudamericana, 1949.

———. *El Perú Frente al Mercado Común Europeo.* Lima: Universidad Nacional Mayor de San Marcos, 1962.

———. *Perú por los Senderos de América.* Second edition. Lima: Imprenta Minerva, 1959.

Romero, Fernando. *Educación y Desarrollo Económico: Movilización Educativa de Nuestro Capital Humano* (*Actividades Productivas del Perú,* Vol. IV). Lima: Banco Central de Reserva del Perú, 1963.

Rosemblat, Angel. *La Población Indígena y el Mestizaje en América.* 2 vols. Buenos Aires: Editorial Nova, 1954.

Ross, Stanley R. (ed.). *Is the Mexican Revolution Dead?* New York: Alfred A. Knopf, 1966.

Roucek, Joseph S. "Peru in Geopolitics," *Contemporary Review,* 204: 310–25 (1963); 205:24–31 (1964).

Rouquette, Robert. "Una Iglesia Reformadora: El Primer Sínodo Episcopal," *Razón y Fe,* 176:439–64 (1967).

Rubio, J. L. "Notas sobre las Centrales Sindicales Iberoamericanas." *Revista de Política Internacional,* July–October, 1961, pp. 161–84.

Ruibal V., Alberto. *Problemas Nacionales: La Evolución Social.* Lima: Gil, 1962.

Saavedra Pacheco, Mauro. *Nuestra Revolución en Marcha: 7 Invocaciones a la Conciencia del Pueblo Peruano.* Lima: Imprenta Minerva, 1962.

Saavedra Rasso, Ladislao. "Análisis Económico-social del Salario en el Perú." Thesis, Universidad Nacional Mayor de San Marcos, 1963.

Sabogal Wiesse, José R. "Las Clases Medias en el Perú," *Economía y Agricultura*, 2:343–52 (1966).

Saco, Alfredo. *Programa Agrario del Aprismo*. Lima: Editoriales Populares, 1946.

———. *Síntesis Aprista*. Lima: Imprenta San Cristóbal, 1934.

Saenz, Moisés. *Sobre el Indio Peruano y su Incorporación al Medio Nacional*. Mexico: Secretaría de Educación Pública, 1933.

Salazar Bondy, Augusto. "Imagen del Perú de Hoy," *Cuadernos Americanos*, 21:104–15 (January–February, 1962).

———, Sebastián Salazar Bondy, Virgilio Roel Pineda, and José Matos Mar. *La Encrucijada del Perú*. Montevideo: Ediciones Arca, 1963.

Salazar Bondy, Sebastián. *Lima la Horrible*. Mexico: Ediciones Era, 1964.

———. "Who Are They?" *Atlas*, 10:170–71 (1965).

Salmón de la Jara, Pablo. *Desarrollo Económico, Desarrollo Agrícola y Reforma Agraria*. Lima: Talleres Gráficos P. L. Villanueva, 1963.

———. *La Reforma Agraria en el Perú*. Lima: N.pub., 1961.

Samamé, Benjamín. "Historia del Partido Socialista del Perú," *Justicia*, October 11, 1952, pp. 2–4.

———. "Manpower Problems and Policies in Peru," *International Labor Review*, 94:127–42 (1966).

San Cristóbal-Sebastián, Antonio. *Economía, Educación y Marxismo en Mariátegui*. Lima: Ediciones Studium, 1960.

———. "El Realismo Peruanista de Víctor Andrés Belaúnde," *Mercurio Peruano*, 39:387–407 (1958).

Sánchez, Luis Alberto. *El Actual Proceso Político Peruano*. Lima: N.pub., 1958.

———. *Aprismo y Religión*. Lima: Editorial Cooperativa Aprista Atahualpa, 1933.

———. "Ha Ocurrido una Revolución en el Perú," *Revista de América*, September, 1945, pp. 337–39.

———. *El Perú: Retrato de un País Adolescente*. Second edition. Lima: Universidad Nacional Mayor de San Marcos, 1963.

——— and others. *Cultura Peruana*. Lima: Universidad Nacional Mayor de San Marcos, 1962.

Santos, Eduardo. "Latin American Realities," *Foreign Affairs*, 34:245–57 (1956).

Sartre, Jean Paul. *Crítica de la Razón Dialéctica.* Buenos Aires: N.pub., 1963.

Schmitt, Karl M., and David D. Burks. *Evolution or Chaos: Dynamics of Latin American Government and Politics.* New York: Frederick A. Praeger, 1963.

Schurz, William Lytle. *Latin America: A Descriptive Survey.* New York: E. P. Dutton, 1964.

Scott, Robert E. *Mexican Government in Transition.* Urbana: University of Illinois Press, 1959.

Seers, Dudley (ed.). *Cuba: The Economic and Social Revolution.* Chapel Hill: University of North Carolina Press, 1964.

Seguín, Carlos Alberto (ed.). *Psiquiatría y Sociedad: Estudios sobre la Realidad Peruana.* Lima: Universidad Nacional Mayor de San Marcos, 1962.

Seligman, Lester G. "Elite Recruitment and Political Development," *Journal of Politics,* 26:612–26 (1964).

Selser, Gregorio. *El Guatemalazo.* Buenos Aires: Iguazú, 1961.

Semana Social del Perú. *Exigencias Sociales del Catolicismo en el Perú.* Lima: N.pub., 1959.

Seoane, Edgardo. *Surcos de Paz.* Lima: Industrial Gráfica, 1963.

Seoane, Manuel. *Nuestros Fines.* Second Edition. Lima: Partido Aprista Peruano, 1931.

——. *Páginas Polémicas.* Lima: Editorial La Tribuna, 1931.

Shapiro, Samuel. "Present-Day Peru: The Economic Situation and the Coming Presidential Election," *World Today,* 16:204–12 (1960).

Siffin, William J. (ed.). *Toward the Comparative Study of Public Administration.* Bloomington: Indiana University Press, 1959.

Silva Villacorta, Pablo. *¿A Dónde Van las Ideas de Haya de la Torre? Una Nueva Visión sobre las Ideas que Conforman la Doctrina del Apra.* Lima: N.pub., 1966.

Silvert, Kalman H. *The Conflict Society: Reaction and Revolution in Latin America.* New Orleans: Hauser Press, 1961.

——. "Nationalism in Latin America," *Annals,* 334:1–9 (1961).

—— (ed.). *Expectant Peoples: Nationalism and Development.* New York: Random House, 1963.

Simmons, Ozzie G. "El Uso de los Conceptos de Aculturación y Asimilación en el Estudio del Cambio Cultural en el Perú." Mimeo. Paper presented at the First International Meeting of Peruanistas, Lima, August, 1951.

Sivirichi, Atilio. *Historia del Senado del Perú.* Lima: Cámara de Senadores, 1955.

Snow, Peter G. (ed.). *Government and Politics in Latin America: A Reader.* New York: Holt, Rinehart and Winston, 1967.

Soares, Glaucio, and Robert L. Hamilton. "Socio-economic Variables and Voting for the Radical Left: Chile, 1952," *The American Political Science Review,* 61:1053–65 (1967).

Solari, Aldo E. *Estudios sobre la Sociedad Uruguaya.* 2 vols. Montevideo: Editorial Arca, 1964–65.

Sologuren, Javier. "Fórmulas de Tratamiento en el Perú," *Nueva Revista de Filología Hispánica,* 8:241–67 (1954).

Sorokin, Pitirim A. *Social and Cultural Mobility.* Glencoe, Ill.: Free Press, 1959.

Sosa Secchi, Hilda C. "Estudio Socio-Económico de la Provincia de Puno." Thesis, Universidad Nacional Mayor de San Marcos, 1963.

Sotelo Ortiz, Guillermo. "La Reforma Agraria dentro del Proceso de Desarrollo Económico del Perú." Thesis, Universidad Nacional Mayor de San Marcos, 1964.

Spota, Alberto Antonio. *El Poder Político y los Grupos de Fuerza y de Presión en la Crisis Contemporánea de la República Argentina.* Buenos Aires: Lecciones y Ensayos, 1955.

Sternberg, M. J. "Agrarian Reform and Employment, with Special Reference to Latin America," *International Labor Review,* 95:1–26 (1967).

Stewart, Watt. *Chinese Bondage in Peru.* Durham, N.C.: Duke University Press, 1951.

Stokes, William S. *Latin American Politics.* New York: Thomas Y. Crowell, 1959.

———. "Violence as a Power Factor in Latin-American Politics," *Western Political Quarterly,* 5:445–68 (1952).

Stycos, J. Mayonne. "Social Class and Preferred Family Size in Peru," *American Journal of Sociology,* 70:651–58 (1965).

Suárez Miraval, Manuel. "Perú: Trasfondo de una Tragedia," *Cuadernos Americanos,* 15:36–63 (September–October, 1956).

———. "¿Vuelve el Perú a la Democracia?," *Cuadernos,* November–December, 1956, pp. 91–94.

Tannenbaum, Frank. *Ten Keys to Latin America.* New York: Vintage Books, 1966.

Tavara, Santiago. *Historia de los Partidos*. Lima: Editorial Huascarán, 1951.

Taylor, Milton C. "Problems of Development in Peru," *Journal of Inter-American Studies*, 9:85–94 (1967).

——. "Taxation and Economic Development: A Case Study of Peru," *Inter-American Economic Affairs*, 21:43–54 (Winter, 1967).

Textor, Robert B. (ed.). *Cultural Frontiers of the Peace Corps*. Cambridge: M.I.T. Press, 1966.

Tomasek, Robert D. (ed.). *Latin American Politics: Studies of the Contemporary Scene*. Garden City, N.Y.: Doubleday, 1966.

Townsend Ezcurra, Andrés. "Frente a la Ley, los Tanques," *Panoramas* (Mexico City), March–April, 1963, pp. 51–60.

Trends in Social Science Research in Latin America: A Conference Report. Berkeley: Institute of International Studies, University of California, 1965.

Trujillo Ferrari, Alfonso. "Análise Ecológica da 'Competicão Económica' numa Comunidade Peruana," *Sociología* (Sao Paulo), 21: 385–417 (1959).

——. "Incidencias Teóricas en el Estudio de las Clases Sociales en Latinoamérica," *Revista Mexicana de Sociología*, 22:543–58 (1960).

Ugolotti Dansay, Humberto. *Las Elecciones de 1963 y la Lección del 62*. Lima: Tipografía Peruana, 1963.

United Nations Economic Commission for Latin America. *The Economic Development of Latin America in the Post-war Period*. New York: United Nations, 1964.

——. *Economic Survey of Latin America, 1965*. New York: United Nation, 1967.

——. *External Financing in Latin America*. New York: United Nations, 1965.

United States Department of Agriculture, Economic Research Service. *Land Tenure and Holding Information: Peru*. Washington, D.C.: U.S. Government Printing Office, 1961.

United States Department of Labor, Bureau of Labor Statistics and Agency for International Development. *Labor in Peru*. Washington, D.C.: U.S. Government Printing Office, 1964.

United States Senate. "Munitions Industry: Hearings before the Special Committee Investigating the Munitions Industry." Washington, D.C.: 73rd Congress, 1934.

Universidad de la Habana (Cuba). *Homenaje a José Luis de la Puente.* Havana: N.pub., 1966.

La Universidad y el Pueblo. Segunda época. 2 vols. Lima: Universidad Nacional Mayor de San Marcos, 1962.

Urdanivia Ginés, José. *Una Revolución Modelo [del] Ejército Peruano.* Lima: Editorial Castrillón Silva, 1954.

Urteaga, Horacio. *El Fin de un Imperio.* Lima: Librería e Imprenta Gil, 1933.

Valcárcel, Daniel. "Fidelismo y Separatismo en el Perú," *Revista de Historia de América,* 133–62, January–December, 1954, pp. 133–62.

Valcárcel, Gustavo. *Perú—Mural de un Pueblo: Apuntes Marxistas sobre el Perú Prehispánico.* Lima: Editora Perú Nuevo, 1965.

Valcárcel, Luis E. *Indians of Peru.* New York: Pocahontas Press, 1950.

——. *Mirador Indio.* Lima: N.pub., 1941.

——. "Nuevas Corrientes Culturales en el Perú," *Cuadernos Americanos,* 26:60–66 (November–December, 1967).

——. *Ruta Cultural del Perú.* Lima: Ediciones Nuevo Mundo, 1964.

——. "La Vida Rural en el Perú," *Revista del Museo Nacional,* 26:3–10 (1957).

—— (ed.). *La Educación del Campesino.* Lima: Universidad Nacional Mayor de San Marcos, 1954.

—— and others. *Estudios sobre la Cultura Actual del Perú.* Lima: Universidad Nacional Mayor de San Marcos, 1964.

Valdés Tudela, Napoleón. "Alcances y Consecuencias de las Reformas Sociales en el Perú," *Revista de la Facultad de Ciencias Económicas y Comerciales* (Lima), 46:40–52 (1952).

Valdovinos, Eduardo A. *La Crisis Moral.* Buenos Aires: Editorial Troquel, 1965.

Vallier, Ivan. "Religious Elites in Latin America: Catholicism, Leadership, and Social Change," *América Latina,* 8:93–114 (October–December, 1965).

Valverde Alvarado, Haydee Manuela. "Estudio Económico y Social de la Agricultura en el Perú." Thesis, Universidad Nacional Mayor de San Marcos, 1962.

Varallanos, José. *El Cholo y el Perú: Perú Mixto.* Buenos Aires: Imprenta López, 1962.

Varela y Orbegoso, Luis. *Los Presidentes de la Honorable Cámara de Diputados del Perú.* Lima: Empresa Tipográfica, 1916.

Vargas Ugarte, Rubén. *Historia de la Iglesia en el Perú.* 5 vols. Lima: Imprenta Santa María, 1953–62.

——. *Manual de Estudios Peruanistas.* Lima: Tipografía Peruana, 1951.

Vásquez, Mario C. *Hacienda, Peonaje y Servidumbre en los Andes Peruanos.* Lima: Editorial Estudios Andinos, 1961.

Vásquez Díaz, Manuel. "Balance del Aprismo," *Combate,* 2:24–35 (July–August, 1960).

Vázquez Varini, Felipe S. *Acción y Pensamiento Económicos de América Latina.* Montevideo: "Palacio del Libro," A. Monteverde, 1961.

Velarde Morán, Ernesto. *Legislación y Jurisprudencia Laboral en el Perú.* Lima: Editorial Ayacucho, 1961.

Véliz, Claudio (ed.). *Obstacles to Change in Latin America.* London: Oxford University Press, 1965.

——. *The Politics of Conformity in Latin America.* London: Oxford University Press, 1967.

Véliz Lizarraga, Jesús. *El Perú y la Cultura Occidental.* Lima: Instituto de Investigaciones Sociales del Perú, 1957.

——. *Principios Fundamentales del Aprismo.* Lima: Instituto de Estudios Apristas, 1956.

Veneroni, Horacio Luis. *La Asistencia Militar de los Estados Unidos.* Buenos Aires: Talleres Gráficos Buschi, 1964.

——. *Fuerza Militar Interamericana.* Buenos Aires: Talleres Gráficos Buschi, 1966.

Vento, Sócrates. *Hacia el Estado Federal Peruano: Fundamentos.* Lima: Editora Médica Peruana, n.d.

Vernal, Andrés. *Guía Vernal del Perú.* Lima: N.pub., 1960.

Vidaurre y Encalada, Manuel Lorenzo de. *Discurso a los Habitantes del Perú.* Trujillo: N.pub., 1824.

——. *Vidaurre contra Vidaurre.* Lima: Imprenta del Comercio, 1839.

Villanueva, Víctor. *Un Año bajo el Sable.* Lima: Empresa Gráfica T. Scheuch, 1963.

——. *Hugo Blanco y la Rebelión Campesina.* Lima: Librería-Editorial Juan Mejía Baca, 1967.

——. *El Militarismo en el Perú.* Lima: Empresa Gráfica T. Scheuch, 1962.

——. *La Tragedia de un Pueblo y un Partido.* Santiago de Chile: Ediciones Renovación, 1954.

Villarán, Manuel Vicente. *Apuntes sobre la Realidad Social de los*

Indígenas del Perú ante las Leyes de Indias. Lima: Talleres Gráficos P. L. Villanueva, 1964.

Villavicencio, Víctor Modesto. *Al Servicio de los Trabajadores.* Lima: Talleres Gráficos Junín, 1959.

Vries, Egbert de, and José Medina Echavarría. *Social Aspects of Economic Development in Latin America.* 2 vols. Paris: UNESCO, 1963.

Whitaker, Arthur P., and David C. Jordan. *Nationalism in Contemporary Latin America.* New York: Free Press, 1966.

Whyte, William F. "Culture, Industrial Relations, and Economic Development: The Case of Peru," *Industrial and Labor Relations Review,* 16:583–93 (July, 1963).

——. *La Mano de Obra de Alto Nivel en el Perú.* Lima: Editorial Senati, 1964.

—— and Graciela Flores. *Los Valores y el Crecimiento Económico en el Perú.* Lima: Senati, 1963.

Whyte, William F., and Lawrence K. Williams. "Structural Dimensions of Rural Development and Change in Peru," Mimeo. Paper delivered at Cornell Latin American Year Conference on "The Development of Communities in Andean Latin America," March 22–25, 1966.

——. "Supervisory Leadership: An International Comparison." Mimeo. Paper delivered at the Conference on Social Change and Assistance in Developing Nations, sponsored by the International Council for Scientific Management, 1963.

Wise, David, and Thomas B. Ross. *The Invisible Government.* New York: Random House, 1964.

Wong L. T., Félix. "Los Barrios Marginales de Trujillo: Posibilidades de Incorporarlos a Nuestra Economía." Thesis, Universidad Nacional Mayor de San Marcos, 1963.

Yepez Miranda, Alfredo. *La Universidad Interamericana del Cuzco.* Cuzco: Editorial H. G. Rozas, 1964.

Zavala Álvarez, Amalia. "La Corte Internacional de Justicia y el Asilo Diplomático." Thesis, Universidad Nacional Autónoma de México, 1952.

Zea, Leopoldo. "La América Latina en el Siglo XX," *Cuadernos Americanos,* 23:73–81 (January–February, 1964).

——. "El Perú, Lima y Belaúnde," *Foro Internacional,* 4:429–52 (1964).

Zeitlin, Maurice. *Revolutionary Politics and the Cuban Working Class.* Princeton, N.J.: Princeton University Press, 1967.

Zuzunaga, Carlos. "Sobre la Tipología Cultural del Perú," *Acta Americana,* July–September, 1947, pp. 151–58.

Newspapers and Magazines

Caretas (Lima)
El Comercio (Lima)
Confirmado (Buenos Aires)
Correo (Lima)
Expreso (Lima)
International Financial News Survey
Leoplán (Buenos Aires)
Life
La Nación (Buenos Aires)
New York *Times*
Oiga (Lima)
Política (Mexico City)
La Prensa (Buenos Aires)
La Prensa (Lima)
Primera Plana (Buenos Aires)
La Tribuna (Lima)
El Universal (Mexico City)
Wall Street Journal

Index